The Complete
Orienteering Manual

The Complete Orienteering Manual

Edited by Peter Palmer

The Crowood Press

First published in 1997 by
The Crowood Press Ltd
Ramsbury, Marlborough
Wiltshire SN8 2HR

British Library Cataloguing in Publication Data

A catalogue record for this book is available from the
British Library.

ISBN 1 86126 095 4

Typeset by Capital City, Swindon, Wiltshire.

Printed and bound in Great Britain by
WBC Book Manufacaturers Ltd., Mid Glamorgan

Contents

PETER PALMER – The Editor

Before becoming the British Orienteering Federation's first Director of Coaching, Peter Palmer taught history in Secondary Schools of all types for 30 years. He is now a school governor, member of the curriculum committee and Chairman of the British Schools Orienteering Association, and is still active with wife Marlene in developing junior orienteering at national, regional and local levels. His publications include *Orienteering for the Young*, *Orienteering in the National Curriculum*, *The Coaching Collection* and *Orienteering Pathways to Excellence*.

CONTRIBUTORS

DEREK ALLISON: Director of Coaching, British Orienteering Association.

STEVEN HALE: Long-standing Number One British Male Orienteer. World Championship Relay Silver medal winner in 1993. Currently ranked in world's top ten.

ANDREW KITCHIN: British International Orienteer, long-standing member of the British National Squad and three times British Men's Champion.

DR IAN McLEAN: Fitness Assessment and Sports Injuries Centre, University of Edinburgh. Orthopaedic Consultant to the Medical Committee of the Scottish Athletics Federation and Medical Advisor to the British Orienteering Squad.

TOM RENFREW: Director of Sport and Outdoor Education at the University of Strathclyde. Publications include *Teaching Orienteering, Start Orienteering, Orienteering for the Young* and *Orienteering* in the Human Kinetics Outdoor Pursuit series. Director of BOF Research Project into Orienteering for those with Learning Difficulties.

SUSAN WALSH: Director of Joint National Coaching Foundation. British Orienteering Federation Research Project into Developing Navigational Skills with Children. An experienced fell runner and long-distance orienteer, Sue is an Accredited Sports Psychologist lecturing at the University of North Wales, Bangor.

ACKNOWLEDGEMENTS

SILVA UK LTD: for permission to use information materials on the Silva Compass and its part in land navigation techniques.

NATIONAL NAVIGATION AWARD SCHEME: for use of fact sheet information on teaching navigational skills through the Orienteering System.

BRITISH SCHOOLS' ORIENTEERING ASSOCIATION: for permission to reproduce fact sheet information on teaching orienteering to children.

BRITISH AND SWEDISH ORIENTEERING CLUBS: including primarily Walton Chasers and Wrekin Orienteering Clubs for permission to use map extracts to illustrate orienteering activities.

DAVID GITTUS MBE, MARLENE PALMER, JONATHON TAYLOR (Cloud Nine) and OLLE PERSSON (Sweden) for providing photographs.

Foreword

PETER PALMER

Orienteering appeals to independent-minded people whatever their sex or ability. Some of them can be suspicious of coaching. Time and again in the pages which follow the authors are talking about 'knowing one's own strengths and weaknesses', 'listening to one's own body', 'devising personal goals' and making competition decisions in the forest without being influenced by others. How does all this match the popular idea of a coach?

The image of the inspirational, opinionated coach shouting on a team or protégé does not fit easily with the running navigator quietly plotting a way round a complicated course in a vast forest. Even in training it is difficult for an orienteering coach to see their athlete and judge performance directly unless they are fit enough to 'shadow' and observe – in which case the coach has to be a much better performer than their charge. If the performer always stays with their coach they can never overtake them. Getting accurate feedback is one of the most difficult problems with orienteering. It is difficult for even the most honest of competitors to be totally objective in analyzing and estimating their own performance.

Having said all this, orienteering is a technical sport as the following pages show. Although in the final analysis, the orienteer who is fit enough to travel fastest over the ground will win, the estimation and execution of route choice and mastery of all the psychological factors involved in making complex decisions while under physical and mental stress can be more significant in orienteering performance than running fitness.

So where does this leave the orienteering coach? Every developed orienteering nation has similar coaching schemes anchored to similar skills and competitive progressions. As in every sport, coaches cover every spectrum from the inspirational disciple ('Do exactly as I say and you will win'), to the empiricist who works from observation and applied experience, to the scientific theorist who is constantly pushing coaching theory forwards in an attempt to keep one step ahead of rivals. Orienteering coaches, like all sports coaches, are trying to narrow their athlete's gap between potential and achievement so that competitors get the maximum out of the orienteering experience.

At the start of Irretain OCS Annual New Year Day Score Event

All, in the final analysis, are justified by outputs rather than inputs – competition success rather than hours spent training.

The orienteering coach, however, is different, in that he or she has to think much more about methods of getting accurate feedback, of analyzing performance without seeing it and of devising learning situations rather than directing or dictating theory. Like colleagues in other sports, they have to be good organizers, motivators, communicators and confident in their specialist field, but more than in most sports they have to encourage competitors to think for themselves, to concentrate on making their own decisions in the forest and to be totally honest with themselves in identifying weaknesses and training to make them their strengths. In one sense, the orienteering coach is working to become redundant in direct coaching terms. While motivating, resourcing and monitoring their athlete, they are aiming to develop a broad role as philosopher, sounding board and consultant in times of injury or stress rather than setting themselves up as an inspirational fount of all technical wisdom.

The coaching themes touched on in this Foreword will be developed by our experts

The Editor as Coach

in the pages which follow. There may be some repetition or overlap but each author from their specialist perspective is trying to give information and advice which will enable orienteers to improve their own performance and therefore get the maximum enjoyment from this multifaceted sport. The book is much more about discovering ways to become a better orienteer at one's own personal level than about laying down immutable rules for competitive success. Judged in these terms, I am sure it will repay the thoughtful reader in an immediate sense as well as providing a repository of information from acknowledged experts in their field for future reference and study.

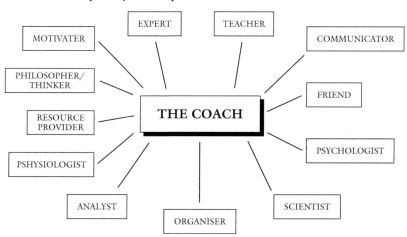

Introduction

PETER PALMER

At various times in this manual our experts seem to contradict each other in describing orienteering as both a simple and complicated sport. Depending on the writer's standpoint it can be both. The basic orienteering format of navigating between fixed control points on a course set in a forest by orienteers for orienteers is indeed simple, but the mix of physical, psychological and navigational factors involved in executing chosen routes effectively can be complicated in the extreme. This manual sets out to analyze what constitutes successful orienteering and to examine ways of developing the specific skills which make for success. Each author is an acknowledged expert in their own field, and some are still competing at the highest levels. All are currently active and successful in their specialist field.

I have put modern orienteering in its historical context to illustrate both the speed of its development and the subtle changes in its

Coaching has it good moments

philosophy from a wilderness sport for hard men to a broad-based family activity with various offshoots into cross-country skiing, mountain biking and watersports. Its flexibility can be both a strength and a weakness. Racing orienteering at the elite end in particular suffers from the blurred focus of the sport. It is difficult to bridge the gap in a sponsor's mind between children map

Orienteering is Head to Head Racing

reading between goal posts on a school field and superb middle-distance athletes competing at 4 minutes a kilometre in a Scandinavian or Scottish forest. Sports like football and tennis have no such image problem.

Another, more personal, reason for putting orienteering in a historical setting is that whatever its form or level I believe that it appeals to the basic human explorer instinct. From the moment it is born, the human child is struggling to extend and come to terms with its environment, but in the hectic, threatening modern world access to the natural environment becomes more difficult in those very years of adolescence and young adulthood when the urge to extend personal limits is at its greatest. Whether a sport, or a recreational or educational activity, orienteering taps the explorer instinct which lies deep in all of us. Its appeal is a universal one. It offers adventure, challenge and competition to the child on a school site, a family in the local park, or the athlete running through a vast forest or on a mountain range, and it demands from all of them a mastery of the same basic navigational skills. 'Hit and Miss' orienteering is no

fun, neither is getting lost in a big forest. Orienteering, like every other sport, has its own skills progression and tested structures for learning relevant skills in an enjoyable way. This book offers advice and information on the assumption that basic orienteering experiences are enhanced by doing it well. It is a philosophy which should appeal to every age and level of experience.

The book's format is largely as bequeathed to me by Tom Renfrew. We both believe that the contributors will not only draw on an unrivalled depth of experience, but will have personal angles on their specialist areas which will provoke interest and thought. I am delighted that Steve Hale and Andrew Kitchin agreed to contribute. Standards and racing technique at the elite end of orienteering are moving so fast that only those fully involved in the current international scene can provide constructive up-to-date material. We have given prominence to psychology because so many orienteering skills involve psychological factors. I am delighted to hear as I write this that Sue Walsh is taking over as Director of the NCF Research Project on Developing Navigational Skills at Bangor University. Dr Ian

Britain's Silver Girl

McLean has worked with the national squads now for several years and I know that he sees sports injuries and health-related matters in a positive way, with prevention taking precedent over cures. As BOF Director of Coaching Derek Allison is the obvious person to explain the coaching system as it relates to adults. Safety is dealt with within specialist areas. Orienteering is not a hazardous sport and most safety issues come down to common sense.

I make no excuse for including chapters on the young and the disabled. No other sport has so many educational dimensions as orienteering; and no other sport or recreation has the potential to be adapted in so many ways to people with different abilities and expectations. As coaches, we must not ignore avenues for motivation. Orienteering offers so many social opportunities to enjoy spectacular natural environments with friends, to collect maps and to relive com-

Britain's Silver Medal Relay Team

petitive adventures by comparing routes with friends. These experiences appeal to every age – but especially to the young – and to families. I have included more detailed information on some of these social and educational areas amongst the Appendices.

I would therefore claim that this is a complete manual for improving orienteering performance. It should appeal to all orienteers of both sexes and all ages at every level, as well as to coaches, teachers, community leaders and those working in the Great Outdoors who see orienteering as an excellent vehicle for teaching and developing navigational skills. Primarily, though, it tackles orienteering as a dynamic sport with high physical and technical standards rather than as a recreational activity.

Finally, I would like to justify the decision to use British practice as the centre of this multinational manual on training and coaching orienteering. Because only one-fifth of the United Kingdom is forested, as against four-fifths of Scandinavia, British teachers and coaches have used a lot of imagination in adapting a Scandinavian forest sport to a wide variety of terrains. They have also used long experience in organizing outdoor pursuits to place orienteering within a supportive context of countryside sport and recreation, which helps access and broadens its appeal. Much of this British experience has a direct relevance to other countries not blessed with the classic forest orienteering terrain of Scandinavia. It is no accident that as the BOF Director of Coaching I was invited to run five of the IOF Development and Coaching Clinics in Sweden, nor that I have been invited to set British practice at the centre of courses that I have run over the last five years in ten countries and four continents. British experience translates readily to the Bush round Perth in Australia, to a Calgary Country Park or the hills and parks of Hong

Orienteering is 'exploring forests' and 'beating friends'

13

Orienteering is 'Finding Control Markers'

examining the 'Hows' and 'Wherefores' of orienteering. I hope some of their enthusiasm rubs off on our readers and that, as Steve Hale recommends, they go out and practise what is recommended. Orienteering in the final analysis is all about 'doing' rather than 'reading' – Cunning Running *not* the Thought Sport.

In sharing our experience with you, I hope we will lead you to some of the pleasures and thrills we have experienced in so many different scenes over so many years.

Kong. The Silver Relay medals of the British men's team in the USA World Championships and the success of two of the British girls in 1996 World Cup Events show too that British coaching practice can achieve results at the very highest international levels as well as in the grass roots of the sport.

It has been a privilege for me to work with such an experienced, knowledgeable team in

1 A History of Orienteering

PETER PALMER

HISTORICAL BACKGROUND

Orienteering is as much an attitude of mind as a sport. Defined as 'competitive navigation', its origins go back to the late nineteenth century when orienteering competitions were held between military garrisons in the then United Kingdom of Sweden and Norway. However, once the definition is broadened to include exploration navigation, we find ourselves returning to the mists of time. Since the word orienteering was first used in military circles to mean crossing unknown territory with the aid of a map and compass, it is not fanciful to start this historical survey back in the ancient world. We will, however, accept that map and compass are prime elements in orienteering navigation and for this reason ignore the navigational achievements of prehistoric aboriginal groups in North America, Asia and Australasia who used animal tracks, stars, winds and dead reckoning of distance and direction travelled to travel vast distances in extreme terrain.

As early as 2000BC Egyptians were using picture maps on which symbols were drawn so as to encourage orientation. We know too that Egyptians, Greeks, Romans and Phoenician mariners had devised rough charts to supplement navigational information from wind, stars and tides. Armies and traders also used primitive maps to make navigation across mountains and deserts a matter of skill rather than chance. European expansion into the Americas, Africa and South-east Asia in the fifteenth and sixteenth centuries gave a big impetus to the improvement of maps and charts, and by this time many ships were equipped with a compass.

Generals – from Hannibal to Napoleon – especially appreciated the importance of accurate maps. The British Ordnance Survey was set up in 1791 as a specialist department by the Army to provide maps of the British Isles and beyond which would assist military movement and thereby help cement together an expanding Empire. German military plans in 1914 for the invasion of France were heavily reliant on maps and communication networks, as were most air, sea and land campaigns of the Second World War. Hitler actually banned the sport of orienteering in occupied Norway because orienteers with detailed terrain knowledge were of great help to Resistance groups. These strong links between the military world and orienteering still exist in many parts of the world.

The Vikings

The history of navigation merits several books in its own right, so for a brief survey we'll accept that the sport of orienteering was a Scandinavian invention and delve back into the past to identify the roots of Nordic fascination with the skills of navigation. This takes us to the eighth century and the legendary voyages of the Vikings to the British Isles, Iceland, Greenland and North America. Nor were all Viking journeys by sea. It was a group of fair-haired Swedes – the Rutsi – who journeyed into lowlands east of the Baltic and first introduced 'Russia' to the vocabulary of world history.

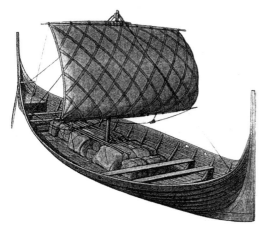

Viking longship.

15th century map of northern waters.

The Vikings were preceded in their exploration of the North Atlantic by Irish monks who had 'island hopped' their way to Iceland via the Scottish Isles and the Faeroes by AD800 in their flimsy wooden-framed, skin-covered *curraghs*. However, although the monks employed expert pilots who used the sun and night stars for orientation, no records exist of maps or compasses, and many days must have been lost drifting uncertain of direction or position.

The Viking instinct for direction is legendary. Even today, elite Scandinavian orienteers are complimented on their uncanny sense of direction. In fact, the Viking navigational instinct, like that of the modern champion orienteer, was solidly based on a body of hard-earned knowledge and the skilful application of known principles. These Nordic explorers were undoubtedly brave and resourceful, but navigation to small inlets in inhospitable coastlines was never a matter of chance for them. They used a mixture of dead reckoning and some form of latitude sailing based on an awareness of the increasing altitude of the noonday sun as they moved southward and vice versa when sailing north. They also used stars, wind direction, tides, changes of sea colour, cloud and ice formations, the presence of birds, fish, whales and from the ninth century a primitive lodestone compass. Their 20-metre single sail longships with steering board were vastly superior to the Irish *curraghs* and in a fair wind were capable of carrying 15 tons at about 150 nautical miles a day. Like the Irish, they were experts in relocating themselves after drifting for days.

The Compass

The Vikings soon became experts in using the compass. Not only was the invention of the compass crucial to the development of navigation but arguably was one of the key inventions in history. It is not clear whether it originated in China, Scandinavia or the

Arab World or whether it developed in all three. We do know that it was in common use in China, the Mediterranean and the North Sea by the tenth century and that it was vital in allowing mariners to move away from landmark-based navigation and towards longer voyages out of sight of land.

Chinese spoon compass with lodestone.

Chinese compass with 24 points.

Chinese spoon compass 100BC.

The Chinese in particular saw the potential of the lodestone to judge direction. From 100BC they were carving lodestone into a spoon shape and putting it on a board or plate to swing on a lacquered or copper base.

The bowl of the spoon pointed north. Later the spoon shape gave way to a fish or a turtle which rotated on a pivot. Twenty-four compass points were set round the rim of the plate.

The first written reference to a compass being used in Europe comes in 1187. It was simply a piece of floating lodestone which lined itself up to point north. The first mention of a compass needle rotating as a fixed pin in a compass bowl was in the thirteenth century. By this time the cardinal points were being shown on maps. In 1338, English ships are recorded as being fitted with sailing needles and dials and by 1375 the first compass rose appeared on a nautical chart. By 1477 north was being put at the top of maps and in 1521 the broad black arrow pointing north was first seen on a Turkish map. Martin Frobisher, an English explorer, noted magnetic variation in 1576 and commented that it increased as one sailed westwards.

The voyages of discovery in the sixteenth and seventeenth centuries, as well as exploration in the eighteenth and nineteenth, depended on the same union of map and compass as the competitive orienteer uses today, but until the work of the Kjellstrom brothers and Gunner Tillander for Silva in the 1930s the compass was a bulky instrument, awkward to use unless fixed to a solid base. Although the first liquid-filled compass was produced in the USA in 1862, it was the development of the liquid-damped Silva compass which really pushed accurate land navigation forward and made possible the evolution of orienteering as a running sport. The Kjellstroms and Tillander placed a compass needle in a housing filled with liquid to

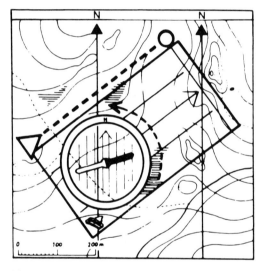

Silva protractor compass.

make it settle quickly. This was fitted to a base plate and protractor with markings around the rim. In this way they combined a magnetic compass, compass card and a protractor all in one precision instrument. With the compass to define accurate direction and improved specialist maps to provide concise ground information, the sport of orienteering could now really advance.

EXPLORING WITH MAP AND COMPASS

This historical survey has jumped on somewhat from the Viking world and ignored navigational developments of the last 500 years like the astrolabe and the invention of printing which allowed the reproduction and circulation of maps. As already noted, the exploration of traders, missionaries and adventurers that opened up new worlds in America, Asia, Africa and the Pacific depended on miracles of navigational improvization and resourcefulness, and it is right that we should remember the link between the adventurers of the past and the modern orienteer. It is time now, however, to turn to the history of orienteering as a specific sport, though we must not forget that deep down in every orienteer there is a David Livingstone trying to escape the constrictions of modern life.

Early Orienteering Competitions

Most modern sports like soccer, hockey or athletics grew from the British public school tradition of *Mens sana in corpore sano*. Orienteering is different. From the start it was a Scandinavian invention, although just as British games have spread throughout the world, so has orienteering. Fifty-one nations are now affiliated to the International Orienteering Federation and no longer do Scandinavians automatically win all World Championship medals. Britain, like other relative newcomers to orienteering, now wins medals and has worked with other orienteering nations to give its own individual flavour to the sport.

The first public – as opposed to military – orienteering competition was held on 31 October 1897 by the Tjalve Sports Club near Oslo, Norway. The course of 19.5km

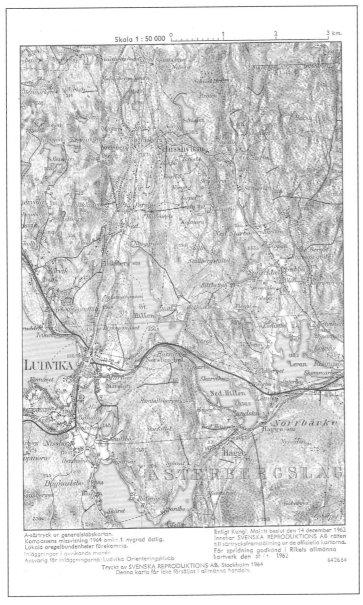

Early Swedish orienteering map.

Stockholm in 1901. Here there were six entries for a 14km course with four control points and the winner took 1 hour, 35 minutes and 34 seconds.

The real birth of modern orienteering racing came in 1918. Major Ernst Killander, President of the Stockholm Amateur Athletic Association, was concerned about the declining interest of youngsters in track and field athletics. He decided to use the natural environment of the Swedish countryside for a new running activity based on his military experience. He devised a cross-country competition where runners not only ran a course but had to pick up and choose their own routes by the application of map and compass. He called it 'Orientation'.

Orienteering in the Killander model demanded stamina, running strength, mental agility, toughness and the application of basic navigational skills in challenging terrain. It proved a great success from the start. The first event had 220 participants, and received a lot of press publicity. The winner over the 12km course with three control points was D.B. Hansson in 1 hour, 25 minutes and 39 seconds. 'Orientation' soon became one of the most popular Nordic

was set in wilderness terrain. There were three control points and the winner, Peder Fossum, took 1 hour, 47 minutes and 7 seconds. A similar competition was organized by the Sundbyberg Club in Sweden outside

SILVA SYSTEM

The world famous Silva system as simple as 1,2,3.

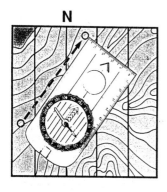

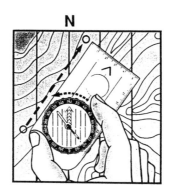

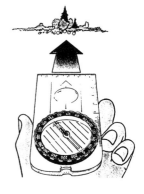

1. Place compass on map with edge along the desired line of travel.

2. Rotate the capsule until the "N" on the compass dial points to Magnetic North on the map. Make sure that the North-South lines are parallel with the map's meridians.

3. Hold the compass level in front of you and turn your body until the red point of the needle is directly over the red part of the North arrow. The direction of travel arrow now points precisely to your destination. Look up, sight on a landmark and walk to it. Repeat this procedure until you reach your destination.

The Silva system for taking bearings.

sports. Ernst Killander went on to lay down all the basic principles of competitive orienteering, including rules, types of courses, choice of control sites, age groups and organization. He is truly recognized as the 'Father of Orienteering'.

In December 1922, the first night orienteering event was held outside Stockholm. In 1922, the first orienteering competition took place in Finland. In the same year, a men's regional championships was held in Sweden and the first ladies event took place in 1925 in Gothenburg. Swedish elite championships started in 1926 and in 1927 a District Relay Championship was organized in Uppsala. Eric Tobe, a member of the winning team, went on to become the first President of the International Orienteering Federation (IOF) when it was set up in 1961.

In the first international competition, Sweden beat Norway in a match held outside Oslo in 1932. By 1934, orienteering had spread to Switzerland, the USSR and Hungary and by the Second World War annual national championships for men and women were well established in Sweden, Norway and Finland. By now, Sweden alone could boast 380,000 active participants.

The maps used by these early orienteers were neither detailed nor accurate. They were black and white – sometimes with blue

Open fell orienteering.

for water features – usually at a scale of 1:100,000 and until the 1950s with hachure lines to indicate height rather than contours. Until the development of the Silva Protractor compass in 1933, compasses were either wooden box types or the conventional 'watch' type. The Silva method was simple to teach and allowed children from as young as six to learn basic map and compass skills without the fear of them getting badly lost. In the post-war years as maps increased in accuracy and opportunities for travel opened up in the west, orienteering spread through Europe, North America, Australia, New Zealand and South-east Asia. This expansion was helped by environmental interest, an urge to find a challenging release from the straightjacket of twentieth century life and the work of orienteering missionaries like Bjorn Kjellstrom and Peo Bengtsson. From 1952 Swedish and Norwegian orienteers have been producing specialist coloured orienteering maps and so many were the new initiatives by the end of the 1950s that the time had clearly come to bring some order and discipline to this energetic – but at times unruly – orienteering adolescent. The many forms that orienteering can take are both its strength and weakness but as a sport it needed clear definitions and guidelines, which only international discussion and co-operation could produce.

The International Scene

The first nucleus for international co-operation was a Nordic Committee for orienteering set up in 1946. In May 1949, the Swedish Orienteering Association held an International Conference in Sandviken in which eleven nations took part. An open international competition held outside Stockholm in 1960 attracted seven nations and the inauguration of the International Orienteering Federation at a meeting in Copenhagen in 1961 was the natural development. The first European Championships for men and women were held at Löten, Norway, in 1962 and from the same time special map committees were set up in Sweden and Norway to regulate mapping styles. International standards were finally agreed in 1965. The first World Championships were held in Finland in 1966.

By this time Britain had enthusiastically adopted this new sport. Because of a shortage of forests, British orienteers imaginative-ly used open fell areas, overgrown industrial sites and town parks to develop the 'Forest Sport'. Britain hosted the World Orienteering Championships in 1976 and will repeat the venture in 1999. Orienteering appears in the English National Curriculum for schools for PE and Geography, illustrating its educational dimension both as a sport and a recreation. Other countries have developed their own variations on the basic formula. France is pioneering Mountain Bike 'O', while in Australia and North America 24-hour 'Rogaines' are very popular.

ORIENTEERING TODAY

In the last 30 years, computer technology, photogrammetrically and computer produced maps and increased personal mobility have encouraged rapid expansion in every aspect of orienteering. The annual Swedish five-day event, first started in 1965 by a group of elite orienteers, now attracts fields of up to 20,000 competitors covering forty age classes. It is mirrored by similar competitions in Europe, Australasia and North America. Standardization of orienteering practice through the IOF and international control symbols means orienteers can use the international language of maps to enjoy competition all over the world. A biennial World Championships, interspersed with the World Cup Series, has seen a dramatic increase in navigational skill and speed at elite levels, just as at the grass roots level many thousands of orienteers compete every weekend in terrain which varies from thick forest to open mountain tops to town parks. National and international courses and conferences develop and spread new coaching expertise and ideas. World Championships now include Juniors, Veterans and Schools,

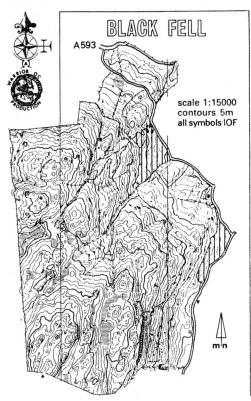

British map of open fell area.

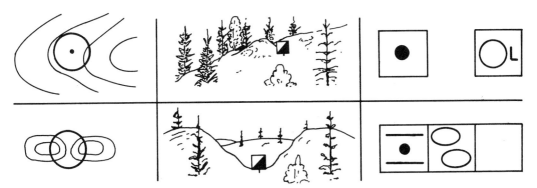

IOF pictograph control symbols.

Finish from the Swedish annual 5 day event.

while orienteering disciplines cover the Classic Long Distance, Cross Country Event, Short Distance, Races, Relays and Mass Start Loops. Ski Orienteering is likely to achieve Olympic status by the turn of the century, while foot orienteering is not far behind. Trail 'O' for the disabled also has its championships and various disciplines. Mountain Bike 'O' is taking off in a big way and is now affiliated to the IOF as an important new discipline. Not only do computers produce instant results for these many thousands of competitors, but computer mapping programmes since 1987 have made possible the production and updating of coloured maps at all scales from 1:5,000 to 1:15,000 for all levels of competition and training. New 'smart card' punching, using a hand-held mini-computer, will soon allow every competitor to record instant results and split times. Orienteering has certainly outgrown its humble Scandinavian beginnings.

LOOKING AHEAD

It is time now to pull the strands of this historical summary together and to examine ways in which coaching can enhance the experiences which every orienteer seeks from this fascinating sport. Every country now faces new pressures from conservationists and landowners in negotiating access for ori-

enteering, and it is easy to be depressed by these negative issues rather than concentrating on new opportunities which modern technology can open up for the sport. Just as improved maps and compasses opened up new worlds to the early navigators and explorers, so up-to-date computerized maps, 'smart cards', electronic tracking displays and wider international travel will widen the horizons for orienteers and open up its secrets to the media. Whatever new paths the sport takes, we must never lose sight of its capacity to tap the explorer in all of us. In an increasingly constrictive world orienteering offers adventure and challenge on the doorstep and opportunities for shared experience in the natural world. The pages which follow describe ways in which navigational skills can be improved and developed so that the experiences become deeper and more satisfying. Like the early pioneers of the North American West, every orienteer knows that in finding your way 'you often find yourself'.

2 Orienteering Equipment

PETER PALMER

Orienteering is essentially a very simple sport. Its arenas are forests or areas of open country. Turning points on a course are indicated by orange and white control markers each with a coded punch to clip a hand-held control card. The competitors use map and compass to navigate from start to finish in the quickest time commensurate with experience, skill and level of physical fitness.

The essentials for pleasurable orienteering have changed little over the years. Primarily they are well designed courses appropriate to the capabilities of the participants planned on interesting terrain, a good map, accurately placed control markers, and organization which is competent to set off and finish competitors in such a way as to record times and finishing positions. Technology has replaced self-inking rubber stamps at control points with pin punches and is now in the process of introducing a microchip 'smart card' which will not only record control

Control marker on trestle.

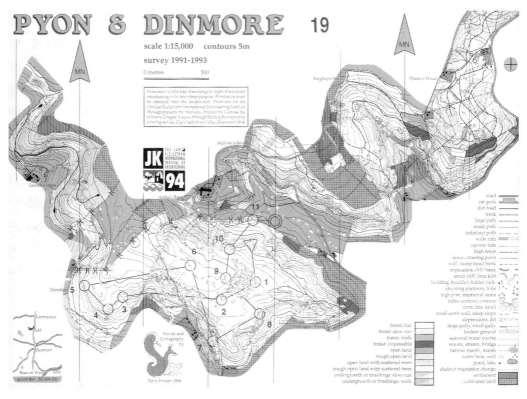

Orienteering map with overprinted course.

visits but leg split times and an instant time at the finish. Computer programmes now cover map drawing, start allocations, control descriptions, timing and results production. Without modern technology, events like the Swedish Five Days with thousands of participants and a final day with chasing start would be impossible to organize. But despite this, the basic spirit of the sport remains unchanged – orienteering offers a navigational challenge in a wilderness environment and the equipment merely provides a means to an end. The section which follows describes personal and event impedimenta within this broad perspective.

NAVIGATIONAL EQUIPMENT

The Map

The orienteering map, whether the competition five colour version or a simple black and white school site map, is unquestionably the most important item of equipment for competitors at every level. Specially drawn and printed to national and international norms, it seeks to depict the terrain as the orienteer sees it. Ground detail is generalized to fit scale and type of event, although orienteering maps show much more ground detail than conventional maps. A 1:2,000 school site map prepared for educational activities, showing details like individual trees or

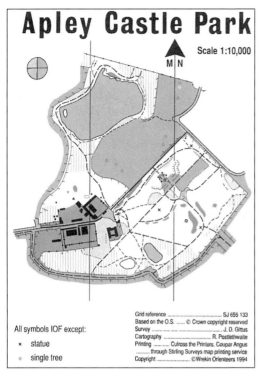

Apley Castle Park

Scale 1:10,000

M N

All symbols IOF except:

x statue

o single tree

Grid reference .... SJ 655 133
Based on the O.S. ...... © Crown copyright reserved
Survey .... J. D. Gittus
Cartography .... R. Postlethwaite
Printing .... Culross the Printers, Coupar Angus
.... through Stirling Surveys map printing service
Copyright .... ©Wrekin Orienteers 1994

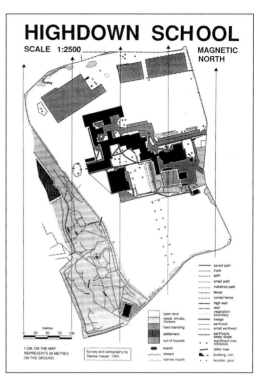

HIGHDOWN SCHOOL

SCALE 1:2500

MAGNETIC
NORTH

metres
0 25 50 75 100

1 CM. ON THE MAP
REPRESENTS 25 METRES
ON THE GROUND.

Survey and cartography by
Denise Harper, 1995.

open land

wood, shrubs,
thickets

hard standing

settlement

out of bounds

marsh

stream

narrow marsh

paved path
track
path
small path
indistinct path
fence
ruined fence
high wall
wall
vegetation
boundary
hedge
earthwall
small earthwall
earthbank,
steep slope
significant tree,
root/stock
fallen tree
building, ruin
boulder, post

Park orienteering map.

Simple school map.

flower beds, would not be appropriate to a 1:15,000 competition map. The relationship between buildings, land forms or other features will, however, be as accurate as the surveyor can make them on both maps. Although there are many professional orienteering mapping companies many maps are still surveyed and drawn by orienteers themselves. Photogrammetry or an air survey base map will provide one aspect of reality, but the imaginative orienteering mapper has to balance clarity against excessive detail to use 'help contours' to accentuate ground shape and sometimes to use 'mappers' licence' to exaggerate a path bend. The final map should certainly look good but above all it should be easy to read and sufficiently accurate at every level of competition to make navigation and control finding tests of

skill rather than luck. The legend for orienteering maps differs from conventional maps. Open forest is white, clearings and fields yellow and graduations of runnability are indicated by colour shades of green to white, for example impenetrable areas of thick forest are dark green to indicate Fight while white means Good Runnability. The competitor's individual course is printed on to the map or copied by the orienteer with a red pen from a master map before the start. The map is the orienteer's basic tool. Protected by its clear plastic envelope carefully folded to assist orientation and thumbing and aligned with compass or balanced against bearings, it steers the orienteer leg by leg round the course. If orienteering is the map and compass sport, then it is the map which has priority. Modern computer

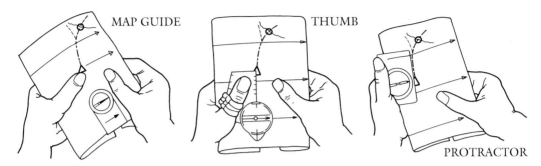

Different types of compass.

programmes for drawing maps like OCAD (Orienteering Computer Aided Diagrams) have revolutionized the production of maps as well as making updating much easier. Computer mapping allied to colour photo-copying allows the smallest of competitions to provide colour maps with or without an overprinted course.

The Compass

The compass often gets a 'bad press' from teachers and coaches. With so many paths and tracks in man-made forests, the compass is not always strictly necessary for what is often very basic handrail navigation. Used properly, however, the modern fast-settling protractor compass, whether used for setting the map, bearings or simply direction back-up, is a vital navigational tool which it is folly to ignore or do without. Put simply, the compass supplies the direction or line of travel along which the competitor reads the map. It should be cleaned, oiled and checked regularly for bubbles or cracks, kept away from excessive heat or cold and handled as gently as possible in competitive and non-competitive situations. Compasses are supplied with a looped cord and should be carried comfortably in the hand with loop around the wrist to avoid dropping. The size of the hand may determine the size of the

compass. Some compasses have built-in magnifiers to show up map detail. The type of compass used will depend on navigational style and cost. Both the thumb compass and the conventional protractor compass are equally effective when used properly. The chapter on techniques (Chapter 3) will deal with compass skills and the most effective ways of teaching and developing them.

Distance Scales

These indicate distance for given scales of maps or the number of double paces a competitor uses to cover a given distance (usually per 100m). They can take the form of a plastic slide clipped to the leading edge of the compass or a stick-on strip. Distance judgement is often linked with direction in a navigational technique called Compass and Pacing. This is dealt with in Chapter 3.

Control Description Sheets

These are provided for every level of competition and include start/finish designations, a list of descriptions for each control point including the control marker code, and the total length and height gain for the relevant course in question. The sheet is either fixed to the map beside the course or provided separately, and occasionally the descriptions

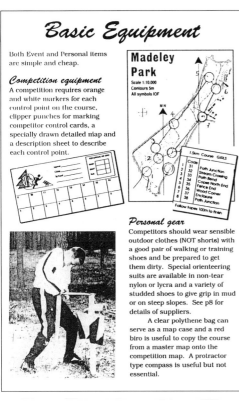

Basic Equipment

Both Event and Personal items are simple and cheap.

Competition equipment
A competition requires orange and white markers for each control point on the course, clipper punches for marking competitor control cards, a specially drawn detailed map and a description sheet to describe each control point.

Madeley Park
Scale 1:10,000
Contours 5m
All symbols IOF

Personal gear
Competitors should wear sensible outdoor clothes (NOT shorts) with a good pair of walking or training shoes and be prepared to get them dirty. Special orienteering suits are available in non-tear nylon or lycra and a variety of studded shoes to give grip in mud or on steep slopes. See p8 for details of suppliers.

A clear polythene bag can serve as a map case and a red biro is useful to copy the course from a master map onto the competition map. A protractor type compass is useful but not essential.

Control card and description sheet in words.

proof that each control on a course has been visited. The competitor uses a punch by the control marker to clip a unique pin-prick code in each numbered box on the card. The punch may be flat on a small trestle or hang by the marker. This is checked at the finish and the elapsed time calculated for results purposes. For most events a tear-off stub which repeats competitor details is handed in at the start. This can then be used at the finish to check that the competitor has left the forest and to record the result on a display. A golden rule for orienteers is that all must report to the finish whether they complete the course or not. Competitors can place the card in the map envelope, or pin it to their clothing during the competition, or more commonly put it in a hand-held plastic case. With electronic punching a hand-held programmed flat disc is held down with the help of a small spike at each control trestle to record the time. Every leg time can be printed out afterwards as well as the finish time are printed on the control card squares, for example in School or Beginners events. Descriptions follow an internationally agreed format. They can be written or put in IOF pictograph form, which is especially useful for international competitions where language can be a barrier to comprehension.

Control Cards

These are used to record name, class and start and finish times as well as

Night orienteers need powerful headlamps.

Specialist Equipment

Ski orienteers, mountain bike orienteers and some disabled competitors have difficulty in competing while holding the map in the hand. For all three, variations on a 'music stand' can be used to provide a rigid map holder. In the case of Ski orienteers it can be fixed to a chest harness, or bolted onto a convenient part of the machine frames of mountain bikes or wheelchairs.

Night orienteers will need a headlamp powered by a battery carried in a back or waist harness. Halogen versions can give powerful illumination but batteries have to be recharged regularly. A hand-held torch is not very satisfactory when trying to use map and compass together.

British guidelines insist that a whistle must be carried for safety purposes in all events except those on benign areas like school sites or town parks. A sports watch which records leg split times at the press of a button is a useful coaching and competitive feedback device.

Orienteer in full kit.

Clothing

Like all sports, orienteering has a distinctive specialist kit – a loose nylon suit (sometimes a nylon top with lycra tights) and stout studded running shoes or 'spikes'. Because orienteering takes place at different times of year and in a variety of climates and terrain types, the kit has to be adapted to competitive conditions. In extreme cold, thermal underwear plus wind or waterproof anorak may be advisable or even mandatory, while even British winters often require a woollen hat and gloves. A peaked cap protects spectacles from rain. In high temperatures clothing can be cut to a minimum of short-sleeved top and appropriate leg cover. Full body cover is the norm to prevent the spread of infections through cuts and scratches from rough undergrowth. In some countries, the wearing of spiked shoes is forbidden in environmentally fragile areas. Clothing is also influenced by the scale and type of event. For a small school competition, competitors may well wear a tracksuit (with or without anorak) and training shoes or even PE kit for a summer event. Even at this level, however, attention has to be paid to extremes of temperature, to which children are very vulnerable. Jeans can act like a cold compress in wet conditions and hypothermia is no respecter of seasons or venues. Less experienced competitors also spend more time standing still and will need more clothing than a more experienced running orienteer. Like course difficulty, clothing has to be matched to competitor experi-

Small children need warm clothes on cold days.

Competitor 'punching' at control.

ence – both tread a delicate line between enjoyment and discomfort.

Competition Equipment

Control Markers

Control sites are usually marked by a 30cm square orange and white three-sided marker kite, indicated by a circle on the map course. The marker is hung on a cane or trestle at a precise point given by the control description, such as Knoll, North Side. For beginners, young children or on limited or exposed sites the marker size can be reduced to 15cm square or even 7cm (for example, for classroom orienteering). Sometimes tapes tied to a clothes peg or punch will be sufficient for a fun activity or training exercise. The important principle for control hanging is to ensure that the exercise relies on skill rather than luck – the size and type of marker should reflect this.

Needle punches

These are the most widely used method of confirming a visit to a control point, although for beginners a pencil or crayon can be sufficient to record the control code on a control card. As technology advances, the smart card now being piloted at elite events may well spread to all regular orienteering competitions as costs reduce and efficiency increases. A 'swipe card' is already familiar on ski slopes. The current needle punch leaves a pinpoint pattern in each control square which can be verified against a master card for the course before the

competitor's time and performance are recorded.

This equipment section does not include work cards, analysis sheets, training logs and other coaching equipment referred to later in this book. Neither does it cover start and finish banners, tape for starts and finish, clocks, results, gantries, club and officials tents, 'portaloos', showers and so on. All the items referred to are available from suppliers listed in the Resource Appendix, from whom current price lists are readily available.

Competitor approaching control.

3(i) Basic Techniques

PETER PALMER

INTRODUCTION

In every sport success requires mastery of a progressive series of skills and techniques. Sometimes these are refined and adapted as the competitor's proficiency increases. The downhill skier's turns, for instance, evolve from stem to parallel as slopes get steeper and speed quicker. Orienteering is no different. Starting with orientated map, path running and pacing for distance the orienteer's 'handrails' change from tracks to ridges and valleys, and distance judgement no longer demands step counting as speed, confidence and technical competence increase.

There is nothing complicated about all this. Orienteering has a straightforward structure and has developed its own navigational systems which have been applied successfully to other outdoor activities. However, map and compass skills have to be applied competently and confidently and levels of physical fitness have to sustain technique. On novice courses, the planner decides route choice for the competitor and line features act as handrails between control points but as he or she moves up the competitive ladder route choices of increasing complexity have to be calculated on the basis of personal strengths and weaknesses. For the fast, fit runner, the best route may be round a path system. For less fit but competent map readers it might be 'straight' with careful reading of the map detail as the route unfolds. For the competitive 'up and go' orienteer it might be a case of running hard for a given distance and then relocating on map and detail near the control. Whatever the personal strategy the basic skills are the same. They are detailed in the Step System illustration. In this chapter we will be analysing them in detail and suggesting ways to learn and develop them. What also has to be stressed right from the start is that there is no way of bypassing them. Young children may start at ground level and move up the steps by age, a fit 30 year old with map-reading experience may start with a red course at levels 2 and 3, while a

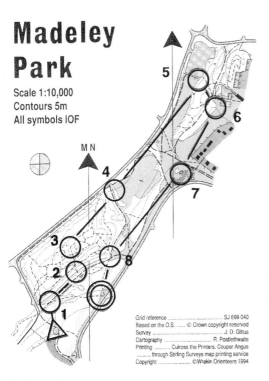

Madeley Park

Scale 1:10,000
Contours 5m
All symbols IOF

M N

Grid reference .... SJ 699 040
Based on the O.S. .... © Crown copyright reserved
Survey .... J. D. Gittus
Cartography .... R. Postlethwaite
Printing .... Culross the Printers, Coupar Angus
.... through Stirling Surveys map printing service
Copyright .... ©Wrekin Orienteers 1994

Beginners' course.

The Step System   STEP

At each level, the recommended sequence of development is:

1. Mastering the individual steps
2. Learning to select and apply the correct technique when just one technique when just one technique is required
3. Learning to select and apply the correct techniques when more than one technique is required
4. Adjusting speed to the difficulty of the orienteering
5. Developing relocation techniques appropriate to the skills level.

Level	Step	Skills	Techniques introduced	Colour	Age class
5+	O	Longer distances from and/or indistinct attack points & catching features		Blue	17+L
5	N	Long legs (1 km +)		Brown	
	M	Using complex contours; generalising contour detail		Green	15A, 17+S
	L	Using simple contour shapes for most/all of leg			
4	K	Using simple contour shapes over short distances on their own or with other information for longer distances	Reading contours	Light green	
	J	Fine orienteering on short legs	Pacing		13A, 15B
	I	Rough orienteering on longer legs (0.6 – 1 km) against catching features	Bearings, collecting features		
3	H	Making simple route choices	Route choice	Red	
	G	Simplification of legs with several decision points	Attack points, absolute distance judgement (eg "100m along")	Orange	11A, 13B
	F	Orienteering over short distances against catching features	Compass directions		
	E	Cutting corners	Aiming off		
2	D	Reading objects alongside line features. Controls just off line features. (Feature and kite clearly visible)	Catching features, spatial distance judgement (eg "halfway")	Yellow	10A, 11B
	C	Linking line features	Check points		
1	B	Following a single line feature	Thumbing, handrails	White	10B
	A	Orientation by compass & terrain. Map colours, common symbols			
Ground level		Understanding the map; getting used to being in the woods		String etc	

Printed 21 February 1997

The Step System.

veteran hill-walker may find more challenge in starting at level 4 with a light green course. All of these, however, are building up techniques on familiar skills and progressing one step at a time. None are jumping in at the deep end and hoping that they will survive. All are using skills on competitive courses for which the navigational challenge extends their grasp but does not exceed it.

In discussing the improvement of personal performance we will be following the Step System model as illustrated. *Skills* are defined as special abilities which can be acquired in practical ways and improved by training. *Techniques* are the selection or integration of skills when tackling a particular task. *Application* refers to strategies adopted to solve particular navigational problems.

At each level the recommended sequence of development is as follows:

(1) Mastery step by step of individual skills and techniques.
(2) Learning to apply skills and techniques selectively as required.
(3) Developing relocation techniques appropriate to each skills level.
(4) Adjusting speed to the difficulty of navigation.

Current age classes and competition technical levels in columns two and three of the Step Diagram are matched to the colour-coded system and the step progression so that the vital relationship between level of skill and competitive course can be clearly seen and understood. At every level and for

Colour	Length	Technical	Control Sites	Type of leg	Time	Age	Step
String	0.8k	Easy	On the line		10	3+	1
White	1-1.5k	Very Easy	Major line features and junctions	Line features minimal route choice	20	6-12	1
Yellow	1-2.5k	Easy	Line features and very easy adjacent features	Line features easy route choice, no compass	30	8+	2
Orange	2-3.5k	Medium	Minor Line + easy point features	Route choice, collecting features near control	45	10+	3
Red	4-5.6k	Medium			50		3
Green		Hard	Small point plus contour features	Fine compass and contours – more physical	50		4
Blue	4.5-6.5k	Hard			60		4+
Brown	6.5+K	Hard			75		4+

Colour-coded system.

every age competition experience must match skill levels. Just as a tennis player chooses who will provide a good game so the orienteer has to choose the right level of course for a satisfying run. In orienteering as no other sport overstretching of technique on a course which is too long or too difficult tilts a challenging experience from bliss to misery in a most dramatic way. Three hours lost in a wet, dark forest is a trauma which often finishes off any further interest in the sport, especially for children brought up on tales like 'Little Red Riding Hood' or 'Babes in the Wood'.

Finally in this introduction we must comment on the arbitrary distinction we make between basic and advanced techniques. To quote Steven Hale 'Basic techniques become

'Basic' becomes 'advanced' under extreme stress. (Steve Hale shows why!)

advanced techniques in extreme terrain or under extreme stress.' Perhaps an analogy with downhill skiing can best illustrate the point. Most orienteers are rather like recreational skiers. They see orienteering as competitive navigation and they test themselves against each other on courses planned to given criteria of physical and technical difficulty – just like the skier on colour-coded pistes with friends. The racing skier, like the racing orienteer, is somewhat different. They are testing themselves and their technique and fitness to the utmost limits, with the one objective of getting from A to B as fast as possible even if it means taking risks and 'playing the percentages'. Steve Hale is one of the world's supreme exponents in getting the most from body, mind and experience on the important occasion. Chapter 3(ii) on advanced techniques deals with this area in elite terms and covers relay and night orienteering as well as the individual classic and short distance disciplines.

There is, however, some 'overlap' between basic and advanced techniques. While preparation for events, organization of equipment and psychology are vital areas for elite orienteers, the average club orienteer also needs systems for organizing map, compass, control card and descriptions. Similarly, he or she has to apply basic technique to different terrains and maps and to analyze performance so as to devise training strategies for improvement. Both the club and international orienteer have to build up concentration drills so as to keep out distractions in the forest. Psychology, preparation and training programmes, physical fitness, damage limitation in identifying high-risk controls and self-analysis will be dealt with in separate chapters, but this does not mean that the grassroots orienteer should not try to learn from the 'stars' of the sport. More skiers have been inspired to take up the sport by watching the stars on television's *Ski Sunday* than by reading coaching manuals. The Step System offers a ladder of opportunity for every orienteer to fulfil their potential within the sport, with or without coaching help, and every orienteer should read and take what they will from the advanced sections on psychology, physical training and advanced techniques. Basic and advanced represent different sections of one continuum. They are not exclusive.

IMPROVING SKILLS

We'll now look at basic orienteering techniques in more detail and suggest some training exercises and tips to develop and reinforce them. To improve at orienteering requires physical effort. Practice makes perfect. It must also be remembered throughout this section that because so much orienteering technique is applied in the forest away from coaching eyes, improvement often comes about through self-analysis and self-help. Indeed, one school of thought believes that the main responsibility of the orienteering coach is eventually to make him or herself redundant. Even if this extreme view is rejected, it remains true that effective orienteering coaching relies on close interaction between coach and athlete to elicit feedback which is not readily observable. On the basis of this, a creative dialogue can help the individual to analyze and understand personal strengths and weaknesses upon which strategies for improvement can be built. Although many of the activities described here assume club or squad training structures, there is nothing to stop the individual orienteer taking them and adapting them to their own circumstances. Nor do most of the exercises depend on access to grade one terrain. Most Scandinavian and

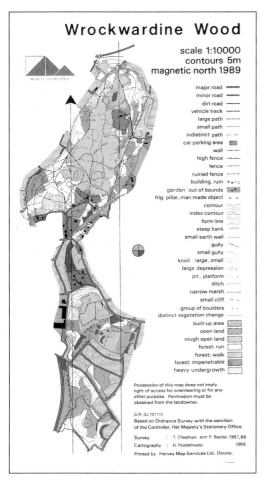

Detailed map of urban mini area.

North American forests can be snowbound for a third of the year and Britain with its normally temperate climate and detailed maps of mini areas offers abundant training opportunities for the motivated imaginative competitor. We will now start at ground level and set off up the 'staircase'.

Map Literacy

Orienteering is *the* map reading sport and from ground level to the top, all skills and

techniques rely on increasing sophistication in reading maps and extracting navigational information from them. The more familiarity that novices can acquire with maps, the better. Confidence in handling legends, scales and map interpretation will grow as practice is gained on map walks with teacher and or coach, on loop handrail courses in familiar environments and by simple mapping of rooms or sites.

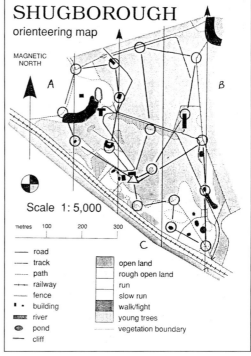

Handrail loop courses on outdoor centre site.

The key skill in all this activity is map orientation with the thumb indicating current correct position on map and ground. Whenever the orienteer stops or changes direction the teacher or coach should check that the map is orientated with the thumb in the correct position. If compasses are available for every individual in a group,

THE BASIC SYSTEM

FIG 3 (7)

All beginners Activity and Competition Programmes should be seen in the context of the following progression for teaching orienteering skills.

LEVEL 1 Using an [orientated] set map to follow line features on the map and ground

a) The map should be **folded** into a comfortable size and then **lined up** to the ground using either a compass or ground features.

b) Then navigate straight ahead where the course takes you **keeping your body behind the map** and turning where necessary to keep it aligned to the ground. If a compass is being used, keep the North [red end of the compass needle] pointing to North on the map and **keep map and compass together**.

• Use paths, buildings, fences and other 'lines' as **handrails** to take you around the course.

• Hold the map with your **thumb** pointing to your position and move it as you travel.

• Keep ahead of yourself. **Think ahead** and always know what should come next.

SETTING THE MAP WITH THE COMPASS

like this............

this............

or this............

SETTING THE MAP WITH THE GROUND

LEVEL 2 Planning 'legs' between control points which include on path and off path navigation

a) Plan fast handrail sections to an obvious **attack point** from which to navigate carefully towards the control point.

b) Use **check points** to keep on line.

c) Employ accurate compass strategies like **aiming off** to one side when aiming for a point on a line feature.

d) Identify **obvious features** like hills or valleys to check direction.

The basic system for teaching skills.

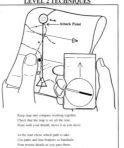

LEVEL 2 TECHNIQUES

Attack Point

Keep map and compass working together.
Check that the map is set all the time.
Point with your thumb, move it as you move.

At the start chose which path to take.
Use paths and line-features as handrails.
Note terrain details as you pass them.
Slow down at the *attack-point* at the wall bend.

....I'm at the boulder......
....I'll pass a building on my left.....
.....a fence on my right.....
...then I'll turn right at the junction.

LEVEL 3 Navigating by the Shape of the Ground – Contour Orienteering

a) Identify and use contour features like valleys and ridges as **handrail lines** to follow towards controls.

b) Link together ground features like knolls and marshes as **checkpoints** to keep on route

c) Use **accurate compass** and **distance judgement** as back up techniques to map reading

d) Use **catching** or **collecting features** beyond or beside your route to contain mistakes or relocate when unsure of position

Try to form a **mental 3D picture** of the control area to help locate the control marker precisely – where you expect it

Look at the ground shape and cut corners to save time.

From the path bend follow the gap between the hills,
then head down the reentrant.
Follow the edges of the marshes as a handrail into No. 4.
The fence will serve as a *collecting feature*
should you over-shoot the control.

orientation is most easily done from the start with a simple compass like the Silva DNS or Clip-on Compass Guide. The orienteer then only has to bother about keeping the movable needle parallel to the magnetic lines and to concentrate on reading the map along the correct direction The main message is to turn yourself and the map around rather than twiddling with the compass bezel. Other skills can then be built on this technique using either a conventional protractor compass or a thumb compass (*see* illustration). The map can be set to ground without a compass by relating it to paths and buildings and other map/ground information. This can be more difficult to establish and reinforce than the compass method, but is equally valid in developing map skills.

Useful Exercises

Map walks and short loops have already been suggested. If the opportunity exists it can be useful to extend the walks into a local park or wood to introduce newcomers to a forest environment and build up confidence. For children, string courses in which they follow a marked route and indicate the position of markers on their map or simple running string courses in which they simply 'punch' as they reach controls can also build up terrain familiarity. Some teachers also like to use 'slaloms', running games and 'hide and seek' to build up confidence and running skills in forested terrain.

Indoor activities should also be included if there is access to a gymnasium or hall. Matching card symbol games, map shuttle

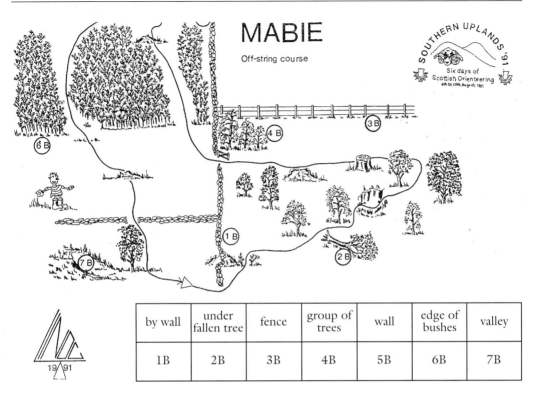

MABIE

Off-string course

SOUTHERN UPLANDS '91
Six days of
Scottish Orienteering
4th to 10th August 1991

	by wall	under fallen tree	fence	group of trees	wall	edge of bushes	valley
	1B	2B	3B	4B	5B	6B	7B

Childrens' string course.

Forest slaloms.

relays and team competitions transforming map information from maps at one side of a room to another can be popular with all ages whether in school or with a club. Board games like orienteering bingo in which players have to match 'called' map sections to those on the card, or snakes and ladders in which they throw dice to complete a course can also reinforce familiarity with maps as well as providing entertainment.

Handrails

The other key foundation skill is the ability to identify and use linear features on a map as handrails between control points. Handrail navigation provides a continuous thread from Levels 1 to 3 and in more sophisticated forms runs through all levels from bottom to top. At Levels 1 and 2, however, handrails mean primarily paths, tracks, fences and buildings. Competitive success on white, yellow and orange courses relies almost wholly on using this type of handrail effectively.

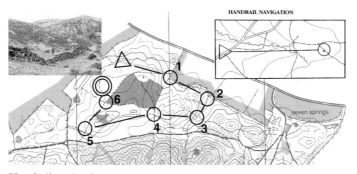

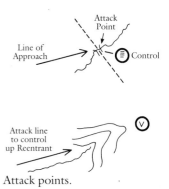

Handrail navigation.

Attack points.

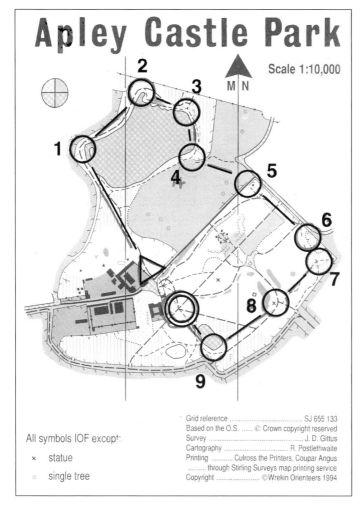

White course.

All symbols IOF except:

× statue

○ single tree

Grid reference .... SJ 655 133
Based on the O.S. ...... © Crown copyright reserved
Survey .... J. D. Gittus
Cartography .... R. Postlethwaite
Printing .... Culross the Printers, Coupar Angus
.... through Stirling Surveys map printing service
Copyright .... ©Wrekin Orienteers 1994

Level 1 courses are white in the colour-coded system. There is no route choice: controls are placed at every decision point and competitors have to follow single line features – primarily paths. Level 2 courses are yellow and can provide controls just off line features which require some basic distance judgement to know when to leave the line. Handrails may now also include features like fences, banks and ditches. Level 3 courses are orange (short) or red (long) and can offer route choice between linear features, as well as a variety of decision points and allowance for corner-cutting between paths. The technique of choosing an obvious attack point on a line feature near the control introduces another important strategy. A more sophisticated use of compass involving bearings is required in using *aiming off techniques* to hit controls on line features. Each new skill and technique develops and builds on those mastered at previous stages.

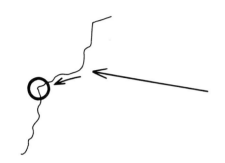

Aiming off.

These first eight steps take the novice up three levels and cover all the foundation techniques. Mastery of these will enable competitors to cope confidently with all beginner courses as well as providing valuable life skills for map reading on walks in the open countryside. Most school pupils taught orienteering on site will not progress beyond this basic level. To go further they will normally have to join a specialist orienteering club or make a conscious effort to improve their performance through self-help or a regional squad system.

Useful Exercises

A variety of handrail exercises can be used within the basic training systems of Star, Loop and Direct courses. Once pace-counting has been taught to enable the orienteer to judge distance by estimating the number of double steps per hundred metres this technique too can be reinforced within handrail training activities.

(a) *The Star System* involves participants visiting a number of control points in turn which radiate out from a central coach or teacher like the spokes of a wheel. Each leg can be divided to test a particular skill, for example a variety of line features to be followed or controls just off lines to test distance judgement. By tackling each leg in turn and returning to the centre, the progress of participants can be monitored and regulated according to competence and speed. No one need get badly lost.

(b) *Loops* are a useful way of splitting up numbers and discouraging following. They can be clover-leaf style or overlapping and test handrail distance or simple attack point techniques in the same way as the Star System.

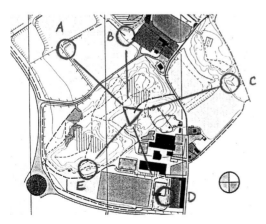

Star exercise.

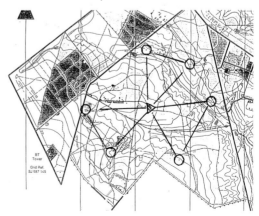

Clover leaf loops.

(c) The Direct System relies on plentiful manpower. Controls on a handrail course are manned so that participants can be reassured and guided on strategies for each leg. In this way, the exercise can be controlled by splitting up following groups and giving help where

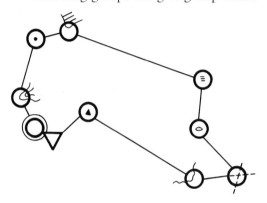

Compass/pacing course on blank sheet of paper.

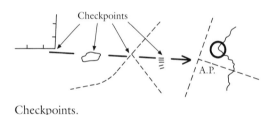

Checkpoints.

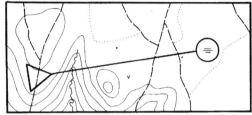

Fence collecting feature upon which to relocate if control is missed

Path or stream can act as collecting features if competitor goes off line

Collecting and catching features.

skills are deficient. Useful distance judgement exercises can be following a marked route and estimating distance between controls on it, or linking distance and compass on a school field or park area by giving a course on a blank sheet of paper with no map information.

Simplification

How can this leg be simplified?

Although Level 4 appears to introduce the difficult new technique of weighing up the difficulty of a leg and breaking it down into manageable sections, it is only continuing a practice started at Level 3 with the identification of attack points. Nevertheless, the step from Level 3 to Level 4 is a big one. Course legs which demand careful (fine) navigation have to be split up into Easy sections and Difficult ones (usually near to controls). For the first time the orienteer is asked to be selective in the information he or she takes from the map and to apply it as part of co-ordinated strategies. Route choice will now be dictated by the best route into the control, that is from the side with the best attack point or 'line approach'. Check points will be identified along the route to confirm progress and collecting features noted to either side which can contain any deviation. Catching features beyond the control will be used if there is an overshoot. For the first time, obvious contour features like hills, valleys and spurs will be used to balance against other map and ground information in deciding and executing route choices. It is at this stage, too, that relocation techniques are taught so that being unsure of position never deteriorates into getting lost. Noting sure points on a route and checking off features on map and ground when unsure fit very easily into this whole process of simplification, identification and verification at Level 4. This is the transition stage from novice to performance orienteering and Level 5 and beyond merely develop the concepts acquired at this level.

Useful Exercises

There are many ingenious and interesting activities which can be used to teach and practise the techniques required for simplification. Many of these slot nicely into squad or weekend training programmes and can give competitive satisfaction and pleasure in their own right for all ages and levels of experience.

(a) *Traffic Light Exercises* mark sections of each leg on a course green, orange or red according to the degree of care and skill required.

(b) *Attack Point/Check Point Courses* indicate with a cross significant features to

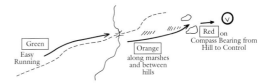

Traffic light exercises.

note on each leg of a course, and/or control markers can be replaced at relevant points.

(c) *Multi-Purpose Technique Courses* can be planned with great variety of leg length and with legs designed to present different simplification problems.

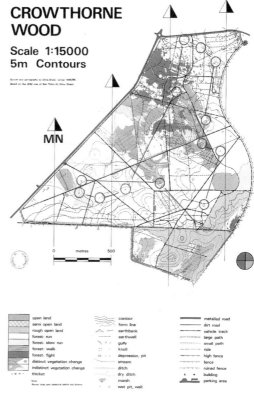

CROWTHORNE WOOD

Scale 1:15000
5m Contours

Multi purpose course.

(d) *Route Choice* competitions can be presented to groups of two or three in

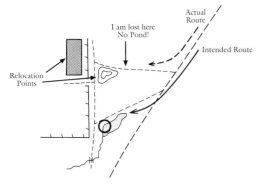

Relocation.

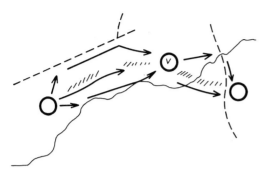

Route choice.

which alternative routes are suggested between controls that can be timed and assessed afterwards.

(e) *Reinforcement of Compass Skills* is also important at this stage. Courses can be designed to run diagonals between path systems, or as compass and pacing courses on blank sheets of paper. Aiming off exercises and corner-cutting courses build up confidence as well as providing fun. Sometimes they can be given a relay or team dimension, such as score events in which competitors have to find as many of a scatter of controls as possible within a given time limit with points gained for each control and a penalty for being late.

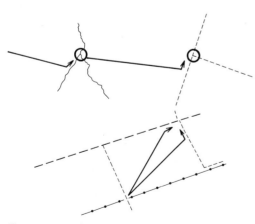

Compass exercise.

(f) *Corridor and Window Exercises* can combine accurate compass work with check point and direct line techniques.

Contour Techniques

Contour Orienteering is the supreme form of navigation. Man-made features like paths or plantations may change or disappear, but the shape of the ground rarely does. The orienteer who runs with an image of the ground shape in their mind extracted from the map will not be put off by unexpected felling or faded paths. Their handrails will be ridges, valleys or the lines of crags, check points will be knolls or spurs and the attack line into a control may be a linear re-entrant or ridge.

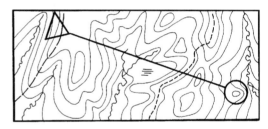

Contours and ground shapes.

Sophisticated contour navigation is built on the handrail and simplification techniques mastered at Levels 1 to 4 but it also relies on the acquisition of other techniques.

Contour Visualization

Contour visualization involves forming a three-dimensional mental image from contour shapes on the map and using this for navigation. This involves not only route information but control identification. The orienteer has a detailed picture of the area around the control feature and the position occupied by the control marker. This is used to navigate accurately to the control point using other ground information to confirm approach. In both 'coarse' and 'fine' orienteering terms this is an advanced technique to which every orienteer should aspire, although it does require a mental faculty which some orienteers never manage to acquire and it demands constant practice. It also needs continual assessment of difficulty on a leg and identification of high-risk controls so that speed can be adjusted accordingly. These skills are dealt with more fully in the chapter on advanced techniques, but they also have a relevance at the basic level.

Map to Ground and Ground to Map Technique

This is implicit in much of what has already been said. The orienteer decides on a route consistent with information extracted from the map and then uses map and compass skills to execute it. This map to ground technique is reinforced by ground information en route which by being related to the map can confirm that the leg is being executed successfully. It is important that the orienteer maintains the navigational initiative by making decisions based on the map and is not dictated to by what crops up on the ground. Although 'ground to map' can be very useful in relay orienteering or running fast on compass with a group, it is much more risky than map to ground, in which the orienteer plans ahead and maintains the initiative rather than waiting for things to happen. All contour navigation involves seeing the skeleton of the terrain beneath other map details such as path systems and vegetation. In a sense, 'contour orienteers' are using another simplification technique by rejecting all map information except that which leads them to the control and confirms their accuracy. At the basic level the

contour information is simple – large hills and valleys. At advanced levels the contour picture can be much more detailed.

Contour Exercises

Many of Britain's forests are man-made and most of its terrain has extensive path networks which simplify navigation. An important training device for accentuating ground shape navigation and providing contour techniques is the *contour-only map*. This is easy to provide by asking the printer to run off the required number of maps from the 'brown printing plate' which shows just the contour lines and ground shape information like depressions or knolls. Failing this, map sections can be redrawn by the orienteer to show ground shape detail only. Contour-only maps can be used for a variety of exercises:

(*a*) Fine 'O' control picking with each control providing the attack point for the next and careful detailed map reading throughout.

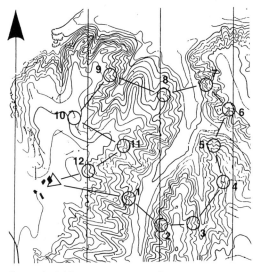

Control picking on contour-only map.

(b) Courses interspersing long legs with two or three short fine 'O' legs to give practice in applying ground interpretation to leg length and reinforcing speed control.

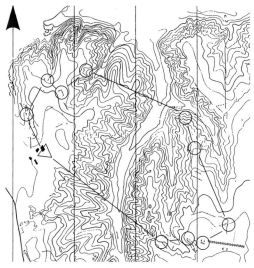

Long and short legs on control-only maps.

(c) A contour line with unmarked controls on the line to be positioned on the map with an accurate cross.

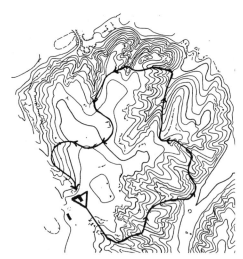

Contour line.

(d) Norwegian style map memory exercises can improve visualization either on complete map sections or contour-only maps depending on experience and the objectives of the exercises.

Mapping contour detail.

(e) The mapping of small map sections in which contour detail has to be added to generalized contour shape is a very useful training exercise which needs little preparation.

Applications of Techniques

Applications primarily involve selection of the correct techniques for the right time and occasion, refinement of relocation strategies and speed adjustment to difficulty of navigation. These are dealt with in detail in the next section, but it is worth mentioning here that pairs working together can give feedback on 'application' as well as providing a social dimension to training. Relocation in particular can be improved by several variations on the pair principle:

(a) One member of the pair hangs control markers on preselected features for their partner to retrieve.

(b) Pairs run a course in tandem, one with the map and one without. A handover of the map takes place within a given diameter of the control feature and the new map holder has to locate the position and find the control.

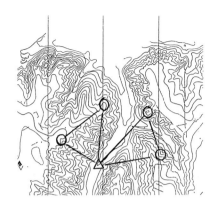

Pairs hanging controls.

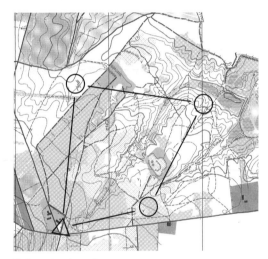

Relocation in pairs.

Physical Training

Although physical training theory and programmes are dealt with in Chapters 4 and 7, it is worth stressing that orienteering is a running sport and that every orienteer benefits from keeping physical condition up with technical levels. Training can include Fartlek running sessions in terrain which intersperses fast sections with recovery jogging; interval 'O' in which the coarse section of a leg is taken fast and the fine 'O' at a recovery walk or jog; and gymnasium circuit training sessions. Army style 'hashes', an environmentally friendly variation on the paperchase, can also combine fun with physical training and keep an assorted pack with varied fitness levels together on a social run.

Since some orienteers use a navigational technique based on continuous relocation, exercise (b) could be given a continuous dimension by the map being handed over at various points on the leg. This could be to a set time. One orienteer sets their watch to beep at two or three minute intervals, as a signal for the map exchange.

Another training exercise is to plan loops which test speed control, such as handrail 'O', fine 'O', and attack points. The participants have to choose the right speed for each loop.

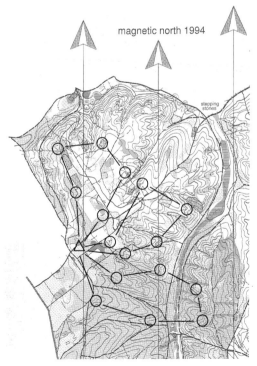

Speed control loops.

Relay Running

All basic techniques are equally applicable to relays and other team competitions like score events, but because they introduce a head to head element in a more direct way, some training exercises can be adapted to produce a relay situation. Sprint 'O' exercises, in which individuals or groups compete against each other on a series of fast short loops, punching relays and straight head to head races over clover leaf loops can be particularly effective in reinforcing concentration and self-discipline when the adrenaline flows fast.

Now we are well into that grey area between basic and advanced skills and it is time for Steve Hale to reveal the secrets of

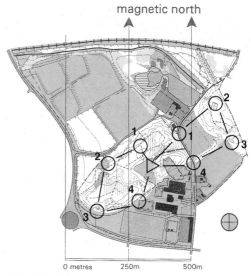

magnetic north

0 metres   250m   500m

Sprint 'O' loops.

Relays introduce a head to head element.

Night orienteering.

the Racing Orienteer. Perhaps we should finish the basic section by stressing that the same skills/technique formula applies to every version of orienteering, including night orienteering, mountain orienteering and rogaines. The same navigational skills also translate to the wider outdoor world of the fell runner, recreational walker, climber or mountain biker. With common sense, application and practice, the Stepladder is there to climb for everyone. Now Steve will guide us up the final rungs to the top.

3(ii) Advanced Techniques

STEVEN HALE

There is no simple recipe for success, no set of rules which will automatically make you a champion orienteer. Orienteering is much more complicated than that. To achieve success you have to develop a personal orienteering style – bringing together all the various aspects of orienteering and becoming the Complete Orienteer. Advanced techniques can be summarized as the art and science of race orienteering.

Above all, you can't learn a technique simply by reading a book. You have to practise and practise until it becomes second nature. Once you've learnt a technique you can't simply rest on your laurels – just to maintain your level of skill also requires constant training. Orienteering is an extremely demanding sport, both physically and technically. Learning and mastering its intricacies takes time and effort – but then if it was too simple it would not be worth doing.

THE MAP

For all orienteers the map is the heart of orienteering. The ability to interpret the map and extract the relevant information is the key to successful orienteering at all levels. Map reading is not just a question of knowing what all the various symbols represent – the map gives a picture of the terrain, and to read the map well is to be able to see this picture. This can take a lifetime to learn – and another lifetime to perfect!

Visualization

The map gives a picture of the terrain.

The skill of being able to visualize the terrain from looking at the map is perhaps the single most important orienteering technique. Instead of running from one feature to the next, you can flow through the terrain. Top orienteers often talk about having a good orienteering 'rhythm' – achieving a flow instead of a stop–start feel to their orienteering. Effective visualization is an essential ingredient in finding your orienteering rhythm. It is also a technique surrounded by an aura of mystique – ask a top orienteer how he uses this technique and he will have trouble giving a clear answer. Top-class orienteers almost certainly use this technique without thinking about how they do it. It is a natural technique which comes from years of running with a map.

Visualization is really being able to form a three-dimensional picture from a two-dimensional map. With practice, this means that you can recognize the terrain when you arrive there by relating it to your mind's-eye picture of the map. To apply this technique successfully requires a great deal of experience in various types of terrain. The amount of map that you can retain in one go is directly dependent upon the amount of detail on the map. In extremely detailed terrain this can mean that you are constantly updating your visualized picture, perhaps every 50 metres or less.

Can you visualize the terrain in the area of the control site?

Central to the skill of visualization are contours. These form the framework of the map onto which all the other features are laid. Contours are much more than their dictionary definition – 'lines joining points of equal height'. The skilled mapper will bend the contours to reflect much more accurately how the ground appears to the orienteer. The skilled orienteer should quite literally be able to read between the lines of the map.

Less experienced orienteers rely heavily on line features such as paths, streams, vegetation boundaries and even valleys and ridges for their navigation. But with experience, the novice begins to stray off these line features, perhaps by cutting across blocks of forest using the compass. In fact, it is possible to come a long way in orienteering simply by

using these basic techniques – reliance on line features combined with compass and pacing, particularly in continental-type terrain. Some orienteers never progress beyond this stage and in the right type of terrain they can be very effective, but when faced by detailed terrain in which line features are scarce the successful orienteer must have additional skills. The orienteer who can master the skill of navigating by visualizing the shape of the land (as opposed to using the 'first on the left second on the right' technique) will have a skill which will enable him to navigate in whatever terrain he is faced with – from the local town park to the toughest Norwegian forest.

Tips and Ideas:

- Survey your own orienteering map. This is perhaps the best single method for improving your orienteering technique and, though a slow and painstaking job, it can improve your map interpretation skills immeasurably as well as producing a map for others to use. It will also give you an insight into limitations that all orienteering maps have. 'Learn-how-to-map' days are often organized by clubs or regional associations.
- Orienteer in as wide a variety of terrain types as possible. Much of being able to interpret a map comes from previous experience in similar terrain. If possible, train as well as race in different and challenging terrain types. For the orienteer who sets his or her sights high, training camps in high quality terrain are a must – places such as Scotland, the English Lakes, Sweden, Norway and Finland should come high in anybody's list of top ten training destinations.

Most countries have at least some pockets of technically challenging terrain.

An example of English Lake District terrain.

- Use contour only maps in training. This will force you to visualize the shape of the ground even in areas where there are many line features. This is particularly useful if you do not have ready access to technically challenging areas. A contour only version of a map can often quite easily be produced using the original artwork of a full colour orienteering map – contact the club/organization which produced the original map.

- 'Visualization' – this eponymous training exercise involves running a normal orienteering course that has been planned without any extremely long or short legs (leg lengths should be between about 150m and 600m). Running in pairs with one map between you, take turns in leading and following. The leader runs without the map using his visualized picture of the map and terrain, whilst the follower prepares for the next leg where roles are swapped. This exercise requires one hundred percent concentration to succeed but it often comes as a surprise how well you can navigate on even very technically challenging terrain by simply relying on a mental picture of the map. To get the most from this exercise the

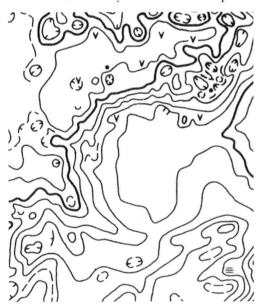

A Contour Only map.

Visualization training.

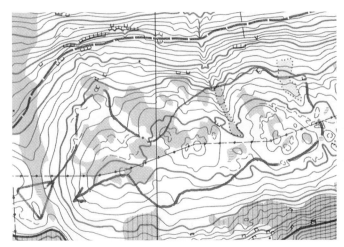

A Line orienteering exercise.

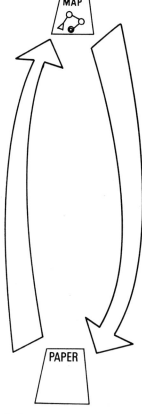

Indoor map memory exercises.

pair should be evenly matched in orienteering and running ability.

- Line orienteering is an excellent way to develop visualization. Try also line orienteering on a contour only map.
- As a supplement to training in the forest or for those without the opportunity to get out into orienteering terrain, practise visualization by placing a map with a course on it and a blank piece of paper about 20 metres apart. Take each leg at a time – memorize (visualize) this leg on the map and then draw in all the important features on the blank paper. Concentrate in particular on the vicinity of the control – this is where it is most important to have an accurate picture of the terrain.

On the Run

Being able to read the map on the run is one of those skills at which it is impossible to train too much. Carrying and using a map should become second nature to an orienteer. Not only can you save seconds by being able to maintain running speed but you can also save minutes of mistakes if you are able to absorb effectively all the relevant information on the map. To the spectator, elite orienteers can often appear to navigate without looking at the map – they need only occasional split second glances to absorb the necessary information.

Tips and Ideas

- Take a map on every possible training run (not just orienteering maps – OS and other leisure maps can be almost as good). If a relevant map is not available old competition maps can be used instead. Route choices from an old competition map can be analyzed, for instance. It can even be beneficial to take normal printed text to read whilst running – newspaper articles, crosswords and so on, but be prepared for some curious looks from passers-by!

- Nearly all types of orienteering training exercises provide practice in map reading on the run, but in particular the 'visualization' training exercise described in the previous section is an excellent exercise for training in map reading at race pace.

- Get your map reading eye tuned in by warming up immediately before a race with a map.

- By improving running technique in terrain you can make map reading easier. Constantly having to look where you are putting your feet means you will not have much chance to read the map. Running in terrain requires balance, strength and co-ordination – in particular ankle strengthening exercises and taping ankles in races can pay off. Weak ankles are the orienteer's equivalent of a boxer's glass chin! Even a simple thing such as using shoes with poor grip can have a knock-on effect on your map reading.

Know Your Mapper

Each mapper has an individual style of mapping. The IOF mapping standards provide a good guideline but they are, of necessity, open to various interpretations. However, one hallmark of a good map is consistency –

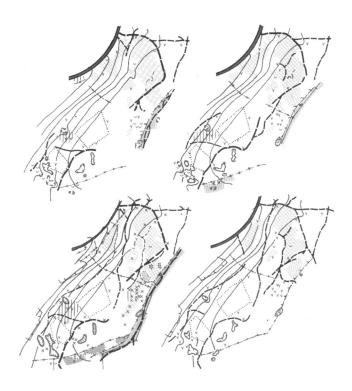

The same area mapped by two different mappers.

similar paths, boulders and vegetation are shown in the same way. For the competitor this means that although every single feature may not be shown on the map, he or she can rely on the features which are shown. The advanced orienteer should not only be familiar with the IOF mapping specifications but also be able to appreciate different mappers' interpretations. During a race, the first couple of legs are particularly risk-filled because the orienteer is not 'tuned in' to the map. With experience, an orienteer should learn to adapt automatically to the map at a very early stage in the race, in the same way that a tennis player automatically adapts his game to the surface he is playing on.

Tips and Ideas

- Map walk – stroll around an area and compare the mapper's interpretation to what you see around you. What rock features are shown? What difference is there between white and green forest? Which paths are shown? Is every small wiggle in the contours shown?
- If you have got a forthcoming race, study other maps which were made by the same mapper. Do they show particular tendencies, for example 'over' mapping of rock features, or ignoring less significant vegetation changes?
- Bear in mind the age of the map – vegetation and small paths can change significantly over a matter of a few years. There can also be significant seasonal variations in vegetation and water features in particular.
- Many major championships have a model event prior to the race (sometimes known as a warm-up event). This model event is usually in similar terrain and, if you're lucky, with the same mapper as the race. Make full use of this opportunity to acquaint yourself with the mapper's style.
- Map scales 1:10,000 and 1:15,000 are the commonest map scales. For a forthcoming race, try to train on maps of the same scale.

THE COMPASS

The compass is the one item of navigational equipment, in addition to the map, which the orienteer is allowed to use – so make the most of it! It is an instrument which is elegant in its simplicity and in recent years there have also been advances in both the stability and settling time of the needle. In skilled hands a compass can prove surprisingly accurate. Over-reliance on the compass, at the cost of map reading, can be a mistake, but it is usually the converse which is the problem – for many orienteers, the compass has a mainly decorative role!

There are almost as many ways of using the compass as there are orienteers. There are also a wide variety of orienteering compasses on the market but in general they can be split into two classes – the traditional protractor compass and the thumb compass. Amongst elite orienteers, traditionalists and thumb compass users are fairly equally represented. The choice of compass often boils down to simple personal preference, choosing one which best suits your individual style of orienteering. Often orienteers who like to keep constant contact with the map favour the thumb compass, whilst orienteers who rely more on taking accurate bearings favour the traditional protractor compass.

The type of compass you choose is not the most important, but the way you use it. In general, it is good practice to get into the routine of using the compass on every leg. Get into the habit of routinely and regularly checking the compass. Thumb compasses encourage this habit. It is also important to learn the limitations in the accuracy of the compass and your use of it. Even in very simple terrain you can shave seconds off your time by avoiding straying too far off the straight line. Often in open moorland ter-

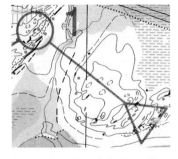

Some examples of aiming off.

rain, for instance, the closer you can run to the straight line, the more time you can save.

'Aiming off' is a popular technique:

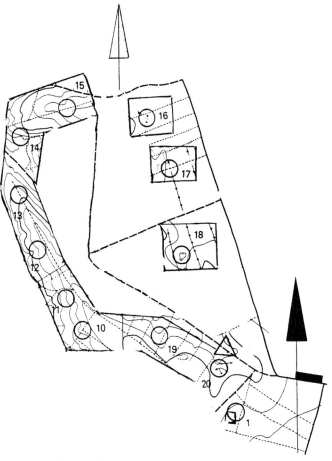

Window and Corridor exercises.

Tip for the Expert

- When aiming off you can also save seconds by aiming off just enough and no more than is absolutely necessary. There are also cases where by combining use of the compass with intelligent interpretation of the map you can avoid the need to aim off at all.

Tips and Ideas

- Use of the compass should become second nature – take it with you on every possible training session.
- Window or corridor training exercises are a good way of forcing the accurate use of the compass.
- Control picking exercises with plenty of direction changes help to develop the routine of using the compass on every leg. The emphasis here should be on leaving the control in the correct direc-

tion – setting the compass for the next leg before reaching the control point.

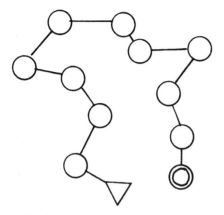

Control picking exercise.

- Learning to take a compass bearing on the run can be practised quite effectively by taking an old competition map on a normal training run, though learning to follow bearings is something which can only be practised effectively in the terrain.
- One of the keys to advanced orienteering is attention to detail – nothing should be left to chance. One of the details which often gets missed is compass maintenance. Learn how to dismantle a compass (if it has a rotating housing) and clean it regularly.
- It is worth investing in a top of the range compass with a fast and stable needle. Compared to a cheaper model the difference in settling time may only be the odd second, but a slow or unstable needle will increase the risk of making an error in following a bearing – and cause you to lose minutes.
- Reserve a trusted compass for important races and change it for a new one at least once a season. 'Natural wastage'

in the forest often means that this happens automatically.

IN THE CIRCLE

The approach and exit from a control is a crucial stage in a race. To find the control you have to be on top of your navigation – at the same time you need to know the control description and code, have your route planned to the next control or at least your exit direction and be prepared to check the control code and punch your card. This is a lot to think about in a short space of time, and it is therefore not surprising that most time is usually lost in the vicinity of the control.

Leaving a control – exit direction pre-planned.

The actual navigation is the important part and so all the other routine actions should be just that – routine. Once again, attention to detail is the motto so the first thing to ensure is that map, compass, control card and descriptions are held in a way that facilitates easy punching whilst not hindering reading of the map and use of the compass. There are many different ways of doing this – map and compass in one hand, control card in the other; map in one hand, control card and compass in the other; or even the whole lot in one hand. Examples of all these methods can be found amongst top competitors. Whilst it is obvious that map and compass should be held in the hand it is perhaps less obvious that the control card should also be held. Many orienteers do pin their card to their chest or sleeve, thus leaving their hands freer to handle the map and compass. However, these methods have disadvantages. If the card is pinned to the chest it can be difficult to reach punches, particularly if they are attached to control trestles – a method which is still uncommon in Britain but almost universally used in other countries. Whilst not sharing this problem, the control card pinned to the sleeve can tend to flap around and be difficult to insert into the punch. This can lead to lost seconds, or at worst to disqualification for poor punching. So find a method of holding your punch card in your hand. Even with this method there is a wide variety of alternatives – a rubber band around the wrist or finger, string around the wrist, or simply held loose with no attachment. You should be able to find a method with which you feel comfortable.

Before running into the circle, you should have already noted the code, description and direction out of the control. This leaves all your concentration for the actual navigating into the flag. It also means that you can punch the control and be away in not much more than a second. Think of flowing through the control rather than to and from it.

The ability to visualize the terrain from the map really comes into its own in the circle. This means that instead of using the run-into-the-circle-and-search method you can recognize all the relevant features and run unerringly to the feature behind which your control is tucked – in theory at least. It also has the advantage that you can spend more time picking out features and a little less time looking at the map. On entering the circle, concentration and alertness should be one hundred percent, and you should be totally aware of your surroundings. Your pace should also be adjusted to your navigation – learn to recognize when you have started to outrun your map reading. This usually means slowing down into the circle, but with a good visualized picture of the terrain this is not always necessary.

Of course, there are control points where there is insufficient map detail to read your way in and here the only method is to rely on the compass from a safe attack point. A good course planner will avoid using such

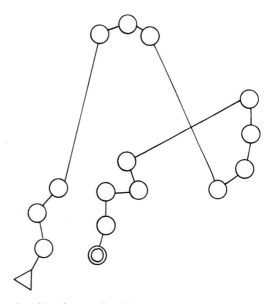

Combined control picking exercise.

difficult control sites which need luck as well as skill to locate accurately but in some terrains the lack of features makes their use inevitable.

Tips and Ideas

- Undertake control picking exercises, preferably with 'proper' controls (flag, code and punch).
- A combined control picking exercise with occasional long legs gives practice in varying concentration and pace – switching into and out of 'control finding' mode.
- Concentrate in less important races on getting your control flow right.
- Set up a control in a park or open forest and practise running in, punching and running out on the compass. Use an old competition map and aim to leave the control in the correct direction for each control, run say 50m, turn and run in to the control again.
- Experiment with new ways of holding your control card – just because a certain method suited you as a novice does not necessarily mean it will always be the most effective method.

ROUTE CHOICE

When route choice is discussed, it usually means choosing one of several alternative routes between controls. There are in fact a whole range of different types of route choice decisions which are made whilst running an orienteering race. At the other end of the scale, the decision of which side of the next tree to run around can also be considered as a route choice. In between these two extremes an orienteer makes a whole range of different route choice decisions.

Route choice in continental terrain.

Macro Route Choice

In continental-type terrain the emphasis is often on macro route choice. This usually means a straight choice between a limited number of plausible routes. Once the choice is made, there is no going back – it becomes simply a question of executing it as fast a possible. So on what do you base your route choice decision and how can you ensure that you have chosen the best route?

In Scandinavian terrain where paths are rare the straight line route choice is often the best, if your technique is good enough to execute it. The good course planner, however, will always throw in the odd leg where it pays off to run round – just to keep you on your toes.

Tips and Ideas

- Mathematical formulae relating distance to height gain or comparing various running speeds in different types of terrain are loved by textbooks, but in practice are virtually worthless. In a race situation there is no time to get out a pocket calculator – you have to rely on personal judgement based on previous experience.

- Try to pick out all the plausible routes – choosing a bad route can often simply be the result of not seeing the best alternative. In some terrain types this can mean considering routes which are a long way off the straight line – here it is important to unfold the map for a clear picture of the whole leg.
- Know your terrain – analyze and save your competition maps. Look at your route choices. Which ones were good, which ones were bad? Did you miss any obvious routes? When approaching a race, review maps and route choices from races on similar types of area.
- Discuss and compare routes with fellow competitors after the race. Take split times and try to co-ordinate this with other competitors (split time watches

with a memory of at least 30 splits are a must for any serious orienteer). At major international races it is normal to have manned controls and split times for every leg. The Regnly electronic punching system also provides split times for every control.

- Take split times during training and plan training exercises with a number of route choice alternatives. As an alternative, train in pairs or threesomes and meet up at each control. This increases the competition element and gives a direct feedback of the time loss and gain on various route choices.
- Know your own strengths and weaknesses. Some people are strong in rough terrain, while others are lightning fast track runners. Choose routes in competitions which exploit your strengths. Then go home and train your weaknesses!
- Calculate the risks. A straight route might look faster on the map but if there is a high risk of missing the control then it might be worth taking the longer, safer route. Choose routes which are within the compass of your technical ability.
- When presented with two or more routes with little to choose between them, it often means that there is very little difference, timewise, between these routes. In other words, don't waste time making the decision but simply choose one of the routes and get on with it.
- Another factor to consider is energy conservation. In a long race or in hot weather taking a slightly longer but physically less demanding route can pay off later in the race.

		1	2	3	4	5	6
	Fastest	1,58	1,02	2,07	0,87	0,92	0,95
	Average of first 5	1,65	1,08	2,27	0,96	0,97	1,02
1	Omeltchenko	1,58	1,02	2,23	0,97	1,07	0,95
2	Mårtensson	1,58	1,05	2,47	0,88	0,98	1,02
3	Valstad	1,67	1,25	2,48	0,87	0,92	1,00
4	Bührer	1,62	1,05	2,08	1,15	0,92	1,05
5	Holmquist	1,80	1,02	2,07	0,92	0,97	1,08
18	Hale	1,67	1,15	2,72	0,97	0,98	1,00

Split time sheet showing the first six controls at the 1995 World Championships Short Distance final.

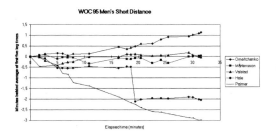

A 'progressograph' is a good way of graphically displaying split time data.

Sub-Macro Route Choice

Now we're getting well into the jargon! 'Sub-macro route choice' is my name for route choice on a smaller scale – but still route choice which is made using the map, as opposed to micro route choice which is described below, where the map is of little or no use. During the execution of a leg, after the main (macro) route choice decision has been made, there are often a large number of small variations and alternatives on this route choice. This means being constantly alert and in contact with the map and being prepared to be flexible. Make adjustments to the route if, for instance, unexpectedly thick forest is encountered. In Scandinavian-type terrain there are often seconds to be won by

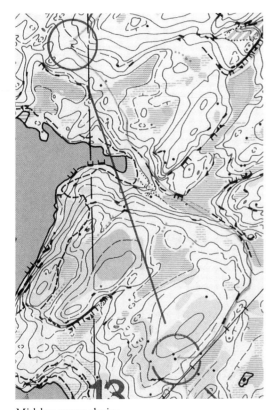

Mid-leg route choice.

reading your way around marshes and knolls rather than blasting in a straight line, although this does require a great deal of practice and concentration to execute at race pace. (See also the section 'Orienteering Styles' below.)

Micro Route Choice

Throughout an orienteering race you will be constantly making what can be called 'micro route choices' – whether to skirt the bramble patch or blast through it; hurdle the fallen tree or run around it; leap the stream or run down and up the banks. Each decision is in itself relatively insignificant but over the course of a race they can add up to minutes. When you've run a race and added up all the time lost due to mistakes and still cannot account for the time you were behind the leader, then the problem could lie with micro route choice.

Tips and Ideas

- Run in terrain with other orienteers – note where you lose or gain ground on each other.
- Improve your strength and 'bounce' so that you can take minor obstacles in your stride.
- Look ahead and pick a good line through the terrain.

ORIENTEERING STYLES

'Constant Contact' versus 'Blast and Ask!'

The two extremes of orienteering styles can be described as 'constant contact' (where the orienteer has constant contact with the map) and at the other extreme 'blast and ask' (running as fast as you can in the direction of the control and then asking some-body where you are). The latter is naturally a high-risk technique! It also breaks all the rules. More realistically, while the blast and relocate technique can be very effective, in practice most elite orienteers aim to run at a speed where they can just keep in touch with the map, both reading ahead and constantly relocating. It boils down to being able to interpret the map at speed and also to pace judgement – running at a speed which is just at the limits of your navigational ability.

Tips and Ideas

- Line orienteering is a good way of train-ing constant contact.
- Run a course with a partner. Each per-son has a map, but with alternate con-trols marked on each map. Take turns to lead each leg.

'Map to Ground' and 'Ground to Map'

These are navigational strategies which over-lap the division between basic and advanced techniques and bear repeating here. Map to ground orienteering is reading the map and then recognizing the feature in the terrain. Ground to map orienteering is the reverse: seeing the feature in the terrain and then pinpointing it on the map. Ground to map orienteering is in effect constant relocation. Few orienteers can achieve perfect map con-tact – always knowing exactly where they are. Top orienteers run at a speed which is right at the limit of their map reading ability, and so a combination of ground to map and map to ground orienteering must be used.

Tips and Ideas

- Line orienteering is a good way of train-ing map to ground orienteering.

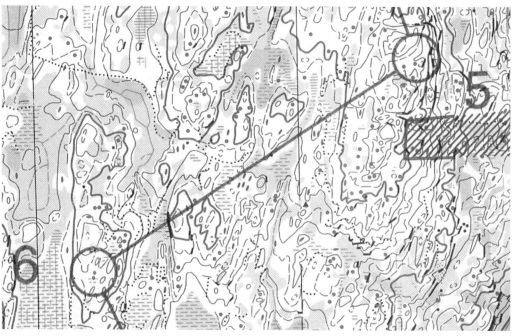

Not much route choice here – compass and pace.

- To practise ground to map orienteering, run a course with a partner. Take it in turns to lead legs. A variation on this is to pass over the lead as you approach the control rather than when you actually reach it.
- Run a course with a partner. Each person has a map but only alternate controls are marked on the map.

Pace Judgement

The classic technique for learning pace judgement is the traffic light system. Another technique is to compare orienteering to golf – drive off the tee (run fast), chip onto the green (ease up on reaching the attack point) and then putt into the hole (run slowly into the control). These techniques can be very useful when learning the skills of pace judgement, but the elite orienteer must learn to be much more flexible. This means constantly adjusting the pace to the difficulty of the orienteering – not just slowing down into the control.

It is important to know your own limitations and to recognize when you are running too fast for your navigation. It is also important to raise your pace when the orienteering is easy. Post-race analysis plays an important role here – look at the mistakes you made which can be attributed to rushing or losing map contact by running too fast or not having time to plan ahead. Also consider the sections of the race where you could have run harder. Learn from these experiences!

Distance Judgement

The textbook method for estimating distance is pace counting. As with the compass, pace counting should never be used as a replacement for map reading. It is a technique to be used as a back-up to map interpretation. As you become more proficient at map interpretation, you will find yourself using pacing much less. Most top Scandinavian orienteers do not use this technique as there is always (or nearly always) sufficient detail on the map to make it unnecessary. In continental terrain, however, pace counting can come into its own when trying to find, for instance, a solitary rootstock in a block of otherwise featureless forest.

Pace counting is an invaluable method for learning distance estimation, although as your orienteering skills mature you should automatically rely on it less and less as the primary means of navigation. Nevertheless, it is always a good weapon to have in your arsenal.

Coping with Different Terrain Types

Orienteering terrain is often classified as either 'Continental' or 'Nordic'. Whilst this is a wild over-simplification it can be useful to think in these terms.

Nordic or Scandinavian

Nordic or Scandinavian terrain is typically broken terrain with many contour and rock features and few line features.

The best technique in this type of terrain is usually constant contact. However, most orienteers will find themselves having to simplify the orienteering and aiming for larger features off the straight line. With experience, you will find yourself being able to hold a course closer to the straight line. Line orienteering exercises are an excellent way of training for constant contact. Orienteers from the non-Scandinavian countries often have extreme difficulty adapting to Nordic terrain, which puts a premium on map inter-

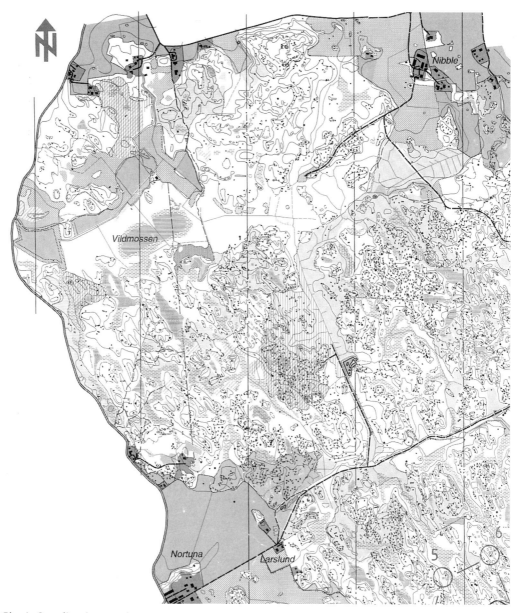

Classic Scandinavian terrain.

pretation skills, in particular visualization and contour interpretation. These are skills which are not usually essential for continental orienteering. They can, however, be developed, particularly by training with contour-only maps.

Another problem for orienteers not used to running in Scandinavian terrain is the intensity of concentration and the unrelent-

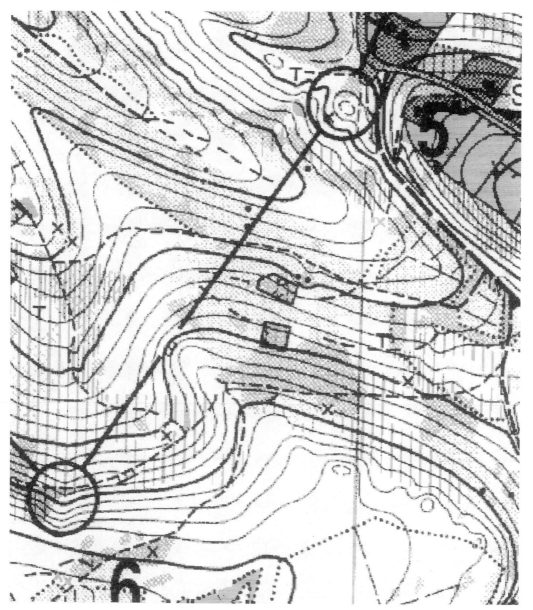

Classic Continental terrain.

ing nature of the orienteering. Here, experience is the important factor. You must feel at home is this type of terrain and that means gaining experience by training and competing in Scandinavian terrain.

Continental

Continental terrain is the classic description for European worked forest. Typically, the topology is large rolling features with little intricate contour detail. Forest roads, tracks and rides are common. The technical challenge in this type of terrain is chiefly route choice.

Just as orienteers from non-Scandinavian countries can find themselves at a disadvantage in Scandinavian terrain, Nordic runners can have major problems adapting to continental terrain.

Runners inexperienced in this type of terrain often miss the best route choices simply by not looking far enough off the straight line. It is also important to use a clear attack point – often not the orienteering style for skilled orienteers in Scandinavian terrain who rely on constant map contact. There is often not enough detail on the map to read the way into the control in continental terrain, so a clear attack point and basic compass and pacing skills can come into their own.

The above description is an extreme simplification. Within the two broad categories there is a wide variety of types of terrain and there are also types of terrain which fall somewhere in between. Whilst Britain is not blessed with an enormous quantity of orienteering terrain, there is a great variety of terrain types.

Sand Dune

Sand dune terrain often provides technically testing terrain combined with high running speeds. Where the sand dunes are forested there can be areas of much slower bushy forest. There are often areas of low detail between lines of highly detailed sand dunes and the key here is pace change – adjusting your speed to the difficulty of orienteering.

This type of terrain can be found on many parts of the British coast. Denmark and New Zealand are also known for their sand dune terrain, as is the Bordeaux region of France.

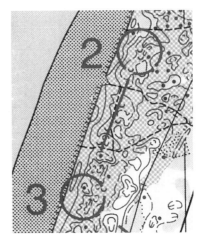

Sand dune terrain.

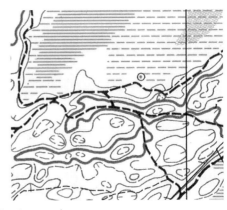

Moraine terrain.

Moraine

Moraine terrain is often similar to sand dune terrain. Moraine is the sand deposits left by the glaciers after the last ice age.

There are a few areas of moraine terrain in Scotland. This type of terrain can also be found in all the Nordic and Baltic countries.

Fell

The lack of forests in some parts of Britain have led to the use of open fell terrain for orienteering. This terrain is often very

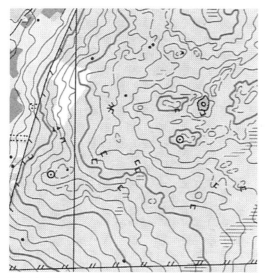

British fell terrain.

detailed and places an emphasis on contour interpretation. As the visibility is high, long legs can often be simplified by looking up and picking out features ahead.

Nordic

Nordic-type terrain can be found in Scotland and the English Lake District.

Outside of Europe, North America and even Australia have terrain which can be compared to the best of Nordic terrain.

Continental

Despite being an island, Britain has its share of this type of terrain!

RACE TACTICS AND TECHNIQUES

Classic Distance

This is the blue riband distance in orienteering – for senior men this usually means a winning time of between 70 and 100 minutes, for senior women between 50 and 75 minutes. Other classes are correspondingly shorter. To race these distances requires supreme fitness and consequently large amounts of time can be lost over the last few controls when energy is exhausted and the brain has stopped functioning optimally. A typical course planner's trick is to throw in a number of short technical legs at the end of a race in a malicious attempt to catch out the tiring runner.

There is also a significant step up to the senior classes from the junior classes, both in terms of course lengths and the strength and depth of the competition. The standard in the senior elite classes is such that even the best juniors can expect to take several years to become established. Very few of the top international orienteers are under twenty-five years old and an orienteer can expect to be at his or her peak at around thirty. To achieve the transition from junior to senior, a routine of training should already be established. It is often the slightly less talented juniors who have worked for their success who go on to be successful seniors. The real high fliers often do not have the background of training and consequently fall by the wayside. No amount of natural talent can compensate for a lack of training when it comes to racing 15km through wilderness terrain!

Over a classic distance race, pacing is important. With the right physical training the distance should not be too daunting – it is important to feel that you really *can* race the whole distance and not just get round the course. You should approach the race with an attitude of controlled aggression.

There are various danger points on the course where the risk of mistakes and time loss are high – we have already named the last few controls when fatigue can lead to costly errors. Early controls, before you have had a chance to tune into the map, are another risk point. Yet another danger point is the spectator control. Orienteers can be rather shy creatures, used to disappearing into the forest and not emerging until they reach the finish run in. Suddenly realising he or she is being watched can turn an accomplished orienteer into a bungling incompetent. TV cameras and press helicopters can have a similar effect. Prepare yourself mentally for these eventualities.

Another point of risk is when you see other runners in the forest (both when they catch you and when you have caught them). It is very easy to become distracted or stressed into making a mistake.

The risk of losing time at the various danger points can be reduced by simply being aware of the risks and preparing a tactic, in advance, to cope with the situation. With the right preparation and attitude a tricky situation can often be turned to your advantage. One of the keys is always to think positively:

- *Don't* think: I must not make a mistake at the first control, or I must not run too fast at the start.
- *Do* think: I must control my running speed and give myself time to read the map.
- *Don't* think: somebody is watching me, so I must not make a fool of myself.
- *Do* think: Somebody is watching me, so I'm going to show them how good an orienteer I am.
- *Don't* think: I'm getting tired and must not lose concentration.
- *Do* think: I'm getting tired and must concentrate on my technique.

Seeing other runners in the forest can be a major distraction and often leads to mistakes. However, these runners can be used to your advantage. Using other competitors

is a grey zone in orienteering ethics. Following is strictly against the rules, but if you find yourself running with another competitor of similar speed and ability then it is almost impossible simply to ignore him. The psychological effect of running with another competitor often leads to an increase in running pace. Two pairs of eyes are better than one when searching for a control. While you should not deliberately run with other competitors, you should make the most of the situation if it occurs – without being distracted into making mistakes.

Blatant following does occur in orienteering. This is a major problem in international races where the standard of fitness is universally high and consequently it is very difficult to shake off a persistent hanger-on. Most people at some stage of their orienteering career are tempted to stick their map in their pocket and hitch a lift with a convenient passer-by. There are many examples of runners having achieved results far above their real abilities. This is a dangerous game to play – not because of the risk of disqualification (which is almost non-existent), but because it is very easy to gain a bad reputation. You only need to do it once to get a reputation as a follower and this label will be almost impossible to shake off. Don't succumb to the temptation!

Tips and Ideas

- Mentally split the course into sections. Instead of running a 9km course, think of it as 3 x 3km – perhaps using refreshment controls as mid-course goals.
- Run training exercises with other orienteers – get used to orienteering with other competitors around you.
- Video film training exercises – both as a valuable feedback on technique and also

to become accustomed to orienteering while being watched and filmed.

- Have a pre-race plan: if a rival starts two minutes behind you think through your tactics for the eventuality of being caught. If you know there is going to be a television crew in the forest prepare yourself for the possibility that they could film you. Think carefully through the techniques that you are going to concentrate on – visualizing in the control circle, running carefully to the first control, always knowing the exit direction out of the control, checking the compass regularly and so on.

RELAYS

Relay running is perhaps the most exciting and intense form of orienteering. Tactics play a major role, and indeed using other runners or even following is an accepted part of the game. Relay running is one of the few forms of orienteering where it is head-to-head racing with the first person over the line winning. Even more so than in individual races, the successful relay runner must be at home running with other competitors in the forest.

To reduce the amount of pure following, relay courses are usually 'gaffled'. This is an Anglicization of the Swedish word meaning 'forked', and is a description of the way the courses are

planned so that runners on any given relay leg do not run exactly the same course. This is usually achieved by having several common controls with different course alternatives between them. At the end of a race all teams have run exactly the same courses in total but each individual runner can have a different course combination. A typical gaffling method is shown in the schematic diagram above.

For the competitor, this means that you can be running together with several other competitors for a section of the course, only for the courses suddenly to fork. You don't

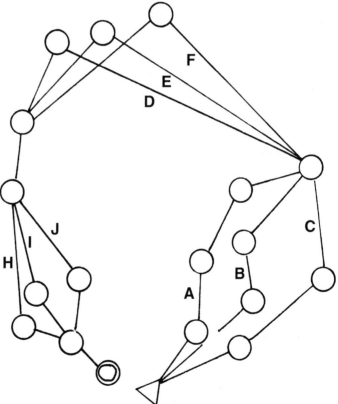

A typical gaffling scheme. The first leg runner might have course combination CDH, the second BFI and the third leg runner AEJ.

know when this will happen – so you have to stay in control of the navigation at all times.

The different legs in a relay race require slightly different tactics – most orienteers find themselves gradually specializing in one of the relay legs (first, middle or last).

First Leg Running

The first leg can often boil down to a pack run. With 'gaffled' courses (runners visit different controls) the pack usually splits into several smaller groups. Many teams put their fast runners, who are perhaps not quite so technically sound, on the first leg. Whilst there is personal glory to be gained by coming back first, the real job of the first leg runner is simply to come back in touch with the leading pack.

Unless you really want to 'do or die', always do your own navigation – even when tucked into a pack. On numerous occasions whole packs have gone walkabout because everybody thought somebody else was reading the map! It takes a very brave first leg runner to pick his own route choice when everybody else takes another route. A disciplined pack will usually hold a higher tempo than a lone runner so you have to be very certain of your route choice.

Middle Leg Running

The second leg runner has to be prepared for anything – if all the first leg runners come back in a big pack then you could find yourself needing all the speed and aggression of the first leg runner. If the field comes back well spread out, you could find yourself running on your own. The middle legs are perhaps the least glamorous, but perhaps more than any other leg require an all-round orienteer.

Last Leg Running

Most teams save their best runners for last – here you need coolness under pressure and a killer instinct. The last leg runner going out in the lead is under terrific pressure – you are being hunted by the chasing pack, and all you can do is lose the race. If you are in the leading pack you will have to decide whether to make an early break and try to defend the lead or rely on a sprint finish. If you go out behind the leader, then you will have to try to take in time on the leaders.

At the top level of orienteering it is very difficult to break away from a pack. Even if you can open a gap, as you slow down into each control the rest of the pack will be able to run straight in at full speed, using you to guide them to the control. This is particularly true in areas of tricky technical orienteering. For the strong runner, a long leg can provide an opportunity to break away but there are also a number of race winning

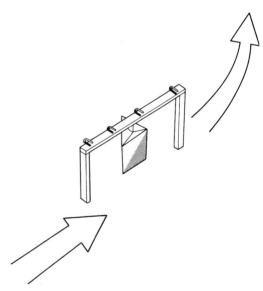

Use furthest punch at last control to make rivals run round you.

strategies if you are with other runners as you near the finish:

- If the race becomes a sprint off between two or more runners, be first to the last control and punch at the furthest punch (i.e. the punch nearest the finish).
- Let the other runner lead – stay cool and wait for your opponent to make a mistake. A 30m gap may be all you need.
- Read the last few legs in advance – at the second to last control, punch and go!

Tips an\d Ideas

- Do not underestimate the importance of team spirit. A relay team can be much more than the sum of its individual members. The club or team coach can play an important role in producing the right atmosphere in the team.
- Run training races with mass starts.
- Run 'match play' training exercises where you start as a group of between two and four and try to be the first to the next control, regrouping at the control.
- Few races are decided on the sprint – in ninety percent of cases the first runner to the final control also crosses the finish line first. Last leg runners should work out well in advance how they are going to run the last two or three legs.
- False starts are not uncommon in major relays – and once several hundred first leg runners have started running it is impossible to call them back. Don't be caught out – be on the start line in good time.
- First leg runners can learn a lot about running in a pack, fast starts and asserting themselves by running in cross-country races.

- Join a club with a number of other competitors in the same age group and standard so that you can form a competitive relay team.
- Last leg runners should be very aware of their own strengths and also know their opponents' strengths and weaknesses. Choose your tactics accordingly. For instance, if you are together with a runner known for his fast finishing, don't wait until the last control to make your move!

Short Distance

This is a relatively new championship distance (it has been included in the World Championships since 1991) and usually takes the form of a 25 to 30 minute race, sometimes with qualifying heats and a final.

One of the arguments for introducing this distance was to give competitors from developing orienteering nations a better chance of success. The idea behind this was that less experienced orienteers who perhaps were not sufficiently well trained to cope with a classic length race would be more competitive at the shorter distance. There is little evidence that this has been the case – short distance orienteering places an extra emphasis on fast, accurate, error-free technique. Developing these skills requires just as much training as for any classic distance race – there are no short cuts to success even in short distance orienteering.

With such relatively short running times there is little or no room for mistakes, and at international level anything over 10 seconds can be regarded as a major error. This means that total concentration is needed from start to finish, and you have to be orienteering at full speed right from the whistle. This does not necessarily mean running at full speed, which will almost inevitably lead to mistakes, but running at the very limit of your technical ability whilst maintaining concentration.

When short distance orienteering was introduced there was much discussion about the best race tactics. Some runners thought that the only way to win a short distance race was to run flat out and take chances – in any race somebody would succeed with these tactics and the slightly more cautious runner would always end up coming at best second. This does not seem to be the case, and the best approach seems to be fast, accurate orienteering while remaining in control at all times.

In short distance orienteering, there are greater changes in pace compared to other forms of orienteering. There is little need to conserve energy so when you reach an easy section you really can afford to open the throttle, but you must have the discipline to slow down again when you reach a tricky section.

Staying in control at all times is not the same as always playing safe. To win a short race requires a certain amount of risk taking – but they must be calculated risks. If your ambition is to win then there is little point in taking the safe route which is perhaps going to be 30 seconds slower. Fortune favours the brave!

A slick technique through the control is absolutely essential in short distance orienteering. A couple of seconds saved at every control gives a total of half a minute saved over the whole course –

and half a minute is a very generous winning margin in short distance racing. Always have a good mental picture of the terrain as you approach the control and always have your exit direction planned in advance.

Short distance orienteering is perhaps the form of orienteering where mental control plays the biggest role. The knowledge that every second counts places an additional stress on the competitor. Most short races are lost because of running too fast and making mistakes rather than running too slowly. It is the speed at which you can navigate which must control the speed at which you run.

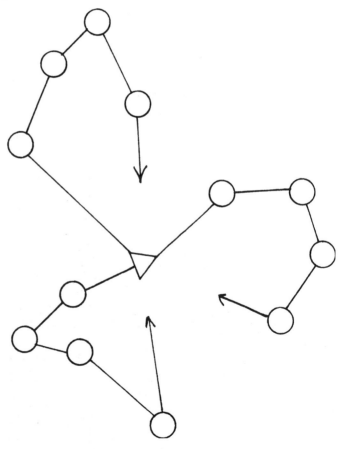

Interval O – can be run as a relay.

Tips and Ideas

- Do not be tempted to rush just because it's a short distance race – orienteer methodically.
- Warm up thoroughly and have a map with you so that your map reading eye is tuned in at the start.
- Control picking exercises are an excellent way of training control flow and fast, accurate navigation.
- Run interval orienteering – several short timed loops (of, say, 500m–1500m) with a short rest between each loop.

Night

Night orienteering is not an international championship event. However, most countries have national night championships and in the two classic club orienteering relay races, Tio Milia in Sweden and Jukola in Finland, night orienteering plays a significant and often decisive role. For this reason, night orienteering specialists are not uncommon in the Nordic countries.

Even for orienteers who have no ambitions for night racing in itself, it can be a valuable part of training. Night orienteering

Night events make good training.

places increased emphasis on accurate navigation and familiar forests assume a completely different character in the dark. Open fell areas in particular usually provide limited technical challenges to elite orienteers in daylight because of the good visibility – but at night it can be a different story!

A prerequisite for night orienteering is an effective headlamp – this means a halogen bulb, rechargeable battery pack and a snugly fitting battery pack holder. There are several models on the market which are specifically designed for orienteering – so buy one (or persuade your club to buy one). A good headlamp can also be a asset for winter training if you don't fancy simply pounding out the miles on asphalt.

Tactically, playing safe usually pays off at night. Even with the most powerful headlamp your field of vision is limited to a few dozen metres, and even within this field of vision the ability to pick out features and discern land forms is severely diminished. This means that pure map reading cannot be relied upon alone, and relocating in particular can be almost impossible. Techniques such as distance judgement (pacing), accurate compass bearings and choosing a distinctive attack point suddenly become essential. It is not uncommon for orienteers who use a thumb compass during the day to revert to a traditional protractor compass for night orienteering.

Dawn legs in races such as Tio Milia and Jukola, and in Britain the Harvester Relay, can present a special problem when it is perhaps not dark enough to need a headlamp to run but you still need a light to read the map. Here, a small pen torch taped to the inside of the wrist can be the solution.

Tips and Ideas

- Train regularly in the winter with a headlamp so that you feel at home in the dark.
- Familiar terrain and even parks can be used to advantage for night training exercises.

Damage limitation

Everybody makes mistakes – even race winners seldom claim to have had the perfect run. However, the mark of the true advanced orienteer is counting mistakes in seconds rather than minutes.

Post-race analysis plays an important role in the learning process. Analyzing a performance after a good result is easy, but after a poor race the map often ends up at the bottom of the plastic bag together with the muddy shoes and sweaty jocks. Reliving a bad race is a painful experience but essential if you are to avoid making the same mistake twice.

Just as no orienteer is infallible, so no map is perfect. Most races include at least one 'dodgy' control – even the World Orienteering Championships occasionally suffers from this syndrome. Nevertheless, the best orienteer nearly always wins anyway. Whilst lesser mortals almost inevitably waste minutes on dodgy controls, top orienteers seem to have a way of hitting lucky. Whilst luck does play a role, there are ways of making your own luck. The key is to be in control of your orienteering and at the same time have the self-confidence and judgement to know when you are right and the map is wrong. One aspect of this is never relying totally on any single technique – back up your map reading with your compass and vice versa.

Racing optimally means running at the limits of your capacity – this means that the potential mistake is never far away. It is therefore important to try to develop a feeling for when things are starting to go wrong.

Tips and Ideas

- Whilst orienteering, constantly consider the possibility that you could have made a mistake – ask yourself 'what if' questions. 'What if I've made a parallel error and run up the wrong re-entrant?' Look for features to confirm your position.
- Routinely and regularly clean and check your compass for bubbles or loss of magnetism.
- If you have made a major mistake, think back after the race to the warning signs which you should have noticed – when should the warning bells have started to ring?
- You run to a control and are about to punch, then suddenly realize it has got the wrong code. Don't panic, or automatically run out to your attack point again, but take your time and relocate – you can be one hundred percent certain that the control feature is marked on the map!

Course Planners' Tricks

The Lure

The obvious exit route from a control is not always the best. Simply running to the nearest path which is heading in the right direction can commit you to taking a less than optimal route. Consider the whole route when deciding which way to run out of a

Which way out of the control?

control and, of course, this should done well before reaching the control.

The Sting in the Tail

Several tricky short legs at the end of the course are a common course planner's trap. If you've had a good run then your mind can already be on the run-in. Perhaps you can already hear the finish speaker – there's nothing worse for the concentration over the last few controls than catching the odd phrase from the finish such as 'and now he has just two minutes to finish if he's going to take the lead!' This is also a stage in the race where fatigue can be starting to affect your mental clarity.

The Diagonal

Controls on slopes are usually tricky, and can be made even harder by trying to hit them when descending or climbing diagonally on the slope. It is nearly always better to drop straight down, climb straight up or contour into a control. Generally, navigating down into a control is almost always easier – the exception being small crags which can be almost invisible from above.

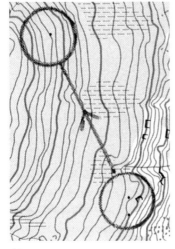

Diagonal leg.

The Short First

The hardest control on the course is often the first one as you're probably high on adrenaline, running too fast and not yet acclimatized to the map. If it is also a short leg you can have real problems. Even worse, on a short downhill leg you can be past the first control before you've managed to locate the start triangle on the map! It's worthwhile always taking it very easy at the start. Don't be worried if you're beaten to the start triangle by a galloping fifty-year-old! Learn to control your arousal level at the start so that you are not too wound up. This

is an area where mental training (sports psychology) can give big rewards.

Short first.

Tips and Ideas

• Gain experience by planning courses yourself – your club will be grateful too!
• If you have an old map of an area being used for a forthcoming race, plan some interesting legs and decide how to run them. Try and put yourself in the course planner's boots. Quite often, you can anticipate some of the legs on a course and already work out how to execute them.

Using Races as Training

Outside of Scandinavia, one of the problems with training for orienteering is getting access to the right terrain. Another problem is that a really good training session requires a lot of effort – gaining permission from land owners, obtaining maps, planning the exercise, hanging and collecting in the control flags and so on, which is why normal orienteering races can be an excellent part of your training – all this hard work has been done for you. This does not mean that simply by going out and racing every weekend you will become a good orienteer. The danger here is that you will end up racing yourself into the ground and keep on making the same mistakes over and over again.

Plan your season, pick the races which are important to you, and really race these. The other races should be seen as stepping stones to your goals. Use some of them to practise particular techniques. For instance, decide in advance to concentrate on visualizing being in the circle, or using a compass on every leg, or planning ahead, or exiting the control in the right direction and so on. Other races can be used as trial races, or dry runs for the 'big one' – but don't fall into the trap of trying to win every race. If you ease down your training for each weekend's race and then spend the next few days recovering from the all-out effort, you will never actually do a full week's training. There are many examples of orienteers being nearly unbeatable early in the season only to run badly when it really counts.

Preparing for the Big One

Achieving your full potential when it counts is an art which is difficult to learn and consistently put into practice. Following these guidelines will not guarantee that you hit form at the right time, but they will give you a fighting chance:

- Avoid injury. Some injuries are simply bad luck, but many can be avoided by training sensibly, avoiding high-risk sessions and taking reasonable precautions (taping ankles, wearing gaiters, and so on). Varied training, including strength training, will help to prevent many injuries. Contact sports such as football are probably not a good idea.
- Avoid illness. This is easier said than done! However, think about what you eat and drink, getting enough rest, personal hygiene and avoiding stress. If you are racing abroad, be particularly careful with what you eat and drink – a runny tummy doesn't improve your chances!

- Plan your training and racing over a season. Your plan might look something like this:

  November: easy training, no specific technique sessions.

  December: start of winter training in earnest. Aim to do one session with a map per week (night sessions with headlamp?).

  January and February: continue winter training as for December

  March: pre-season build up. Train basic techniques – one to two sessions per week plus the occasional race. Concentrate on orienteering smoothly rather than going flat out and making mistakes. Have a technique training weekend.

  April and May: spring season – races most weekends plus two technique sessions per week. More advanced training sessions with, perhaps, time-taking.

  June and July: summer break – holiday multi-day races plus training camp. A good time to really concentrate on technique training.

  August, September and October: autumn season. Races most weekends plus one to two technique sessions per week.

- Gear your training to the type of terrain on which the race will take place. Think about what techniques will be important and train them. Try to find other races in similar terrain.

Week	Date	Event	Location	Comments
10				Winter training
11	18/03 *	Spring Cup	Denmark	International standard race
	19/03 *	Spring Cup	Denmark	
12				
13				
14		Training	Cumbria	
15	15/04 *	JK	Yorkshire	
	16/04 *	JK		
16	22/04 *	Vårstafetten (relay)	Norway	International standard race
	23/04 *	Vårspretten (classic)		
17		Training Camp	Germany	
18	07/05 *	Tio Mila (relay)	Sweden	
19	14/05	Närke dubbel	Sweden	Training race
20	21/05	Siljanskavlen (relay)	Sweden	
21				
22	01/06 **	Nordic Open Championships	Sweden	Peak
23	11/06 *	Jukola (relay)	Finland	
24				Training period
25				
26		Training week in the hills		Final build up
27		Training race		
28				
29	22/07 *	Selection Races	Germany	
30		Training in the hills		
31		Training race		
32				
33	15/08 **	World Championships	Germany	Peak
34				
35				
36	10/09 *	Swedish. champs classic	Stockholm	
37	15/09 *	Swe. champs short	Stockholm	
	17/09 *	Swe. champs relay	Stockholm	
38				
39				
40				
41				
42	21/10	Blodslitet (long distance)	Noway	
43	29/10 *	Smålandskavlen (relay)	Sweden	End of season

* Important race
** Major goal

A typical plan for an international season. Note that the racing period is end of March to the beginning of June, and again from late July to mid October.

A typical training week during low season (early March):

Monday: Easy run 40 mins + 60 mins weight training
Tuesday: 40 mins easy run + 75 minutes night orienteering
Wednesday: 110 mins long run with map. 30 mins weight training
Thursday: 60 mins intervals
Friday: 40 mins easy run
Saturday: am 75 minutes technique training, pm 65 mins night O
Sunday: 100 mins long run with map + 40 mins cycle.

This week included five sessions with a map. This is only possible if you live somewhere with easy access to orienteering terrain.

Excerpt from Steve Hale's year plan.

- If you miss some training due to injury or illness, don't be tempted to try to make up for lost time by squeezing three weeks' training into two weeks. In particular, as the big race approaches it can be very tempting to squeeze in that extra interval session. Don't!
- Ease down your training in the two weeks up to the race so that you are fresh, though it is important to keep ticking over. Your diet in the last few days up to the race is particularly important – plenty of carbohydrates and liquids. This is the fuel you will be running on, so don't start the race with empty tanks!
- Learn to listen to your own body – learn what training suits you in the approach to a race.
- Prepare yourself mentally. The benefits of mental training are often underrated.

GETTING THE BALANCE RIGHT (FITNESS AND TECHNIQUE)

Most of us know somebody who is the 'best technical orienteer in the world', but simply can't run fast enough. There is a basic fallacy in this line of thinking – navigating accurately at 10mins/km is a whole world away from navigating accurately at 6mins/km. Running speed and technique are intimately related and one of the hardest things when training for orienteering is achieving the right balance. Improvements in technique must match improvements in fitness. This is one good argument for maintaining a basic level of technique training even during the 'off season'.

Conversely, lack of fitness can lead directly to navigational errors. The textbook course planning trick of setting a number of short technical legs at the end of a course is designed to catch out the tiring runner. Anybody who has 'bonked' on an orienteering course (what marathon runners call 'hitting the wall') will know that the next control is not easy to find. If you are not used to running in rough terrain then your map reading will suffer when you come up against just that. This is just one of the reasons why continental orienteers have such a hard time in Scandinavia. The answer is, of course, to train in sufficient quantity and quality so that you can take all the physical challenges of an orienteering course in your stride. Increasing your physical fitness will also enable you to cope with a greater quantity and better quality of technique training. Fitness and orienteering technique must go hand in hand.

TRAINING TOGETHER

Orienteering is often a solitary sport. Some of the real value-added training sessions, however, can be those done with another orienteer. Few things are more conducive to improving your orienteering than a bit of friendly rivalry. The quality of your training almost always improves when you train together with somebody else. You can discover weaknesses by direct comparison as you run in the forest and you can discuss and analyze the training together afterwards. There are many good training sessions which are specifically designed for pairs or small groups:

- Match play: training exercises where you start as a group of between two and four and try to be the first to the next control, regrouping at the control.
- Route choice: train in pairs or threes and deliberately take different route choices, meeting up at each control.

- Visualization: running in pairs with one map between you, take turns in leading and following. The leader runs without the map using his visualized picture of the map and terrain, whilst the follower prepares himself for the next leg where roles are swapped.
- Conducting: running in pairs with one map between you, take turns in leading and following. In this exercise the follower has the map and 'conducts', that is, gives instructions to the leading runner.
- Relocation: running in pairs with one map between you, take turns in leading and following. The leader passes over the map in the region of a control. The follower relocates and navigates the final bit into the control.

ARMCHAIR TRAINING

Not everybody has easy access to orienteering terrain. Good quality technique training also requires a high level of fitness and the volume of training you can cope with is therefore limited. 'Armchair training' can be an important complement to your training in the forest.

The basis for much of your armchair training is the map folder – the ring binder where you archive the maps from your past races. This is a valuable library of your experiences and it can be both beneficial and enjoyable to look back on some of your previous races. In particular, when preparing for a specific race you can gain a lot by studying past maps of the competition area and similar forests.

Another form of armchair training is mental training. This is not easy to do but it is worth trying to get into a routine of perhaps 5 to 10 minutes of mental training each day. Try:

- Visualizing yourself on the start line for a big race. How does it feel? How are you going to run to the first control?
- Visualize your routine for running into a control, punching and running out.
- Imagine yourself approaching the finish of an important relay. You are together with a rival – what tactics do you use?

The possibilities are endless – use your imagination!

THE ROLE OF A COACH

The orienteer must learn to be self-reliant. When out in the forest, whether training or racing, there will not be a coach shouting instructions. Perhaps the main role of a coach is to help to teach the athlete to be his or her own coach. This is a philosophy through which Norwegian elite sports have achieved remarkable success. The personal coach should be there to help the athlete plan his own training; he should offer advice and be ready to answer questions. No coach can be an expert on all aspects of elite sport, but he should at least know which direction to point the athlete in order to find the answers he's looking for. A coach can also provide a shoulder to cry on and a ready ear to listen.

A club or team coach can help in many practical ways. Planning and setting out training exercises is perhaps the basic bread and butter of being an orienteering coach. Observing and giving feedback to the athletes is another important function. Video filming exercises and shadowing runners are two good ways of doing this. Of course, the runners can be encouraged to shadow each other and give constructive criticism themselves.

As a motivator the coach can be invaluable in creating the right team spirit. The team coach must get to know the individuals in a team, and learn what they best respond to. Some people require constant encouragement whilst others respond better to the honest truth, even if this can seem harsh at times. In getting the right atmosphere in a team – encouraging friendly rivalry and discussion after exercises – the most valuable coaching advice will often come from the team members themselves. The coach should be a catalyst, rather than doing all the work himself.

REACHING THE TOP

As with all sports, to reach the top you need one hundred percent commitment. The 20/80 rule is a very good approximation!

With twenty percent commitment you can expect to reach eighty percent of your potential. This is good news for the keen club orienteer with only a limited amount of time available; but it also means you have to work very hard if you want to achieve that last twenty percent!

To reach the top, you don't just have to be one hundred percent committed, you have to train intelligently. Optimal training is, contrary to common belief, not simply the most training. It is sometimes said that you can train twice as much as you think you can, and ten times as much as your mother thinks you can. This may be true but it is very easy to end up overtraining. Listen to the signals from your body and adapt the training load accordingly.

The 20/80 Rule.

Reaching the top requires a great deal of hard work and nobody else is going to do it for you. However, there are a number of ways that you can make life simpler. First and foremost, make sure you live in an environment which is conducive to training. If you have the luxury of being able to choose where to study or work, then consider the possibilities for training when you make this choice. Another important factor is choosing a club which actively supports elite orienteering. This support can be both practical in the form of training sessions, training camps, group travel to races; it can also be financial, either through training grants or assistance in obtaining grants and sponsorship from other organizations.

For any junior, the transition to the senior class can be a big shock. This is not just because the courses are longer and tougher. The level of competition in the senior class is such that very few, if any, juniors can expect to achieve success in their first year or two as a senior. It can be good experience to encourage top-end juniors to occasionally 'race up', that is, enter the senior class. Short distance races are particularly good for this. One of the dangers of 'racing up' in longer races is that it can encourage juniors to adopt a too steady orienteering style – playing safe and not risking running at full pace in case they can't last the distance. In this case it can be better for top juniors to race their own class but to compare their minutes per km to the top seniors' speed.

One of the keys to reaching the top in orienteering is gaining as wide an experience of different terrain types as possible. Often

Reaching the top.

access to terrain is limited and the amount of technique training you can cope with is also limited by your physical capacity. It is therefore important to make the most of your technique training sessions. Spend a few minutes before starting your training session preparing yourself, almost as if it were a race. Concentrate on the purpose of the exercise and what techniques you will be training. Start the exercise fully concentrated on the job in hand. In order to maintain concentration throughout the session it is often better to run shorter, intensive technique sessions. Two 40-minute technique sessions will almost certainly be better than one 80-minute session.

It takes a tremendous amount of experience to reach the top in orienteering. Most orienteers reach their peak in their early thirties. A lot can be learnt by listening to more experienced runners. Do not be afraid to ask somebody how they train or how they ran a certain race or what route choice they took, but avoid simply copying the approach of your idol. Listen and learn and adapt the best ideas and tips to your own needs. Finally, remember that nobody reaches the top of their sport without experiencing setbacks. The real winners are those who learn from their setbacks and return stronger and faster.

4 Orienteering Fitness Training

ANDREW KITCHIN

I have decided to write about training with a different approach from some popular manuals that are very prescriptive with lots of training sessions plans and regimes. *I want you* to understand what is going on when you train to get fitter. If you understand what happens then you are in a position to plan and build your own individual training programme. There is a great deal to know about fitness, training, exercise and related physiology. All of it links together and is applicable to many different aspects of fitness training.

As you read this, you should try to concentrate on the biological processes (the physiology) that contribute to your level of fitness. Having done so, you should be able to take a sensible, educated and successful approach to fitness training.

FITNESS

The *Oxford English Dictionary* defines 'Fit' as meaning 'Well adapted or suitable for some purpose ...in suitable condition.'

"Why do you train so hard?" asked the man behind the camera. "It's the same as with any sport, the fitter you are the more you get out of it." said the man in front.

To me, this seems a most simple and valid expression of why fitness, and the training necessary to achieve it, is worthwhile. If orienteering is a joy, then orienteering when you are feeling fit is sublime. Gliding through the woods, powering up a hill, rip-ping through controls, are uniquely exhilarating experiences.

In orienteering improved fitness has perhaps greater competitive payoffs than in many other sports. You cannot only move more quickly when fit, but in addition you will be able to move more accurately, saving even more time. Through training, you become more comfortable with physical exertion. It is less of a distraction and you can concentrate more on navigation. More of your attention can be given to route choice and execution, so that they are performed more clearly and correctly. Even for those orienteers who derive satisfaction from accurate navigation rather than racing, improved fitness will allow greater enjoyment because it will improve navigation.

To me, the sport of orienteering is a navigational race involving physical effort. Racing round a course is a great pleasure, even if no-one else is running. This is because a race provides the spur to navigate without error. It provides the urgency for accuracy. There must be no time loss from either the physical or the navigational aspects of the course. If you are not pushing for the fastest time then there is no urgency and concentration begins to lapse. Thus, paradoxically, by taking it easy you make more mistakes. The more you put in the more you get out.

That is why I believe fitness improves enjoyment and performance in orienteering, especially if it is specific to the demands that orienteering running places on the body. Although an endurance sport, orienteering

Orienteers run through marshes and over broken ground.

response to a repeated physical demand the body adapts so that it becomes more able and efficient at performing that physical task. To understand how the training stimulus works it will help to understand the physiology of exercise, that is, how muscular work is achieved. This will help you to understand your training and the effects that it has on you, both pleasant and, dare I say it, occasionally unpleasant. An understanding of exercise physiology is central to the training ideas covered later in this chapter and will help you to plan and adapt your training to best effect.

EXERCISE PHYSIOLOGY

Muscle and Movement

Muscle only does one thing. It shortens or contracts and when it does that it moves things for us – arms, legs, fingers, any part of the body – and this movement is called physical work. To lengthen again one muscle needs a second, an opposing partner. When the second muscle shortens it pulls the first out to its full length so it is able to shorten again.

A body of muscle such as the biceps in the arm or the calf muscle in the lower leg is a large collection of muscle cells. These cells are quite long and thin and they all run in the same direction so that when they contract they all pull in the same direction. The many cells are held together in position by connective tissue. Inside each muscle cell there are many muscle fibres made of protein. There are two types of fibre, thick

involves running through marshes, up hills and over broken ground. It demands bursts of speed, exceptional leg strength, and suppleness to dodge obstacles and sway through trees and undergrowth. Put in crude terms, orienteering fitness needs a subtle balance of Stamina, Speed, Strength and Suppleness. Let us now return to the exact nature of fitness.

'Well adapted for some purpose' is a good definition for human athletic ability. A fit person is well adapted to perform physical work. Repeated physical training is what provides the stimulus for adaptation. In

fibres and thin fibres. Thick and thin fibres are arranged to interlock. *See* figure 1.

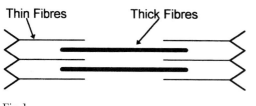

Fig 1.

When a muscle contracts thick and thin fibres interact and move over each other so that the amount of interlocking is greater. This shortens the muscle cell. *See* figure 2.

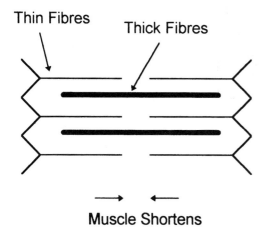

Fig 2.

Muscle Contraction

It is important to understand where the energy for muscle contraction comes from. When a muscle cell is relaxed each side body carries an energy rich molecule called ATP (Adenosine Tri-Phosphate). *See* figure 3.

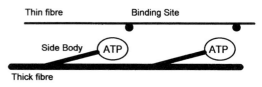

Fig 3.

When the muscle cell is stimulated to contract the side bodies of the thick fibres attach to the binding site on the thin fibres. At this point the side body takes energy from the ATP molecule to allow it to do the work of movement. In releasing its energy the ATP molecule is broken in two and released from the side body. *See* figure 4.

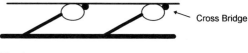

Fig 4.

Next, the side bodies move, pulling thick and thin fibres over one another, shortening the muscle cell and achieving bodily movement through physical work. This uses up the energy from the ATP. *See* figure 5.

Fig 5.

Finally, the side bodies must let go to get into position for the next cycle of movement. To let go, the side body must get a new molecule of ATP. Unless this happens the side bodies cannot let go and the contraction of the muscle cannot continue. *See* figure 6.

Fig 6.

86

For example, if you were climbing a ladder and had totally run out of energy, you would not take another step until someone had given you a chocolate bar. It's a little worse than that for the thick fibres, however, because the side bodies actually stay stuck to the thin fibres until they get more ATP for energy. They really cannot let go. In a dead body this leads to rigor mortis, in which muscle becomes stiff and solid.

There is also a consequence in living, exercising muscle. Imagine a situation where you are running low on energy so the supply of ATP is not quite up to the needs of the muscle. Lots of side bodies are getting ATP and are keeping moving while a few are stuck. What happens then is that the movement of the majority of the muscle tears off the side bodies that have been left attached.

- *An important point.* If you exercise without an adequate energy supply, or sprint into a large oxygen debt by running so long that you 'hit the wall', you do more damage to your muscles, which is not much good if you are trying to improve your fitness. When you are training regularly it is therefore important to pay attention to eating enough of the right food (see below).

ENERGY SUPPLY

The energy carrier known as Adenosine Tri-Phosphate collects energy from the parts of a cell where food is broken down and carries it to the proteins where the energy is used. When ATP interacts with proteins such as muscle this energy is released and the proteins are able to perform the millions of processes of life in our bodies. Proteins form all the structures in our bodies that actually do things, and doing things always requires energy.

The available supply of ATP is limited. There will usually be enough in a muscle cell for about 4 seconds of contraction. To provide for muscle contraction lasting longer than this it is necessary repeatedly to recreate new molecules of ATP, by recycling broken down ATP. This takes place in a part of our cells called the mitochondria. In the mitochondria chemical reactions are designed to take energy from food stuffs and to pass that energy to ATP. A source of energy is needed to enable ATP to be continuously reformed. There are several.

Creatine Phosphate

This is a molecule similar to ATP though it acts more as an energy store than an energy carrier. Creatine Phosphate provides a short-term supply of immediately available energy for the recreation of ATP, sufficient to resupply muscles with ATP for 6 to 8 seconds of contraction. Though it is a very important energy store for sprinting and other short, intense bouts of exercise, Creatine Phosphate does not provide the long-term solution needed for prolonged exercise of the orienteering type.

Carbohydrates

These include such things as sugar, pasta, rice and potatoes, and all are stored in our body as the sugar glucose, either in our muscles or in the liver. The store of glucose in our bodies is very changeable and depends on recent exercise and diet. By eating a high carbohydrate diet it is possible to store enough glucose for 90 to 100 minutes of exercise.

By using carbohydrates we can have an energy source sufficient to support prolonged exercise such as running. Unlike Creatine Phosphate the energy stored in glucose cannot be used directly for the re-creation of ATP. Glucose must undergo a complex series of chemical reactions, many of which require the presence of oxygen. These reactions take place in the mitochondria. So, although it provides a good energy store glucose is not an immediate energy source, and Creatine Phosphate exists to bridge the energy gap between ATP/Creatine Phosphate stores and getting the glucose system going.

Fat

This provides a very large store of energy that is virtually limitless in terms of its ability to supply energy for exercise, enough for many hours of running. Like glucose, fat must undergo a complex series of chemical reactions before its energy can be used to recreate ATP and, in the case of fat, oxygen is essential to the whole process. These reactions also take place in the mitochondria. Fat provides a very reliable but slow source of energy for exercise – it is a slower source of energy than glucose. There are two reasons for this. The first is that there are fewer mitochondria in muscle cells capable of using fat than are capable of using glucose, and therefore there is simply less capacity for the use of fat in exercise. Secondly the release of energy from fat requires more oxygen than the release of energy from glucose.

To release one unit of energy, 1kJ:
from fat requires   0.512 litres of oxygen
from glucose requires   0.495 litres of oxygen

Thus fat is a less efficient use of the oxygen available in our muscles.

The supply of oxygen to muscle is central to our ability to perform exercise. We breathe more in exercise, so as to get more oxygen into our blood, and our heart beats faster so that the oxygen is then carried more quickly to our muscles, where it is used to release as much energy as possible, preferably releasing energy from glucose. When the energy used for exercise has been released from fat or glucose through reaction with oxygen we call it *aerobic exercise.*

When you are exercising at the limit of your ability to supply oxygen to your muscles – at maximum aerobic capacity – then all the energy being released will be from glucose. Of course, it is possible to exercise below this limit, which allows some of the energy to be released from fat because there is spare oxygen available. Glucose stores can therefore be conserved. The further below your maximum aerobic capacity you exercise the more energy comes from fat and the longer you can maintain continuous exercise.

It is also possible to exercise beyond your maximum aerobic capacity. This is called *anaerobic exercise* because it does not use oxygen in the release of energy.

Where exercise is so intense that the energy demand exceeds our maximum ability to supply oxygen to muscles (called the maximum aerobic capacity) for a time glucose can continue to supply ATP without oxygen but at the cost of creating lactic acid. Lactic acid is probably something that you have heard of and undoubtedly you have experienced it. When you run too hard lactic acid leaves you with heavy, burning, painful muscles; gasping for breath whilst your heart goes wild. Lactic acid hurts.

Whenever you experience pain it is a warning that you are in danger of physical damage. A build-up of lactic acid in your muscles generates pain as a warning that damage is imminent and because of the pain you slow your exercise, allowing the lactic acid to be removed. The damage is due to

Lactic acid hurts.

the substance's acidic nature. Too much acid is damaging to proteins; in fact, it pickles them just like vinegar would!

A second reason why it is preferable to avoid anaerobic exercise is that high acid levels affect the nervous system. In terms of orienteering running over broken ground this causes a loss of co-ordination so that movement is less efficient, even leading to trips, stumbles and falls. Of perhaps greater relevance to orienteers is that it affects clarity of thought and concentration levels and this of course will lead to more navigational errors.

Anaerobic energy release is also a waste of the energy that is available from a molecule of glucose. The anaerobic stage only releases enough energy to re-form two out of a potential thirty-six molecules of ATP from aerobic exercise. By using up glucose in anaerobic energy release your glucose stores will run out far sooner and this means you will not be able to run so fast for so long.

Consider the Various Facts

- Glucose gives a rapid energy release.
- Glucose gives a substantial energy store.
- Aerobic energy release from glucose is the most efficient use of oxygen.
- Anaerobic energy release wastes energy store.
- Anaerobic release disturbs co-ordination and concentration.

The conclusion has to be that for an orienteering race, it is best to gain energy by aerobic release from glucose. We have seen that this requires sufficient oxygen and takes place in the mitochondria. To improve our ability for aerobic exercise we need to improve the oxygen supply to muscles and increase the number of mitochondria.

TRAINING AND ENERGY EFFICIENCY

I do not want to spell out specific training programmes for you to follow. Training is an individual thing. Your programme depends on what you want from the sport, what you already do as training, the time you have available, and your ability to cope with volumes of physical activity. I want to give some rules of thumb and the principles on which you should plan and progress your own programme.

The human body always tries to save energy. We have evolved from a lifestyle thousands of years ago where the next meal could never be guaranteed, so the body will tend to store energy whenever it can – hence give it a lot of food and it gets fat, storing it

up for when the food runs out. The other side to saving energy is not to use it. Maintaining the human body is a full-time job: bone, protein, muscle and enzymes are always breaking down and must be replaced and recreated. This, of course, uses up energy from our daily food intake. If there is less body to maintain, then less energy needs be used and we save energy. As a result of this, our bodies do not replace or maintain any part that is not used regularly, such as a muscle. Unused muscles waste down to a small size, whereas a muscle maintains its size if used regularly. Muscles become bigger and stronger if worked harder than usual for a few weeks, or if trained repeatedly by overloading them.

The same process for improving and maintaining muscle strength applies to aerobic fitness: the number of blood vessels in muscle and lung and the number of mitochondria in muscle increase. If they are not used, then the body does not waste energy to keep them. Used regularly, they are maintained. Pushed beyond their capacity – overloaded – and blood vessels and mitochondria will increase in number to meet demand. This increase of capacity in response to a regular overload is consistent with saving energy, because it allows exercise to be aerobic and that, as we know, is more efficient than anaerobic.

Training uses the tendency of the body to save energy by adapting so that the capacity for regular exercise is aerobic. Should you fail to exercise and maintain your fitness you will fall foul of the other way in which the body saves energy, by not maintaining unused fitness.

'USE IT OR LOSE IT'

Improving Aerobic Fitness

Training for aerobic fitness aims to improve the body's capacity to transport oxygen to exercising muscles and to increase the rate at which it can use glucose and fat. The effects of such training on oxygen transport are to:

- improve oxygen uptake in the lungs by increasing the blood vessels in the lungs;
- improve the rate of blood circulation around the body, by strengthening the heart;
- improve the oxygen supply to muscle cells by increasing the number of blood vessels in the muscles;
- increase the oxygen carrying capacity of the blood by increasing the number of blood cells and iron content.

The effects on energy release are to:

- stimulate an increase in the number of energy releasing mitochondria;
- increase the ability to remove lactic acid that is generated during exercise.

These changes along with the increased supply of oxygen raise your ability to exercise at a steady rate over a prolonged period of time.

TRAINING AEROBIC FITNESS

Giving your body the stimulus it needs means exercise. In orienteering terms this primarily means 'running'. To improve, you must make demands on your body that are greater than normal. The normal adapted level of exercise for your body is fully aerobic, because it is the most efficient. Beyond that level, the harder you try, the more anaerobic and inefficient your exercise becomes. To stimulate an increase in your aerobic capacity you must push your body beyond its normal limit and into anaerobic exercise, to a level of exercise that raises the level of lactic acid in your muscles above normal.

It is often easy to think of aerobic and anaerobic exercise as two sides of a coin: you are on one side or the other, using one system or the other, aerobic or anaerobic. This is not the case.

Because biological systems are complex and made up of many thousands of parts, thousands of muscle cells, thousands of fibres, thousands of mitochondria, thousands of blood cells, thousands of oxygen molecules, thousands of ATP molecules; the system as a whole is never one or the other, but more or less of either. Some parts will be aerobic, others anaerobic, and the balance shifts as the intensity of exercise changes. Which is more, or less, depends on the balance of factors between what is available in oxygen and energy and what is needed in exercise rate. As your rate of exercise increases there is a gradual change starting with all energy being released aerobically. Then a transition begins; most energy is released aerobically and a little anaerobically, then more is anaerobic. Finally, too much is anaerobic, leading to lactic acid overload – at which point you stop or slow down. Importantly, though, there are the transition levels of exercise where some energy is from anaerobic release. At these levels exercise can be maintained for quite long periods of time without ever leading to lactic acid overload. The reason for this is that the lactic acid, after being created in the muscle, is released into the blood and circulated to the liver where it is removed. In the liver, lactic acid is converted back to glucose through aerobic processes.

Anaerobic energy release and the accompanying build-up of lactic acid is, as has been described already, a waste of energy and bad for your ability to compete in an orienteering race.

The reason that we have the ability for anaerobic exercise when it seems like such a poor process is that it provides a very important way of meeting a short, sudden, very rapid increase in our need for energy. For example, you are running along through the woods and suddenly a lion appears and starts chasing you – or in orienteering terms, you jump a fallen tree or run up a hill, run across a marsh and suddenly your legs are burning with lactic acid. You could not instantly breathe deeper and pump blood faster to get the oxygen needed into your muscles, because that takes at least a few seconds, and the appearance of the lion produced an instant demand for energy. Anaerobic exercise provided the immediate energy and bridged the gap between instant demand for energy and delayed supply of oxygen. Once you have outsprinted the lion your muscles hurt because of the lactic acid, but after a brief time the feeling subsides. This is because our physiology is not so hopeless that it does not have a mechanism for removing such a nasty but natural thing as lactic acid.

The removal of lactic acid takes place in the liver and it is achieved by converting lactic acid back into glucose. This rebuilding process and the fact that it uses oxygen gives the term 'oxygen debt'. The term is a very good one. When we use anaerobic exercise we are in effect borrowing energy from glucose without paying for it with a supply of oxygen and the energy debt remains as lactic acid which is carried in the blood to the liver. Once in the liver the loan is paid back with oxygen and we get our glucose back. However, as with any loan there is a price

and that price is the glucose energy used up in the liver during the removal of lactic acid.

In the muscle, when there is not sufficient oxygen:

$$Glucose \longrightarrow Energy + Lactic\ Acid$$

Lactic Acid circulates through the blood to the Liver, where:

$$Lactic\ Acid + Oxygen + Glucose \longrightarrow Glucose$$

This process of reforming glucose in the liver is less efficient than the direct aerobic use of glucose for energy in muscles. It does, however, prevent the build up of lactic acid and it saves some of the energy that would be wasted as lactic acid by reforming glucose. In effect, the liver acts as a back-up to our muscles by taking on some of the burden of releasing energy aerobically.

Lactic Acid Levels

Lactic acid production in our muscles depends on how hard we are exercising. It is possible to measure the amounts of lactic acid in the blood and produce a graph of lactic acid against heart rate or against running speed. There is always a low stable level of lactic acid being produced in our bodies. At low levels of exercise, there is no increase in blood lactic acid, because there are enough mitochondria being supplied with sufficient oxygen for all our energy requirements to be met by aerobic energy release.

As exercise effort gets greater, we reach a point where all the energy that our muscles require cannot be provided aerobically because not enough oxygen and mitochondria are available. So we begin to produce some energy anaerobically. As a result, blood lactic acid level rises. The point at which this begins is called the *aerobic threshold* – there are not enough mitochondria and/or they are not receiving sufficient oxygen. In this zone, we have a raised blood lactic acid but in fact our exercise is still overall an aerobic process. Lactic acid is being converted back to glucose in the liver as fast as the muscles are producing it; the lactic acid level is stable. The liver acts as a back-up to muscles to achieve more energy release aerobically. In this zone, though the level of lactic acid in the blood is raised to a degree it is actually stabilized by the activity of the liver and exercise can be maintained for a long period.

As we exercise harder and harder, the muscles produce more and more of their energy anaerobically, releasing higher levels of lactic acid into the blood. The liver works harder and harder at removing the lactic acid. Blood lactic acid is stable at a steady level of exercise but the harder the exercise the higher the blood lactic acid. Eventually, a point is reached where the liver is removing lactic acid as fast as it possibly can. This level of exercise is called the *anaerobic threshold*.

As effort increases beyond this point, the muscles produce lactic acid at yet greater rates but the liver cannot keep up. Blood lactic acid spirals upward quickly because lactic acid is produced more quickly by the muscles than the liver can remove it. If exercise continues at this level, we rapidly reach lactic acid overload and exhaustion – burning muscles, breathlessness and finally collapse.

AEROBIC ENDURANCE TRAINING

To increase aerobic fitness you need to stimulate your body to adapt by pushing it beyond its aerobic capacity. There are certain levels of exercise ideal for providing this stimulus – these are the levels between the *aerobic and anaerobic thresholds*. It is these levels of exercise upon which you need to concentrate to improve your aerobic endurance fitness for orienteering. When aiming for these levels of exercise you come up against some conflicting requirements.

When I talked about ATP and muscle fibres I mentioned the damage that can be done by tearing fibres that are not supplied with ATP. To stimulate adaptation through anaerobic exercise you will therefore need to exercise at levels where energy supply will be insufficient, thus there will be some damage to muscle fibres. What this means is that in the process of getting fitter you will do a little damage to your muscles. This damage is felt as stiffness after exercise, and that brings us on to the important matter of rest and recovery.

You want to get fitter so:

- you have to exercise beyond your aerobic threshold;
- which means you are bound to cause some degree of damage to your muscles;
- which means you had better let the damage repair itself;
- which means rest and recovery – as essential a part of any training programme as the exercise itself.

If you don't rest, your body never has the opportunity to repair damaged muscle, so you have less useful muscle and become less fit. Training requires overuse, but overuse without recovery will lead to a reduction in ability, a state of fatigue – so you must have periods of *rest and recovery*.

How to push just enough but not for too long is a fine and difficult line to tread and part of the art of training.

A rule of thumb here is the rule of three:

- never do three hard days on the trot, nor three hard weeks, nor months, nor even years.

That's a guide to try to avoid damage and fatigue, but you must always be aware of how your body is feeling. If your muscles are stiff and sore when running then they need a rest to recover.

HOW HARD TO TRAIN

I should perhaps start by naming and defining some types of training. These are: Recovery, Maintenance, Aerobic Endurance and Speed and Anaerobic Tolerance.

Recovery Training

Recovery training means rest, though not necessarily doing nothing. It allows your body to recover and build a higher level of fitness. It is very light, and it doesn't hurt, but often it means doing something. Doing a little will mean that you are in a better position to resume serious training once your recovery is complete. It avoids you stiffening up, you retain flexibility and mobility, and the processes of digesting and storing food to maintain a high level of exercise continue.

Recovery can be nothing but a bit of stretching, a jog, a swim, or a cycle ride. The main requirement is that it should not hurt. Remember that pain warns of damage, so if you can jog without hurting stiff muscles then that's fine, but don't do more and don't be tempted to say 'well its not that sore'. If it's sore, it's sore, and you should slow down or stop. Also be wary of running through a pain barrier because that is cheating. Your body will suppress pain if it has to

and this means that sometimes if you keep running pain subsides (the suppression of pain allows you to keep your sanity), but you are still doing damage. With pain, the rule must be that if a muscle or joint is tender and hurts, *stop now*.

You can also feel fatigued without anything specific hurting. It is not only important to rest to allow repair but to allow the process of developing new tissue, more new muscle, more new blood vessels, more new mitochondria. This too requires time and energy, so if you are not able to get going, or to get up speed on a run as you would like to then it is probably that you are tired from building new tissue and enzymes. As you become a more seasoned runner it is more likely that you will experience this kind of fatigue than muscle damage fatigue. The key to avoiding this is not only rest but also good nutrition.

Maintenance Training

This is not too hard. It is running at a comfortable level that you can maintain for a substantial time without having to push or force yourself to keep going. It is running at effort up to your *aerobic threshold*.

What this type of training does is to maintain the adaptation, the increased fitness hard-earned in past training sessions:

- the powerful heart;
- muscular strength and tone;
- the dense, fine network of blood vessels in lungs and muscle that allows rapid and efficient transfer of oxygen;
- The high number of mitochondria in muscle to supply ATP.

You could say this is 'Use it or lose it' training.

Aerobic Endurance Training

This is where the work is done, where you push your body beyond its comfortable capacity and ask it to do more, to which the response will be increased fitness. The level of effort is above your *aerobic capacity*. Training at this level of effort raises the level of lactic acid above normal because the supply of oxygen to the muscles is not sufficient to supply all the energy needed by aerobic means. The conditions that this creates stimulates the body to adapt, increasing:

- the heart's power;
- muscular strength and tone;
- the dense, fine network of blood vessels in lungs and muscle that allow rapid and efficient transfer of oxygen;
- the number of mitochondria in muscle to supply ATP;
- the capacity of the liver to convert lactic acid back to glucose using oxygen.

These adaptations have the effect of increasing your aerobic capacity so that you become able to exercise comfortably at higher levels of effort. You will become able to run faster and still be comfortable, and you will be able to maintain this running speed for longer. In short, your endurance at higher speeds increases by raising your aerobic threshold and increasing your liver's capacity to remove lactic acid. It is this level of training that will do most to increase your endurance fitness.

Speed and Anaerobic Tolerance Training

From the above you will realize that for distance running the key to going faster for longer is to increase your aerobic capacity, and that to go anaerobic is not desirable. However, you will also understand that anaerobic exercise is unavoidable. In the aerobic training zone lactic acid levels are raised by anaerobic energy production but stabilized by removal in the liver. But sometimes in an orienteering race you will be forced into an extra effort which will tip you over your anaerobic threshold, generating a pulse of lactic acid that the liver is not capable of removing immediately. These are the levels of effort that you will experience when racing and to avoid the effects of lactic acid such as impaired co-ordination and thought, it is essential to be able to tolerate brief periods of lactic acid generation.

Such tolerance can be provided by adjustments in body fluids, blood, plasma and cell fluids. Put simply, the amount of bicarbonate and the proteins in these body fluids can adapt to help neutralize the acid effects of lactic acid. To train this tolerance, effort needs to be pushed to the anaerobic threshold and just beyond. The effort is maintained for a short time and then a recovery period allows the liver to clear the lactic acid. This level of training will significantly extend the limits of your running ability.

Judging Effort

I have explained what I consider to be the relevant levels of training effort. They relate to levels of blood lactic acid. To achieve a certain training effect you need to push your blood lactic acid to a certain level. Describing various levels of training is all very well, but the important question is what kind of effort does this mean for you as an individual? The effort for a given level of training is specific to *you*. There are various ways of determining the right effort, and one is running speed.

The level of your blood lactic acid can be related to running speed. For example, your aerobic threshold might be 4 minutes per kilometre on flat grass. Judging your effort by speed is fine if you are training over consistent ground, for example flattish roads or grass, but if you start running through rough terrain, or up and down hills, then your speed drops greatly despite maintaining the same or even greater effort.

One way around this is to use heart rate as a measure of effort, which has been found to be an extremely reliable indicator of blood lactate levels. Lactate levels provide the stimulus for adaptation to training, heart rate is an excellent guide. One very useful aid in judging effort, and which is becoming more and more affordable, is a heart rate monitor. Basic, good-quality models are now little more expensive than a pair of training shoes.

The training zones are: *maintenance* which is below the aerobic threshold; *aerobic endurance* which is between aerobic and anaerobic thresholds; *anaerobic tolerance* which is around the anaerobic threshold. You need to be familiar with your aerobic and anaerobic thresholds. There are several rules of thumb that can help you to determine them. For all the guides described below, you should try to become familiar with the level of effort and how it feels, either by running or by recording heart rate with a monitor.

Finding your Anaerobic Threshold

A common rule of thumb is to say that your effort over a 10km road race or a cross-country race when run to the best of your ability throughout is just below the anaerobic threshold. If you don't run any such races, you will need to do several practices before you can decide on your best speed.

A useful way of defining your appropriate running speed is proposed as follows:

- Do a series of 1km repetition runs on the flat, for example 4 x 1km with 3

minutes rest between. Do them as evenly but as fast as you can, so that at the end of each rep you should be gasping. You may need to do this a few times to get used to the feel and get reliable times. Once you are getting consistent times and feel that you are putting in maximum effort you will be familiar with the level of effort required to reach your anaerobic threshold. Calculate your speed or measure your heart rate towards the end of the rep. Taking this speed as a marker, you can calculate the target speeds for your other levels of exercise.

Finding your Aerobic Threshold

This is much more difficult to judge through the feel of the running effort, but try to get a feel for the following description:

- Once warmed up (20 minutes), increase your running speed gradually and go a little faster every couple of minutes for as long as it is comfortable to do so. You will settle at a speed that is your aerobic threshold – to run harder takes a concentrated effort. The effort that pushes you over your aerobic threshold and into your anaerobic endurance training zone is indicated by two effects: to maintain a higher effort requires continued concentration; and running harder requires a marked increase in breathing.

Maintenance Speed

At speeds more than 30–35 percent slower than your maximum aerobic speed, for example around 4 minutes per kilometre, you will be in the best area for maintenance training, though your maintenance running will be this fast only if you are feeling good and fresh. Maintenance training will likely be effective down to sixty percent slower than maximum aerobic speed.

Anaerobic Tolerance Speed

The target speed for this kind of high-intensity shorter interval training would be five percent faster than maximum aerobic speed.

Recovery

Using speed to judge effort is fine over regular ground or over regular routes, but it has its limitations in very variable terrain and over unfamiliar training routes. You could solve this by finding out your maximum aerobic speed over rougher/hilly ground and then doing similar calculations. If you use a heart rate monitor you can record your heart rate when running over flat, even regular ground at various levels of effort. These heart rates at certain levels of effort are then the same in whatever terrain you choose to train in.

If you want to be as certain as possible about judging your effort level by relating heart rate to blood lactic acid then a lactate profile test on a treadmill will give you very good indications of your aerobic and anaerobic thresholds. For this you will need to find a sports science laboratory that can run the tests for you. As your fitness improves further tests may be useful.

Training to Improve Fitness – Sessions for Aerobic Endurance.

There are a range of sessions that can be done to work on aerobic endurance. Those that are just above the aerobic threshold will be longer and steadier than those just below

the anaerobic threshold – the latter are more like long repetitions.

Here are some ideas, for you to use or adapt as you feel suitable:

- *Long steady effort:* the effort level in this run would be just above your aerobic threshold. After a decent warm up of 10 to 15 minutes, you should up your effort over your aerobic threshold and maintain this steady effort for 20 to 30 minutes. Follow this with a warm down and stretch. For our examples 3:40 minutes per km is twenty to twenty-five percent slower than your maximum aerobic speed.
- *Tempo Runs:* warm up. Raise your effort level to the middle to upper range of your aerobic zone; maintain this as a steady effort for 15 to 20 minutes. For our examples the speed would be 3:25 mins per km. That is ten to fifteen percent slower than your maximum aerobic speed. Warm down and stretch.
- *Long Repetitions:* warm up. Set a route of 4 to 7 minutes. Repeat the course until you have done a total of 15 to 20 minutes effort – say 5x4 minutes or 3x6 minutes. Between reps your rest need only be around 2 or 3 minutes. Warm down and stretch. For our examples the speed would be 3:10 mins per km or around five percent slower than your maximum aerobic speed.

SESSIONS FOR SPEED AND AEROBIC TOLERANCE

These sessions will help improve your maximum running speed, your control and efficiency at high speed and your ability to maintain control and speed through spells of extra effort when you generate a brief pulse of lactic acid.

Interval Training

Here your target level of effort is at or just above your anaerobic threshold. After a suitable warm up of at least 15 minutes and some stretching and striding your intervals of running should total 12 to 15 minutes of effort. The distances covered will be between 400m and 1km. You can do a set of repetitions all the same distance, build up where you do a longer distance each rep, step down, or pyramid where the repetitions get longer then shorter again. Recovery between the repetitions should be just enough to regain your breath and feel ready to go again, but do not hang around. Aim to achieve a consistent speed throughout the repetition session. Progressing an interval session can mean making the running faster if your aim is more speed, but reducing recovery times if your aim is better endurance and lactic acid tolerance.

After the session warm down and stretch well. Intervals such as these are not recommended for children and young teenagers, until the main growth phase is finished, at about seventeen to eighteen years old depending on individual rate of maturation. Since all junior training should have long-term objectives it is better to be conservative with interval running for juniors rather than to seek short-term success (*see* Chapter 7(ii)).

Caution should also be exercised by veteran orienteers. As muscles and tendons lose flexibility it is easy to tear muscles with too much speed or in heavy impact training; calf muscles especially are at risk for those over fifty years old.

Circuit training

Circuit training not only helps improve all-round body strength, but for an endurance athlete it also helps improve speed and co-ordination. If the circuit is well designed it can also improve lactic acid tolerance. The leg muscles are our largest set of muscles and as such they can generate more lactic acid. To help lactic acid tolerance control and co-ordination use leg exercises to generate a pulse of lactic acid through the body. These are followed by arm and abdominal strengthening exercises where you work through the lactic acid.

Make a Circuit of Twelve stations

Four sets of leg, then abdomen, then arm exercises:

(1)   *Running on the spot,* knees high and fast.
(2)   *Short-range sit-ups,* knees bent and small movement range, touching the knees but not lying all the way back.
(3)   *Bench Pressing.*
(4)   *Single sprints,* in the squat thrust position but with one leg forward and one back. Step your legs back and forth as fast as possible.
(5)   *Back raise,* feet, hands and bottom on the ground. Raise your bottom to level with head and knees. Do this slowly to use all your back muscles. Don't throw your bottom in the air.
(6)   *Jump pull-ups,* pull up to a high bar – get off the ground with a short jump, then pull up as fast as possible.
(7)   *Step run,* on a one or two step bench, run up step by step with both feet and back down step by step with both feet as fast as possible.
(8)   *Chins sit-ups,* from lying down raise one leg at a time and turn the oppo-

site shoulder towards the knee as fast as possible.

(9) Arm circling, hold your arms out horizontally and circle steadily around a circle about a foot across.

(10) Shuttle runs.

(11) Knee raises, from a frame raise your knees to horizontal.

(12) Finally *Press-ups* – arrrgh!!

If you do not have regular access to a gym you can still do most of these exercises at home.

Start with a couple of easy familiarization sessions. Then move on to doing 15 seconds at each station. Move quickly between exercises and do not delay in starting again. Do two laps. You can build up the time at each station to do as much as 30 seconds. If you then decide to go for three circuits drop the time at each station and build up again.

Building Training – Progression

The body will adapt to cope with the demands put upon it. For a certain level of demand the body will adapt and increase fitness until it is able to cope efficiently with that level of effort. Once adapted, your fitness will become steady at that level. Should you want to get fitter still then you must increase the demands of your training programme. It is a basic fact that training needs to be progressive. Increased fitness is achieved step by step, progressing from one level to the next in a steady improvement. Short cuts are not possible because excessive demands will wear your body down, causing fatigue, injury or illness. The progression must be judged properly. It is better to fall a little short with the effort than to push too hard, ending up injured, ill and unable to train and so less fit, or in a state of 'over-training syndrome' (*see* Chapter 6).

Rate of Progression

Expect a training programme to cover about three months. Your body will usually adapt fully to a steady and maintained programme in ten to twelve weeks. If you think in terms of three months that gives you a couple of weeks off to rest at the end – maybe to freshen up for that big race, or maybe just to feel good about it all.

During the three months you may pass through various phases:

• You will feel fine and fresh for the first couple of weeks.

• Next you may experience some muscular stiffness and fatigue as your muscles begin to feel the pressure of the new maintained demand. This will pass. Your muscles will build more active fibres and mitochondria to cope, and blood vessels in the lungs and muscles will increase. Another very important adaptation is an increase in the collagen connective tissue that binds muscles together. Collagen has very powerful elastic and shock absorption properties, so increased collagen connective tissue helps protect against muscle damage and stiffness. You will notice increased collagen as an increase in firmness and tone in your muscles. Another tissue that will be increasing in strength will be bones.

• After several weeks you may experience a more general feeling of tiredness and fatigue. This is a sign that your body is working hard at building up new tissue – muscle, collagen, bone and enzymes to cause the chemical reactions that release energy from the mitochondria or the reactions in the liver that remove lactic acid. If you do feel this fatigue don't let it put you off. This strange tiredness and lack of energy, which is not like having stiff or sore legs after a hard run, can be very confusing. Ease off a little and pay particular attention to good nutrition. Eat plenty of everything, and build yourself up again. Of course, good nutrition is important throughout your training and careful attention to diet will help avoid this fatigue phase (*see* Chapter 6).

- Finally, your body will adapt and you will no longer get stiff. The tiredness has passed and after a couple more weeks you will have no problem training at your current level. This is the time to enjoy your fitness and make the most of it. Do that big race, run that epic route in the hills, take on your friends and rivals.

Planning Training

How much running should you do? This must be a personal decision and it is impossible to give precise advice. But first ask yourself some questions. How much do you do already? Perhaps you go orienteering at the weekend and do one or two other runs a week. If this is so, then before you begin any of the quality sessions, I have described which target specific improvement in your aerobic fitness you will need to build up your basic fitness. Basic fitness is your ability to go running several times a week, say to do 3–3½ hours of running over five sessions a week. This is running at maintenance levels of effort within your aerobic ability.

The reason you need to work on basic fitness is to avoid injury. Until you are used to running for 3–3½ hours a week your body will not be strong enough to stand up to the impact and stresses of hard running sessions. A basic fitness build-up is necessary to strengthen your bones, tendons, ligaments

and muscle connective tissue before you begin quality training, otherwise you will get injured. The more of this running you can do on paths and terrain the better. Tarmac puts a lot of strain on the body and it is not so relevant to orienteering. A forest sport demands as much forest training as possible.

Building up Basic Fitness

The target for a basic level of fitness would be three hours of running or more done over five days a week, with two days off. This might consist of an hour of orienteering and four half-hour steady runs. If you presently do less than this, then you will need to build up to it. Remember that each step in the build-up is three months. It might seem like a long time to keep the same weekly training but be patient, you will get there soon enough. Building step by step means adding one run at a time. If you only do two runs a week, an orienteering race and, say, club training night, start by adding one more run per week for the first three-month phase. In the second phase add another run and so on. When you add another run it is a good idea to drop the length of your other runs so that at first you are doing the same amount of training.

Example:

- from three runs of 30 minutes = 90 minutes
- move to four runs: three at 20 minutes plus one at 30 = 90 minutes
- build the 20-minute runs back up to 30 minutes each gradually over the weeks until you are at four runs at 30 minutes = 120 minutes.

Once you are doing five runs a week, build up the time of the runs, until you are totalling 3–3½ hours of running. It is a good idea to vary the distance of your runs as well as the terrain. You might do one run of 50 minutes, one of 40 minutes, two of 30 minutes and one of 20 minutes. Doing runs that are all the same speed over the same route can lead to injury as they always work the body in the same way. Variety of route and surface avoids this by working and stressing the body differently each time. Try to spread out your runs evenly through the week so that you have a regular pattern of run, rest, run, rest and so on.

Rest

On the subject of rest, remember how important this is to allow recovery and adaptation. As well as planning rest days you should plan rest weeks within a training phase. Weekly patterns of hard, medium or easy running will be different for different people, and you need to find what suits you best. Some examples are:

(1) hard, hard, easy, hard, hard, easy;
(2) hard, medium, easy, hard, medium, easy;
(3) hard, easy, medium, hard, easy, medium;
(4) hard, easy, hard, easy, hard, easy.

In an easy week you should not force yourself to do a certain amount. Do what you feel comfortable with without being lazy. Typically, you might end up doing fifty-five to sixty-five percent of a hard week's effort. For youngsters it is important to take into account a busy school life which may include of other sports and recreations and the fact that as they are growing there are extra demands on their bodies. Teenagers should not increase their training in large steps. The common limit given is not to exceed increases of fifteen percent in one year (*see* Chapter 7(ii)).

Quality Training

Once you have reached a basic level of fitness where you can regularly run five times totalling 3–3½ hours in a week you can introduce some quality runs to improve your aerobic endurance and speed. These are sessions like those described in the section on training to improve fitness. How much should you do? Start with one quality session a week – be it a tempo run, long repetitions or intervals.

As you progress through training phases you can do more quality sessions but you should *limit the amount of your running that is hard quality work.* Sensible limits are:

(1) Only one run in three should be a quality session. Remember to include races.
(2) The total time of quality training should be no more than twenty to twenty-five percent of your total training in a hard week.

All of the quality training sessions that I have described are valuable and differ in how they improve your fitness. Obviously, you cannot do all these sessions in a week but you can alternate sessions across the weeks. Do a tempo run or a race one week, the next week do long repetitions and maybe if there is no race do a long steady effort run. Training plans need not be a weekly cycle. You should think about finding a pattern of training that suits you best, and the more orienteering-specific you can make it the better. You will then be better able to keep your training going and so will get the most out of it.

The core of training is to do lots of what you enjoy – if you enjoy it, you are more likely to do it, will put more effort in and get more out of it. Think about how you can adapt the training you enjoy to improve your weaknesses. Make up your own new

Orienteering running has to be skillful, strong and flexible.

Jörgen Mårtensson, World Champion.

session that bridges the gap to your weakness. The essence of this chapter is to try to get you to think about your training, how it works, how to plan it and how to adapt it to your needs and goals. In this way, you are more likely to get it right for yourself and gain more satisfaction.

So here are some more ideas to think about:-

Some of your training should be specific to orienteering – not navigation technique, but the terrain that you cover and the length of time you are running. Running over rough ground, up hills and through marshes places different demands on parts of the body than steady-state road running. Just look at an elite orienteer running on a track. Why is he overstriding and sometimes rolling? Look at Jörgen Mårtensson's thighs and upper body as compared with a track or distance runner's physique.

You could include hill repetitions as one of your quality sessions. Do a tempo and/or maintenance run on terrain. There are different types of terrain. If you have a big race in mind and it's on very fast or very slow terrain practise on something similar. As for time or distance you need to develop sufficient stamina for the courses that you do. Personally, I do a long run every two or three weeks that is one and a half times my race distance. Path running is very fast going but uneven and winding. All these things should be considered and though they cannot all be done weekly they can be done occasionally or as part of a specific build up.

There may be a time of year that you can best concentrate on certain aspects of your training – for example through the winter you develop your hill strength, stamina and aerobic endurance. Running in snow is excellent for leg strength and balance. Many orienteers, especially in Scandinavia, also include weight training in their strength programmes to build up specific muscle groups for the summer demands of tough terrain. Only use weights, however, in collaboration with a coach who can provide precise guidelines on size, repetitions and so on. Orienteers are not into body-building!

Come spring, you may want to develop speed and terrain running in time for an important race. The strength, stamina and endurance gained over the winter can be maintained by the occasional run every four weeks while your more regular quality runs concentrate on speed, skill in terrain running and the type of running likely to be demanded by imminent 'peak races'.

Depending on your goals and aspirations your training can build through the years. As you increase your training you may reach a point where you run more than once a day. You may end up training twelve times in a week with runs built around job or lifestyle. If you do build up to these levels you will

obviously need to think very carefully about how you put your training plan together. Always remember the importance of rest and recovery and limit the amount of quality running you do in high-volume, hard weeks to twenty percent and to one in three runs. Spread your training loads and build up gradually. Though you may be thinking about and planning your training it is always helpful to have a coach to bounce ideas off, to give a second opinion and to point out if you are getting it wrong or out of proportion, such as during periods of persistent illness or injury. The cautious approach is better than the headlong rush. High levels of fitness are a long-term goal and need a long-term commitment. Do not be impatient. You will enjoy getting there as much as finally being as fit as you can – and in the process you will discover a lot about yourself. More information and advice on training programmes specific to age and ability is included in Chapter 3(i) and 3(ii), and 7(i) and 7(ii).

5 Psychological Skills in Orienteering

SUSAN WALSH

INTRODUCTION

Orienteering is a complex sport which requires the orienteer to solve problems and make critical decisions whilst running at speed through very diverse physical environments. Success requires a fine blend of physical fitness, technical expertise and psychological skills. Orienteering is also almost unique in that it must be one of the few sports where the coach does not see the performance. This in itself poses an interesting problem for both coach and athlete because, in order to be effective, the coach relies on feedback *from* the performer. This is in contrast to the situation in other sports where the coach watches the performance and is able to give direct feedback *to* the performer. However, the fact that the coach does not see the performance may have an advantage because it does mean that, generally, as the orienteer acquires expertise, he or she takes more control of their performance and it is the *interaction* between the coach and the performer which then is critical to the feedback process. It follows logically from this that an awareness of the factors which affect per-

A complex sport – critical decisions at speed.

formance and the strategies and skills which may be used to enhance or cope with these factors should become an integrated part of the training programme for the orienteer and his or her coach.

This Chapter presents an overview of those factors which may affect performance and then introduces the psychological skills which may be used to enhance performance both in training and competition. The different skills will be described alongside the way in which they may be incorporated into training and competition and used as fundamental skills by both the orienteer and the coach. This is followed by some examples of methods for a more structured approach that the orienteering coach or sports psychologist may adopt in developing a training programme. The relationship between athlete and coach is vital, with the coach fulfilling a key role at all levels of performance from beginner to elite. However, the good coach will recognize the limitations of some aspects of their expertise and will, where appropriate, make use of the additional knowledge offered by sports scientists. In Britain, there are sports psychologists and physiologists who are accredited by BASES, the British Association of Sport and Exercise Scientists. The contact address for BASES and information about accredited sports scientists in the different regions is listed at the end of the Chapter. Similarly, there is a contact address for the National Coaching Foundation which provides a structured programme of core courses for all coaches; some of these include elements of psychological skills training (for example, Mind over Matter). A list of references appends this Chapter for those who would like to study psychological skills training in more depth.

FACTORS WHICH AFFECT PERFORMANCE

Both external and internal factors can affect performance. External factors include things such as the weather, the terrain, travel arrangements, other competitors, previous performance (particularly a previous performance on a similar terrain), injury and recovery from injury, personal interactions (at school or work, with parents, boyfriends, girlfriends and so on), and the importance of the competition (for example, selection races, club and regional competitions), to name but a few. Internal factors are things such as levels of physical fitness, psychological/mental skills ability, as well as the psychological state which may be influenced by certain personality traits, but more particularly by mood state at the time of performance. Moods such as anger, fatigue and confidence will inevitably influence reactions to any given situation and will, of course, vary from one situation to another. The important thing to remember is that everyone is influenced by these factors to a greater or lesser degree.

TRAINING

A well balanced training programme should enable the orienteer to cope with both the external and the internal demands of competitive performance and should involve physical, technical and psychological components. For the sake of clarity these three components are considered separately within this coaching manual. There is, however, a strong argument for incorporating different components simultaneously within training, so that training conditions are closely related to competition. For example, because orienteering requires a high cognitive element (decision-making and interpreting visual information from both the map and the terrain), it is logical to practise these more technical skills in parallel with aspects of physical training. Psychological skills and strategies may be used to improve and enhance physical and technical training. Additionally, it is important to consider psychological skills training in parallel to physical and technical training which must be practised on a regular basis. Just as improved speed through complex terrain is linked to regular physical and technical training, being able to cope with the pressures of competition may be linked to psychological skills training (PST). If psychological skills become an integral part of a training programme then they can also become integrated into competitive performance.

The fundamental benefit of PST is in helping to develop those skills which will allow the orienteer, where possible, to be in control and therefore minimize the effect of those factors which may have a negative affect on performance. Obviously, there are some factors which are almost impossible to control, but it should be possible to develop other, more generic psychological skills which will enable the orienteer to use some sort of 'damage-limitation strategy' to cope with most situations.

PSYCHOLOGICAL SKILLS

Psychological skills are the mental techniques which may be used to enhance performance. They can be incorporated within a multi-disciplinary training programme to enable the orienteer to optimize performance within competition. External and internal factors which affect performance may potentially have a positive or negative affect on performance. For example, an orienteer may carefully prepare for a particular competition and may feel confident and in an appropriate state of readiness but, because of the unpredictable elements inherent within the sport, the level of arousal may be inappropriate for the change in competitive conditions. This is further compounded by the individual competitor's own response to the changing competitive situation. The successful orienteer, therefore, is the one who has a wide repertoire of strategies which can be used to optimize performance. It is the mismatch between the orienteer's perception of the needs of the competition and his or her readiness for the competition which creates feelings of anxiety.

Anxiety

There are basically two forms of anxiety which a competitor may experience: somatic anxiety and cognitive anxiety. Somatic anxiety is normally recognized through the perception of physiological responses, for example a dry mouth, yawning, wanting to go to the toilet frequently, a feeling of 'butterflies' in the stomach and sweaty palms. Cognitive anxiety, or worry, may have a negative effect in terms of fear of failure or performing badly but, more importantly, it may be handled in a constructive way, enabling the orienteer to channel anxiety so that it has a positive effect on performance both in training and competition. For example, an orienteer may feel anxious because a close rival is starting one minute behind. Instead of focusing on this in a negative way, the orienteer can use the information to concentrate on aggressive running and flowing cleanly through the controls.

Anxiety before and during competition is probably the most commonly experienced feeling for all orienteers. It is closely linked to state of readiness or level of arousal and is a very individual thing which may be further exaggerated or diminished depending on the perceived importance of the competition. Some orienteers seem to thrive in competitive situations and perform very well, whilst others seem to 'fall to bits' and underperform. Recognizing the optimal state of readiness or level of arousal for performance is important both for the individual orienteer and for the coach. This is quite difficult for those coaches who have limited contact with their performers because of geographical constraints and who therefore rely heavily on telephone communication. There is also a difficulty for coaches who are trying to work with large groups of individual performers. For example, a member of one of the elite squads may be resident in the south-west and rely on telephone communication with a coach who lives in the Midlands, whilst a regional squad coach will often be coaching a large group of youngsters of different ages and of varying levels of ability. The important point is that the coach and orienteer should be able to recognize that levels of arousal will depend on both the competitive situation and individual differences in response to the situation. This may best be thought of as an arousal–performance interaction. Every individual orienteer, in any given competitive situation, will have an optimum arousal–performance level. Therefore, logically, being under- or over-aroused will have an effect on performance. Although being under-aroused may equate with underachievement, over-arousal does not necessarily equate with overachievement.

The arousal–performance interaction is best described by the catastrophe model. This, in its simplest form, predicts that as the level of arousal increases so performance is enhanced up to an optimum level of arousal and that after this optimum level is reached

any further increase in arousal will have a catastrophic effect on performance. The performance 'falls to bits' and simply reducing the level of arousal does not restore the level of performance to an optimum level. However, using appropriate coping strategies to reduce anxiety does have a positive influence by restoring confidence and rebuilding the arousal–performance interaction towards an optimum level (*see* diagram).

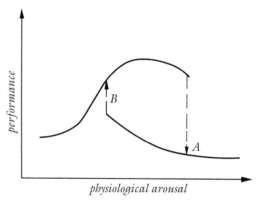

physiological arousal

Catastrophe curve. Diagram of a catastrophe curve illustrating performance decrement A as a result of high cognitive anxiety and high physiological arousal. Use of PST reduces arousal and allows for performance recovery B.

The important point is that optimal arousal–performance interactions are dependent on the individual performer and his or her reaction to a particular competition or competitive situation. An example might be time lost at a difficult control site when an orienteer loses concentration because a rival is close behind and then compounds the time loss by making another error in trying to make up time afterwards. In this scenario, the damage is done, although using psychological skills would enable the orienteer slowly to regain the original level of performance. The ideal would be to construct a training programme, to enable the orienteer to learn to recognize potential problems before they occur and then make use of psychological skills to control them.

Anxiety Control

There are several strategies which may be used to control anxiety and these should form an integral part of training so that they then, in turn, become integrated into the competitive routine. It is just as important to develop and use appropriate anxiety control as it is to develop routines for the pre-start and entering, punching and leaving control sites.

Relaxation

Orienteering, by its very nature, places the competitor in stressful situations. Although the orienteer may have prepared very carefully for an event, the actual course is unknown until 10 seconds before the start. The skill then is to make the right decision for this course based on map interpretation. Although this may be supported by previous experience, it is still a potentially stressful situation, even for elite performers. Relaxation techniques may be used to help to control anxiety to an optimum level for the best performance. For example, the feeling of flowing through controls is often characteristic of a relaxed run, and can be practised mentally before the start.

There are two main forms of relaxation to consider – mental relaxation and physical relaxation. Use of either of these will allow the orienteer to have more control over levels of anxiety and the way it affects performance. This does *not* mean *total* relaxation, but a sufficient level of relaxation to reduce anxiety. This will differ from individual to individual. Generally, mental relaxation techniques are used to control cognitive anxiety, whilst physical relaxation techniques are used to control somatic anxiety.

Orienteering requires a high physical component, but it is predominantly cognitive in nature, particularly in terms of decision-making and map–terrain interpretation. If we consider these alongside the pre-start to start process, then the difference between a good and poor performance may be substantially influenced by the way in which an individual copes.

Mental Relaxation

Mental relaxation techniques which refocus the thoughts may be triggered by a verbal or visual cue which enables the orienteer to have a more controlled approach to performance. This requires specific practice and is normally linked with a slow, controlled breathing routine. An example of when this may be used would be at the pre-start when there are a lot of people around as well as the many associated distractions. Using the well practised cue (such as silently repeating a chosen word) cuts out all the distractions while the orienteer focuses on preparation. Similarly, around the first and last control site, when there are a large number of other competitors around, it often helps to focus on a simple practical activity (for example looking at the compass or checking the control code) in order to eliminate the external distractions. The cueing and accompanied breathing routines should initially be practised in a controlled situation and then, when the technique becomes familiar, the practice should be in simulated competition situations. It is also possible to use the slow, controlled breathing technique without the cues and often performers skilled in this type of technique are able to feel relaxed and in control after only two or three breathing cycles.

Physical Relaxation

Physical relaxation techniques are probably more familiar to orienteers. One of the most commonly used and widely written about is that of Progressive Muscular Relaxation (PMR). This technique uses a method of systematically tensing and relaxing individual muscle groups. Through practice, it is possible to tense and, more importantly, relax specific groups of muscles very quickly when needed. For example, often after hard hill climbs through rough undergrowth immediately followed by fast descents, the thigh muscles become quite tense, and selective muscle relaxation may allow for a quicker recovery. Probably a more obvious scenario in orienteering would be the use of PMR to control anxiety at the pre-start in individual events and handover sections in relay competitions. The process of tension and relaxation of muscle groups in this situation may act as a focus or readying routine for the orienteer and helps in cutting out other distractions.

Relaxation techniques should be incorporated into a physical and technical training programme so that it becomes natural to use them in competition. It is also important to experiment with the different techniques to find out which of them suits a particular individual. There are other relaxation techniques (for example yoga and massage) which are sometimes used to a greater or lesser extent, but they are not really psychological skills. However, they are techniques which the orienteer may develop to supplement the other relaxation routines used in a training programme.

Positive Thinking and Self-Talk

The successful orienteer is confident and thinks and talks positively about perfor-mance. Positive thinking and self-talk is a strategy which helps to restructure negative thoughts before, during and after competition. For example, rather than focusing on the negative effect of how nervous and apprehensive the competitor may feel about a particular competition, this nervous apprehension could be viewed in a positive way; that is, as indication of readiness for the competition. The skill is to focus nervous energy into the physical demands of the competition whilst, for example, clarifying and refining the details of route choice. Self-talk is often used automatically as a method of increasing effort, particularly near the end of a long, tiring course or as a method of focusing in intricate terrain which requires high levels of concentration.

Often, negative thoughts can be interrupted or stopped by using a cueing action or word to stop the negative thoughts. This then triggers a conscious change to positive thinking. This is sometimes referred to as *thought stopping*. It may be triggered by simply using a word, for example 'stop', or by the use of a physical signal, such as slapping the thigh or clicking the fingers. It may also be a visual image, for example a stop sign.

Another technique, called *countering*, is to present a counter-argument or statement in response to a negative thought. For example, an orienteer might worry about not performing well in intricate terrain because of an earlier poor performance. This could be countered with the argument that, because of that poor performance, the orienteer has developed the fine navigation skills which will allow them to make the best of intricate terrain. This is a much more positive approach!

Positive thinking is a method of *restructuring* anxiety feelings so that the orienteer perceives them in a more positive way. Not all anxiety symptoms have a negative effect on performance, but again this will vary from individual to individual and from situation to situation. An individual may perceive a situation differently on two separate occasions! It is a good idea to develop a method of evaluating responses to the different demands inherent in competition and practise focusing on these in a positive way so as to always feel in control.

One way of doing this is to make sure that some training is done under competitive conditions. Many orienteers use small local events and Badge events as part of their training programme. They establish a clear training goal for these events which allows them to train and practise the different skills under competitive conditions. The preponderance of research in this area suggests that negative self-talk is linked to poor performance or losing whilst positive self-talk is linked to success and winning. Many of the top-level orienteers use self-talk as an inherent part of their decision-making process when they, for example, go through the 'if I do this... then...' scenario when making route choice decisions. In fact, many of the young elite orienteers who used self-talk techniques within the Developing Navigational Skills Project reported that the self-talk helped them to focus on their performance.

Imagery

There are two aspects of imagery to consider – *imagery* and *mental practice*. Imagery is a mental process whereby an individual creates the mental image of both the perceptual and sensory image of a particular action. Mental practice or rehearsal is more about the rehearsal or visualization of a particular technique or sequence of techniques. Imagery may be from an internal or an external perspective. An internal perspective produces an image from the orienteer's own viewpoint, such as seeing the terrain as if they were actually viewing it; whereas an external perspective is as if the orienteer were an outside observer seeing the image as others would see it.

Normally, imagery is used to recreate or reconstruct a good or ideal performance, that is, to create a positive image. This is often used in relationship with relaxation techniques. For example, in training, without the stress of competition, if the orienteer can visualize what it feels like to flow through a control point then they are more likely to recreate this 'flow' through the control during the actual performance. Some elite orienteers have made audio tapes of their own positive self-talk to support this use of imagery and they are able to reinforce and reconstruct the perfect performance whilst they are driving to and from work. In this way, they promote confidence and positive thinking about their orienteering.

There are different ways to incorporate imagery and mental rehearsal into a training programme. For example, if the orienteer lists the thoughts or emotions felt in a typical competition and then divides those that have a negative effect from those that have a positive effect on performance, it is possible to target those negative images and work on strategies to make them more positive (for example through positive self-talk or thought-stopping techniques). Alternatively, if the orienteer uses positive images of self in relation to other higher ranked performers, then these can be used to create confidence that opponents can be outperformed.

It has been suggested that the positive use of imagery techniques may have some influence on recovery from injury. Similarly, it is possible to prepare for the difficult parts of the competition (for example the pre-start, the first control and the last control), by imaging the associated distractions and ways of coping with them. Likewise, it is possible to relive successful runs as a means of reinforcing the techniques used to achieve success.

Visualization

Mental practice and visualization techniques are often the fundamental orienteering strategies for map interpretation. Some people find these easier than others, although they do improve with practice. Imagery scripts are often used to help performers develop vivid images by presenting them with written 'scenarios' linked with their sport. This enables them to develop appropriate coping strategies for potentially difficult situations in a controlled environment. Imagery scripts in orienteering are often used as part of technical training practices. For example, the coach or another individual would ask the orienteer to create an image of and then verbally describe a control site or a set of features from a small piece of map.

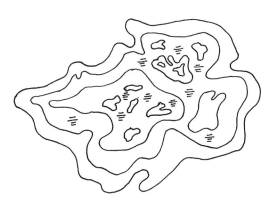

Visualization. The control site is on top of a knoll which has small marshes to the NE and SW. There is a long spur running away to the W and smaller knolls to the NE, E and SW. Which knoll is it?

Alternatively, the orienteer could listen to a verbal description of a small mapped area or a control site and then try to reproduce the map from that verbal description:

- This sausage-shaped hill has two summits, one at each end of a narrow east-west trending ridge. The ridge has two knolls making a col somewhere midway between the summits. From that col a steep-sided valley runs northwards. The eastern summit is higher than the western one and has steep slopes on the east, a large broad spur running away to the north and gentle slopes to the south. The western summit has gentle slopes to the north and west, and a long thin spur running south.

Both these skills help develop visualization and, although not everyone has the artistic talents demanded by the latter example, it is an important skill to practise.

These visualization skills are fundamental to orienteering. The ability to visualize the control site or a given area of the map should improve with practice. Practice, however, should not be limited to training or competing at events. There are other opportunities for both indoor and outdoor practice. For example, careful study of maps of familiar and unfamiliar areas and then visualizing specific control sites based on the mapped information could precede an actual visit to the mapped area. It is quite common to hear an orienteer say 'that wasn't what I expected' during a discussion about a particular control site or mapped area. Another idea used by some orienteers is to carry a map of another area whilst running on home terrain, and to try to visualize specific terrain detail from it while running. This may seem rather bizarre but it is a very good exercise in concentration.

Motivation

The high levels of commitment and the concomitant high levels of motivation that orienteers have has been fundamental to the development of orienteering in Britain. In comparison to many other orienteering nations, Britain has remarkably few 'good technical areas'. Orienteers who are committed to the sport have to be highly motivated as, in order to compete at a high level, they have to travel vast distances both within and outside Britain. This means that an orienteer may travel for many hours to compete in an event which lasts between 45 and 60 minutes and then may not know their official result until many hours or even days later. If they are lucky there will be a second day of competition followed by an equally long journey home.

What motivates orienteers? Motives are considered to be either intrinsic or extrinsic. Intrinsic motives do not have external reward, but are linked with enjoyment, satisfaction and feelings of achievement and are often associated with mastery of a given task. Extrinsic motives are linked to external rewards such as prizes, winning/losing, peer and parental pressures and are generally associated with outcomes. Individuals are said to be either high or low in their levels of intrinsic or extrinsic motivation. Elite orienteers, to be successful, are normally high in both intrinsic motivation, in terms of mastery of their sport, and in extrinsic motivation, in terms of their will to win. Winning will create a sense of achievement, which in itself is highly motivating. However, not everyone will win and therefore it is important to develop intrinsic motives which allow the orienteer to have more control over their training and performance by focusing as much on the mastery of skills as on the outcome of performance. Goal setting is a powerful technique in the development of intrinsic motivation. However, it is important to recognize that goal setting may have a negative effect as well as a positive effect on motivation. Goals that are appropriate, that is, they are specific, challenging, achievable, measurable and personal, may become inappropriate through injury or some other change in circumstances. For example, the orienteer may have established a clear set of goals leading up to a series of national selection races, then is injured a few weeks before the start of the series and as a result has no chance of achieving what has become an unrealistic goal (of selection). This, in turn, will affect self-confidence, which in its turn will affect training and performance. This situation should not arise, or at least the effect may be minimized, if goals are carefully structured.

Goal Setting

Goals should be specific. It would be inappropriate to set goals that are about 'running as fast as you can' or 'hitting all the controls', as these are very general goals. Specific goals, such as 'select an attack point' and 'concentrate on fine map detail around the control site' are more appropriate and within the orienteer's control. Making goals challenging but realistically achievable is also important. If the goals which you set are too easy then there will be no sense of achievement, but if they are too difficult then there will probably be very little chance of succeeding. It is important to remember that success builds confidence, which in turn affects performance. This is another reason why it is important for the orienteer to set their own goals *with* the coach's guidance. If the orienteer sets their own goals, then these will be accepted, whereas if the coach or someone else dictates the goals then there is a strong chance of rejection and therefore less chance of achievement.

What are appropriate and realistic goals? Short-term goals, for the day or the week, or a particular competition, allow the orienteer to focus more clearly. The competitor will generally use more effort and be more persistent if the goal is perceived as realistic and achievable. Success will boost confidence. Therefore it is more appropriate to set a lot of short-term goals which are realistic and within the orienteer's control. These then lead towards a set of mid-term goals, which in turn lead to a long-term goal which may be two or three years away. These short-term goals should not be limited, but should include all aspects of training and performance – physical, technical and psychological. The important point is that orienteers should set their own goals and not be pushed into setting goals that coaches or parents see as desirable. This way, the orienteer will be in control of their own training. However, it is important for the orienteer to talk through goals with coach or trainer as this will help *both* to monitor their appropriateness.

There are three types of goals – outcome goals, performance goals and process goals. Outcome goals are about winning and losing and are really out of individual control. No matter how well prepared the orienteer, the outcome of a competition is really dependent on the other competitors. Performance goals are about achieving specific standards, for example, running at 6 min/km in a particular terrain. This is measurable but does not depend on the perfor-

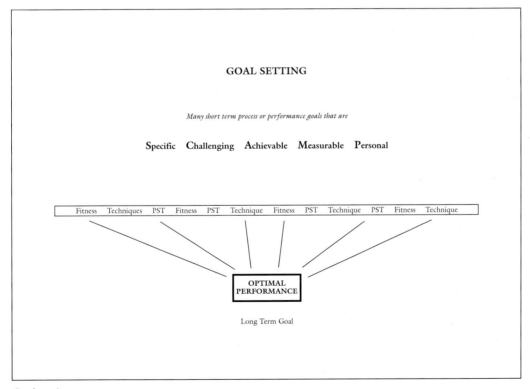

GOAL SETTING

Many short term process or performance goals that are

Specific   Challenging   Achievable   Measurable   Personal

| Fitness | Techniques | PST | Fitness | PST | Technique | Fitness | PST | Technique | PST | Fitness | Technique |

OPTIMAL PERFORMANCE

Long Term Goal

Goal setting.

mance of other competitors. Process goals are goals that are not so easily measurable but are more about technical expertise and the way psychological skills might be incorporated within performance. For example, the goal for a particular event may be to concentrate and clearly focus on fine orienteering into the first and last control sites; that is, the part of an event which causes the most problems. However, it is true that orienteers do set themselves combinations of these three types of goals in competition.

The problem is that orienteers who are highly extrinsically motivated cope with competition as long as they are winning or achieving recognition in some way, but often find it difficult to cope with losing. On the other hand, intrinsically motivated orienteers generally manage to cope more effectively because their goals tend to be about the mastery of skills. However, it is possible to be both intrinsically and extrinsically motivated. For example, during training the orienteer may be highly intrinsically motivated but in competition motivation may be more extrinsic. Whatever the motivation for competing, it will influence the way that different individuals train and prepare for competition. The elite orienteer will certainly have different motives to the recreational/social orienteer.

To be successful, the competitive orienteer has to be both intrinsically and extrinsically motivated. Creating a fine balance between the desire to win and to be in control through mastery of skills and techniques demands high levels of commitment as well as the development *and* practice of appropriate psychological skills.

Attention and Concentration

Orienteering is about quick decision-making based on information extracted from the map and related to the physical environment. Usually there are route choice options to be considered and the orienteer has to make a trade off between the different route choices based on personal levels of fitness and technical expertise. The correct execution of the route choice depends on the ability to concentrate and attend to the appropriate cues on the map and in the environment. The amount of information that can be absorbed is not limitless and so it is important to develop the ability to attend selectively to those cues which are going to enhance performance.

Selective Attention

The number of informational cues that an individual can cope with, and therefore use effectively, is influenced by a number of factors. When the orienteer is relaxed and confident he or she will be able to attend to a broader range of environmental information and will therefore be able to select or 'pick up' a wide range of cues. However, when tense and anxious, for whatever reason, then the range of cues that the orienteer will be able to select from the attentional field will be much narrower. This will obviously affect performance. For example, when relaxed and confident it is relatively easy for the orienteer to monitor map information and match it to the terrain while running between controls. In this situation, it is easier to make minor adjustments quickly within route choice and therefore minimize errors. However, when the orienteer has just made a huge error or has been distracted in some other way, and is not so relaxed and confident, then it is easier to overlook important map and terrain information because of the narrowing of attentional focus. This in turn can lead to errors which take longer to resolve. There are situations, however, where the orienteer may need to narrow the attentional focus and concentrate on a more limited number of informational cues. For example, as the orienteer approaches a control site, it is important not to be distracted by other runners or irrelevant information. In this situation, it is vital that a competitor selectively attends to the appropriate cues to encourage flow through the control. It would seem, therefore, that rough orienteering requires a broad attentional focus to pick up helpful cues, whilst fine orienteering demands a narrow attentional focus. This, however, will be influenced by the ability to concentrate.

Concentration

Concentration is about focusing on specifics and not becoming distracted. It may be that the focus is on a particular physical action, on internal factors, or on external factors. The important issue is that, whatever the focus, the orienteer should be concentrating on those factors which enhance performance. Concentrating on factors which are inappropriate and outside the orienteer's control can only have a negative effect on performance. For example, concentrating on running smoothly through terrain, or concentrating on the fine map and terrain detail close to a difficult control is much more appropriate than concentrating on the way another runner is performing and the route that they are following.

There are simple indoor exercises which can be used to improve concentration and attention (for example the 'concentration grid' in which sequences of numbers have to be matched by memory); however, one of the most widely used techniques is simulation training. This reproduces the competitive environment in training, complete with all the stressors and distractions. As mentioned earlier, most of the top orienteers use competitions, such as national or badge events, as part of their training. This way, they are able to practise their technical and psychological skills simultaneously. However, it is possible to recreate specific aspects of competition as part of training outside of actual competition. For example, elite orienteers select training areas because of the similarity of terrain to a forthcoming important competition. This often means that they may live and train abroad. There is no reason why training for individuals at club level should not incorporate simulation training in the lead-up to major events, by recreating the situations which will 'test' concentration and attention. It is important for the coach to present situations where the orienteer is able to practise and refine routines which help in coping with situations where concentration can be difficult, for example at the pre-start and at control sites.

Self-Confidence

Success and failure both affect levels of self-confidence. Success, and repeated success, will positively affect self-confidence and, although a single failure may have a negative effect, repeated failures will have a drastic effect. The way an individual perceives success and failure is also important and, more often than not, this will be closely linked to the type of goals set. For example, orienteers who have outcome goals, and repeatedly fail to achieve those goals, are likely to lose all confidence in their ability and frequently will drop out of orienteering altogether. Similarly, the orienteer who has set goals which are unrealistic and too difficult will fail and lose self-confidence. This is one of the most important reasons for setting appropriate goals.

The orienteer's perception of success and failure will also be influenced by performance feedback; that is, feedback from *both* training and competition. This is usually at a personal level in terms of the outcome of the performance, both from the technique used as well as the ability to cope psychologically. This is problematic when the individual is reliant purely on outcome measures which place great emphasis on comparisons with others. However, if the orienteer uses feedback in a constructive way to develop their training programme then feedback reinforces self-confidence. The individual who is full of self-doubt and lacking in self-confidence is easily distracted and this limits their ability to concentrate and focus on the cues relevant to performance. They are likely to make more unforced errors.

It may, however, be that an orienteer who is generally confident and positive about their ability to produce an optimum performance may be lacking in confidence in specific situations. For example, if an orienteer made a serious error or was injured during the last competition in a similar sort of terrain, he or she may be lacking in confidence when confronted with a competition in a similar terrain. In this situation, it is important to set appropriate goals and to develop positive intervention strategies to enhance self-confidence. This may be reinforced by manipulating the training environment to recreate a specific situation and thus enable the orienteer to achieve success. This is easier to do when an orienteer is still acquiring skills and techniques. The elite performer may often use a restructuring technique initially developed in training in a positive way to build on a strategy for coping with problems. The use of role-models plays an important part in the development of self-confidence. Quite often a less experienced performer will gain confidence from observing

another competitor's good performance during an event. This is particularly significant in orienteering, where there is a wide range of ability across performers within a competition. However, it should be emphasized that the confidence gained through vicarious experience from role-models is most effective within peer groups. This more readily enforces the 'If they can do it then so can I' argument, thus helping to develop a positive self-image and therefore confidence.

DEVELOPING AN INTEGRATED TRAINING PROGRAMME

Training programmes come in all shapes and forms but, to be effective, they should all be based on an evaluation of the needs of the performer within the specific demands of the sport. Unfortunately, there are many programmes that are based purely on the notion that they should include certain physical and technical elements because that is what everyone else seems to be doing. There are four basic questions to ask when designing a programme:

(1) What skills are needed to meet the demands of the sport?
(2) Which of these does the performer already possess?
(3) How might these skills be developed?
(4) Which new skills must the performer acquire?

All of these questions require the assessment and evaluation of both the individual and the sport. There are standardized psychometric assessment and evaluation techniques which are available, but most of these should only be carried out by an accredited sports psychologist who would be able to analyze and, more importantly, interpret the results and recommend appropriate training schedules. However, it is possible for the orienteer and the coach to develop basic training schedules based on some quite simple mechanisms.

The simplistic approach would be to assess all those factors which the individual recognizes as having an effect, either directly or indirectly, on performance. This should include the period before competition, competition itself, and the period following competition. The pre-competition factors should include lifestyle events at home, school or work, the days leading up to the competition and the time spent travelling to the competition. The competition factors should include registration, changing facilities, warm-up routine, going to the start, the pre-start, the course itself and the finish. The post-competition factors would be all the other factors following the event itself. Within any of these areas, it is possible to list all the factors which influence performance under three headings – positive, neutral and negative. Presumably the factors in the positive column are 'working well' and probably only need continued reinforcement through practice. The neutral list may not be problematic as these events may in themselves be fairly neutral in effect. However, it is worth considering these neutral factors in a similar way to the negative factors. Any factor which has a negative effect on performance is a problem.

The next step is to distinguish between those factors which are within or outside the orienteer's control. Those that are within the control of the orienteer can be worked on and the appropriate coping strategy used to 'move them to the positive list'. However, there will be some factors which are outside the individual's control and it is for this group that the orienteer, with their coach, must develop effective coping strategies to minimize their effect on performance.

It would be impossible to carry out a training programme which addressed all these issues at once so it is important to prioritize the most debilitating factors and work on one or two at a time. If the orienteer, with appropriate advice from the coach, develops their own coping strategies then they will feel more in control of the problem. This simplistic approach may become more structured if the orienteer differenti-

Problem	PST technique
Lack of motivation	Goal setting
Anxious and tense	Relaxation / positive thinking / imagery
Too nervous	Relaxation / positive thinking / imagery
Worried about other competitors	Concentration and attention
Importance of competition	Concentration / goal setting
Easily distracted	Concentration / cueing

Some common problems and PST techniques.

ates between physical, technical and psychological factors.

Performance Profiling

A more formalized and structured method for assessing, evaluating and developing a training programme is to use a technique called performance profiling. This requires the orienteer and coach to brainstorm all the attributes which they believe make for elite performance. These will include physical, technical and psychological factors.

The *orienteer* then:–

- ranks these attributes;
- selects the top fifteen to twenty; and

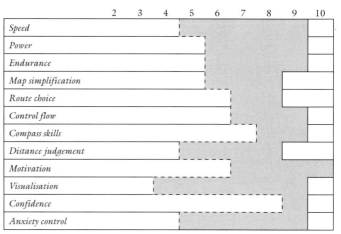

	2	3	4	5	6	7	8	9	10
Speed									
Power									
Endurance									
Map simplification									
Route choice									
Control flow									
Compass skills									
Distance judgement									
Motivation									
Visualisation									
Confidence									
Anxiety control									

A performance profile in a table format: the shaded area represents the discrepancy between actual and ideal profile.

- then rates each of these top fifteen to twenty on a scale from 1 to 10 concerning their relative importance for elite performance.

The orienteer then rates their own performance on these selected attributes. They then transfer the two sets of scores to a profile sheet and this provides a visual guide to the discrepancy between actual and ideal score for each of the selected attributes. This information can then be used as a basis for developing a skills training programme for that individual orienteer. It is very important to recognize that each profile is very personal and 'belongs' to the individual orienteer.

Performance profiling can be a very powerful diagnostic mechanism. It allows the orienteer to fine-tune strengths and raises awareness of weaknesses as well as forming a basis for effective communication between the coach and orienteer about the development of a training and competition programme. The profile may be used for assessing physical, technical or psychological skills in isolation but this would seem inappropriate when considering the development of a

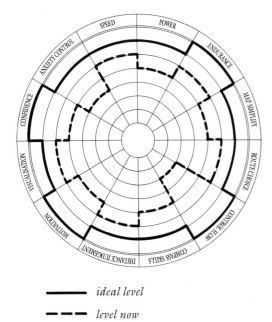

————— *ideal level*

– – – – *level now*

A target format performance profile.

realistic training programme for orienteering. As orienteering training requires both cognitive and physical elements, it is important to create a careful balance between all three of the skill areas within a training programme.

Competition Preparation

The way that an individual prepares for competition will inevitably affect performance. Overall preparation may start days, weeks or even months before a competition, but this will depend on the goals set for that competition. Although the format and the intensity of preparation will vary, there are several elements to good preparation. These include setting appropriate goals, practising and refining technical routines and psychological skills, the development of strategies to cope with and therefore minimize the effect of the uncontrollable elements of competition, a structured pre-competition routine, and, finally, lifestyle.

Goal Setting

Goal setting has been discussed earlier in the Chapter, but it is important to remember that individual competition goals are part of an overall long-term goal. For example, the goal for competition A may be to focus on concentration techniques through the first three or four controls, with the goal for the subsequent competition B being to refine and extend these techniques through the final controls.

Technical Routines

Technical routines will include routines for handling route cards and descriptions: the pre-start, including information gathering in the pre-start boxes; the start from map pick-up to the first control; a protocol for entering, punching and leaving controls; and smooth run in from the last control to the finish. Relays have other technical elements to them (such as mass starts and the changeover) and these should also be considered. The most successful orienteers will have practised a variety of different techniques and routines before refining those which work best for them. These may be practised initially as isolated technical training exercises, but they must also be practised in simulated competitions. The golden rule is that if something is not working then it must be refined or changed until it does work.

Event-Specific Strategies

There are other vital aspects of technical preparation. It is important to find out as much as possible about forthcoming events. Details such as the map scale, who the mapper is, terrain details, any specific peculiarities to that type of terrain, the course length and the climb involved will all influence individual preparation. Other details such as the distance from the parking area to the start, how far it is from the finish back to the start, and something as simple as keeping an eye on the weather forecast are all part of good preparation.

Psychological Skills Training

PST, as discussed earlier, should become an integrated part of training and competition. Initially, these skills may have to be practised in a very controlled way but they should, as soon as possible, become integrated into the orienteer's performance routines. For example, the orienteer who is sufficiently relaxed and able to focus their attention at the pre-start and start has an immediate advantage over another orienteer who is chatting to officials and other competitors. The benefit of PST becomes even more evident when the orienteer has to cope with adverse situations, which may be either technically or emotionally focused. For example, the orienteer may have lost contact with the map and need to relocate or may have been caught up by another competitor who started 4 minutes behind. Both of these situations are difficult to handle so it is important to develop and practise routines for coping with them. The successful orienteer is the one who, together with their coach, has thought through the different elements of the competition and has developed and refined the appropriate coping strategies through a structured PST programme. Of course, there are always situations which are completely unpredictable. However, there is still a strong argument that the trained orienteer will cope better than the untrained orienteer. The secret is to practise, and practise in simulated competitions until training becomes integrated into the optimum performance.

Pre-Competition Routines

Pre-competition routines are fairly diverse and will include packing clothing and equipment, registration, changing, physical warm-up and psychological preparation and getting to the pre-start. Most orienteers keep a mental check-list of the clothing and equipment they use, but there is no harm in using an actual checklist. All equipment should be regularly checked for wear and tear. These seem such simple things but it is this attention to detail which is important in creating a relaxed and confident performance! This attention to detail should apply to all aspects of competition preparation. Physical warm-up routines (and warm-down routines) are important for injury prevention, but more importantly they should be viewed as quality time for physical and mental preparation for the event. This allows the orienteer to approach the pre-start in a state of physical and mental readiness which enables focus and concentration on the relevant cues and strategies for the competition.

Finish routines are really a form of preparation for subsequent training and competition preparation. However, an important element of the post-finish is the warm-down routine. This will minimize the physiological after-effects of exercise, but it is also a time which can be used to focus on performance in preparation for some form of structured performance evaluation. Evaluation is vital and it becomes almost meaningless if it is only carried out in an *ad hoc* group setting.

Lifestyle Events

Lifestyle events in the days leading up to the competition will also have an effect on performance. The quantity and quality of training done in the week before a competition are obviously important, but work and social commitments are equally vital. These events should be considered carefully as they will influence the amount of rest and sleep in the lead-up to the competition, and in some instances they will have an influence on the amount and type of food and fluid intake. It is also important to check all clothing and equipment before the competition day. The simple fact of finding out that there is something missing or wrong with equipment or clothing after arrival at an event will have a devastating effect on confidence. All equipment and clothing should be checked and ready at least the day before a competition. Other lifestyle factors to consider are work and social commitments in the week or days immediately prior to important competitions. Both will bring stressors and distractions at different levels and these will have an effect on competition preparation and, inevitably, some of these will be more controllable than others.

Competition Evaluation

Feedback and evaluation are fundamental to learning and, in order to be most effective, they should take place as soon as possible after the event. As stated at the beginning of the Chapter, orienteering is unique in that the coach does not see the performance and therefore relies on feedback from the orienteer. It is obvious from this that self-evaluation and analysis of performance are critical skills for the orienteer to develop. These should include all aspects of the performance. However, it is very difficult to present this type of information in a structured format unless there are some basic guidelines agreed between orienteer and coach.

Feedback may be in a verbal format or in the form of written sheets. Different styles of evaluation sheets are commonly used, especially by the more experienced and elite orienteers. Whatever the format of this feedback, competition evaluation should be directly related to the overall goal for that particular event. The first question should be 'Did I achieve my goal?' Then through a series of questions and answers the orienteer should be able to evaluate the positive aspects of their performance, that is the things that worked, and only then consider the negative aspects of the performance, that is the things that did not work. Because orienteering is about decision-making, route

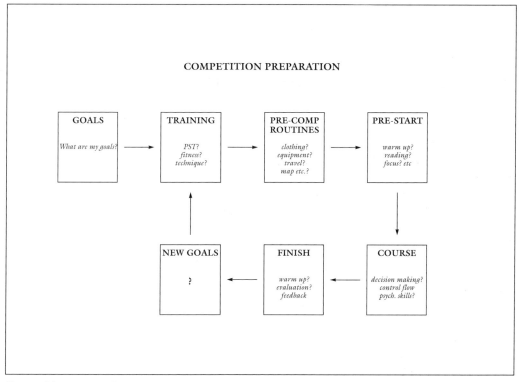

Competition preparation.

An Example of an Event Analysis Sheet

Event: Date: Course:

Length: Climb: Type of terrain:

Personal time: Winner's time:

Goal for the event:

Strengths: *(physical/technical/psychological)*

Weaknesses: *(physical/technical/psychological)*

Errors: *(physical/technical/psychological)*

Leg   Why/how initiated   Recovery technique   Time lost

1

Finish

Total time lost

Training changes based on event analysis: *(physical/technical/psychological)*

Other special comments: *(weather/opposition etc.)*

Example of an event analysis sheet.

choice and minimizing errors, the initial evaluation, depending on the overall goal, may be related to the whole course or to the individual legs within the course. The coach and orienteer, after this initial evaluation session, are now in a position to use an interactive feedback mechanism to discuss ways in which the positive elements of the performance may be refined and enhanced. Similarly, they will also be in a position to discuss the ways in which they may resolve or minimize the negative elements of the performance. This may then influence the short-term goals for subsequent training and competition. It is this interactive discussion which creates confidence and is vital if the coach and orienteer are going to communicate effectively. The orienteer is learning to take control of his or her own performance and the coach is thereby becoming more effective.

CONCLUSION

This Chapter has presented an overview of the basic psychological skills that an orienteer can develop within a well structured training programme. However, like any skills training programme, it is important to continue to practise and refine these skills until they become an integrated part of performance and this all takes time and a high level of commitment. Knowing how to think positively about training and competition and the feeling of being in control means that the orienteer who uses well thought-out psychological skills has a head start over other competitors!

Useful Addresses

National Coaching Foundation
114 Cardigan Road
Headingley
Leeds LS6 3BJ

BASES
114 Cardigan Road
Headingley
Leeds LS6 3BJ

Further Reading

Bull, S.J., Albinson, J.G., and Shambrook, C.J., *The Mental Game Plan: getting psyched for sport*, Sports Dynamics, Eastbourne (1996).

Butler, R.J., and Hardy, L., 'The Performance Profile: Theory and Application', *The Sports Psychologist*, (1992) 6, 253–64.

Hardy, L., Jones, G., and Gould, D., *Understanding Psychological Preparation for Sport*, Wiley, Chichester (1996).

Morris, T., and Summers, J., *Sports Psychology: Theory, Application and Issues*, Wiley John, Queensland (1995).

6 Injury Prevention and Treatment for Orienteering

IAN McLEAN

Orthopaedic Consultant to the Medical Committee of the Scottish Athletics Federation

INTRODUCTION

Health promotion and injury prevention should be amongst the main aims of any sport. The attitude that injuries are a necessary consequence of hard training is unacceptable. Prevention is better than cure. I strongly recommend an approach to training which minimizes the risk of injury, especially through overuse. However, evidence-based medicine is in its infancy and evidence-based sports medicine has barely been conceived. Therefore, systematic and infallible advice about how to prevent injury does not yet exist. Successful coaching depends on effective communication of theory, strategy, tactics and technique. This system is appropriate for medical advice also.

'Theory' covers the therapist's body of knowledge and general approach to treatment, and distinguishes between sports physicians and chartered physiotherapists on one hand and complementary therapists on the other. 'Strategy' and 'tactics' relate to the details of diagnosing and treating specific problems and are outside the scope of this Chapter. 'Techniques' are the exercises, precautions and equipment used to treat and prevent injury.

What follows is a guide as to what works best for me in preventing injury and illness while orienteering. Exercise is safe but the element of competition involved in sport and any hard training regime of over 4 hours a week increases the risks of injury dramatically. Exercise physiology is on the verge of some exciting advances. The days of hours of long slow distance training with some quality work sustained by a high carbohydrate diet may be over. Fat and free radicals are the future.

Health and fitness are not synonymous. Health is a state of complete physical, mental and social well-being. Fitness is the ability to perform a specific task.

Regular aerobic exercise has physical, mental and social benefits. The quality of exercise necessary to enjoy these benefits is thought to be three or four 30-minute sessions each week at an intensity which produces a heart rate of about seventy-five percent of an individual's maximum. (Maximum heart rate is approximately 220 minus your age beats per minute.) Whether the activity is running, swimming, cycling or aerobics the health benefits are similar.

Fitness in its capacity to perform a specific activity depends on strength, speed, suppleness and stamina. Successful orienteering requires endurance running fitness with strong muscles to stabilize the pelvis and ankles to prevent excessive sideways movement. Disregarding the possibilities of injury and staleness, the ideal training for orienteering is to run in a forest at racing pace for the usual race time as often as possible combined with exercises designed specifically to stress those muscle groups used in running across rough country.

Human biology is based on balance between six interacting physical systems – cardio-respiratory, locomotor, endocrine (hormones), neurological, homeostatic (fluid balance and temperature control) and immune. Homeostasis, the maintenance of a balanced internal environment, is the keystone. The effect of fitness training is often to disrupt the balance by aiming for a lower heart rate for the same workload. If the disturbance is not excessive, adaptation occurs and the system operates about a set point. The athlete becomes fitter. If the disturbance is such that it exceeds the capacity of a part of the body to adapt by ignoring the other interactive systems, the body breaks down. Activity which has benefits for heart function may have adverse effects elsewhere. The athlete is injured. An overuse injury results if the breakdown is insidious, an acute injury if it is sudden. Staleness, stress-fractures, shin splints, anterior knee pain and overtraining syndrome are part of a spectrum of overuse conditions. Most of them are due to faulty training – particularly emphasis on an inappropriately competitive approach to training. In many such cases coaches must bear the blame. Competition is conflict! Training should be co-operation. A balance between the two is the key to success.

Elite orienteers regularly train for 10 to 14 hours each week. Such commitment necessitates mental and social deprivation. The aim of this training is to induce changes to physique and physiology. An alternative definition of physical ill health is variation from normal. Extremes of height, weight and blood pressure are considered unhealthy, likewise unusually rapid heart rates and low oxygen uptake. Does the same apply to the low heart rate and high oxygen uptake found in highly trained endurance athletes?

It is relatively easy to achieve ninety percent of one's physical potential. Competitive success depends on being more ready to achieve the extra ten percent than your opponents. Unfortunately, that extra ten percent is disproportionately hard to achieve. The increased training load raises the risk of injury, when suddenly performance is twenty percent or less of one's potential. At an elite level it is important to have a clear idea of the balance between realistic goals and possible problems.

Orienteering has the significant advantage that for the average orienteer the greatest improvement will come from technical rather than physical training. Most orienteers can, therefore, enjoy the considerable benefits of sustained aerobic exercise in beautiful surroundings without the need to run the risks of physical overtraining. Some physical training is necessary, however, because attempting to do something for which one is totally unprepared is also risky. This applies particularly to veteran competitors. Orienteering is an excellent activity for the over-fifties but in middle age tissues become less elastic, weaker and more prone to damage. For this reason it is probably wise to avoid high impact training like aerobic intervals and circuit training. Stretching to maintain flexibility and careful warming up and down also become essential components of all training and competitive sessions.

In summary, realistic aims and achieving a balance are the keys to maximizing health and fitness and avoiding illness and injury. An experienced coach should be capable of offering personalized advice for anyone who wishes to fulfil their orienteering potential safely.

Finally, the importance of *warming up and down in* injury prevention for both competition and training must be stressed. The warm up for competition should take 30 to 40 mins and consist of four phases:

- Slow jogging, aiming for a heart rate of 110–130 beats per minute to warm muscles and tendons, gently stimulates heart and lungs and starts the switch to the appropriate metabolism (time: c. 10 minutes).

- Stretching – *slow* and sustained for muscles and tendons, non-weight bearing 'ballistic' for joints (time: c. 10 minutes). Be careful that the stretching is gentle rather than sudden, pushing or straining. It is easy to aggravate a minor muscle tear or to desensitize nerves in muscle joints and tendons by aggressive stretching so that they no longer warn properly of possible injury.

- Faster strides – greater stimulus for heart, lungs and metabolism (time: c. 5 minutes).

- Terrain running ('event-specific activity') – alerts joint position sense and reflex pathways (time: 5 to 10 minutes).

The aim of warming up is to ease the body to a state where the oxygen transport system is at full capacity to allow a maximum rate of aerobic exercise. The gradual stepwise approach avoids generating excessive lactic acid and the heat generated by the exercise speeds up the chemical reactions which release energy and generate movement. Other important reasons for warming up

properly are to get into a confident but alert state of mind which comes from carrying out a regular pre-competition routine, and to avoid injury. Warming up before hard exercise warms up the plastic collagen tissue which binds muscles to tendons and to bones, thereby allowing easy free-flowing movement of muscles, tendons and ligaments that might otherwise snap from the stretch and strain of hard running.

Gradually returning to normal after running by warming down is also important (*see* Chapter 4). A warm down should include about 10 minutes of gentle running and jogging to keep the circulation to the muscles going and to allow time for lactic acid to be cleared. It also helps clear out the debris of enzyme muscle and other molecules damaged during the run, leaving muscles in a better state for repair and replacement. This means less chance of injury in the future. After warming down it is safe to do some gentle stretching to maintain flexibility and range of movement in muscles which may be stiffening up.

WHAT TO DO IF YOU SUFFER ILLNESS OR INJURY

The key figure in the National Health Service is the family doctor or general practitioner. It is to that person that you should first turn if you require medical help with a problem that is not an emergency. Seeking direct access to a specialist can cause problems with medical ethics, confidentiality and communication and should not be encouraged.

Other professionals allied to medicine can of course be consulted. A fee-for-service may be payable, however. Beware that the term 'physiotherapist' is not a protected title. A Chartered Physiotherapist is a member of a strictly controlled profession, however, and must conform to the Chartered Society's standards. I have little experience of the abilities of sports therapists.

For an emergency problem, the Accident and Emergency Department of your local hospital should be useful. The priority of the staff in this department is the immediate care of your problem and any A&E department which arranged supervised rehabilitation would be exceptional. An injured sportsperson will require rehabilitation to a high level after injury. Be prepared to take responsibility for your own well-being to achieve this. Do not expect it to be provided automatically.

Background

What follows is some information which will permit an intelligent conversation with your doctor or therapist. It is not an exhaustive summary. The sections on first aid are possibly most relevant but as with any practical skills this is far better learned by supervised experience than by theoretical considerations.

The commonest problems for orienteers are shown in Table I.

Overuse musculoskeletal injuries are due to the repetitive microtrauma of distance running training or racing. Acute injuries are due to the sudden application of an unaccustomed force and are more common during races. Most acute injuries which affect orienteers are not severe and usually heal uneventfully aided by suitable treatment. They will be considered later.

Overuse injuries are more of a problem. Their frequency is difficult to estimate but they can cause recurring problems and long-term disability. As injured tissue cannot be relied upon to heal as strongly as the original

Overuse musculoskeletal injuries	Foot and tibial stress fractures Achilles and tibialis posterior tendonitis Exertional leg compartment syndromes Ilio-tibial tract friction syndrome Patellofemoral joint pain Hip and groin pain Low back pain
Acute musculoskeletal injuries	Ankle ligament sprains and peroneal tendon subluxations Knee ligament sprains Calf strains Hamstring strains
Skin and eye complaints	Blisters Cuts and grazes Eye injuries Insect stings and tick bites
Environmental problems	Heat-related collapse Cold-related collapse
Other problems	Over training Cardiac arrest

Table 1

and as an injury can require many frustrating months of recovery, injury prevention is the priority.

TYPES OF INJURY PREVENTION

Preventive medicine has three components: primary, secondary and tertiary prevention:

- *Primary prevention* means avoiding injury in the first place.
- *Secondary prevention* means limiting the damage of an injury after it has happened by prompt and appropriate first aid. Injuries have an irritating tendency to become worse if not handled properly in the first place.
- *Tertiary prevention* applies after initial treatment for the injury. It is equivalent to rehabilitation which should be appropriate and sufficient to ensure full fitness before returning to sport. The US College of Sports Medicine has published guidelines for fitness in sport. For orienteering one should have no pain, swelling or tenderness in the lower limbs or back, a full range of joint movement and the ability to run forwards and backwards, to hop, walk forwards while squatting, 'run and cut' at full speed to right and left and run figures of eight at speed without a limp. An orienteer who cannot do these requires further rehabilitation before participating in the sport.

OVERUSE MUSCULOSKELETAL INJURIES

Intuitively, primary prevention seems to be the ideal method. However, despite exhortations to stretch and warm up properly and to eat a suitable diet, overuse injury rates are still too high.

This failure of primary prevention has two explanations. Either the advice is incomplete or the people who should be following that advice fail to comply with it. Both reasons are probably true. First, to give suitable personalized advice for injury prevention demands accurate estimation of internal joint and soft tissue forces exerted by all training and racing activities. Such information does not yet exist reliably. Second, most injury prevention routines are time-consuming and dull. An orienteer who asks, 'Why am I doing this to achieve a state which I already have?' will probably not comply with that routine for very long. In other words, traditional primary prevention of overuse injuries requires too much effort to achieve unclear goals.

The approach I have adopted to this problem of the failure of primary prevention is to say, 'Assume that you are currently injured and do not start running again until you are fit enough to do so!' In other words, progress straight to tertiary prevention or rehabilitation. This has the advantage that goals are more concrete. 'Fitness' is the specific ability to perform an activity and so a detailed analysis of an activity is required to determine when one is fit enough to perform it.

The nature of running and injury

Overuse injuries amongst runners are caused by bad anatomy, bad footwear or bad training. Improving these can improve performance as well as minimizing injury.

Anatomy

There is little that can be done easily to correct knock-knees, bow legs or pigeon toes.

Imbalances of muscle strength and flexibility can be corrected, however.

Footwear

Avoiding wearing shoes which are excessively or unevenly worn and choosing shoes with sufficient padding are essential for avoiding injury.

Training

Training errors are probably responsible for most overuse injuries. Realistic goals for training are important. If one takes part in orienteering merely to stay healthy, the only training that is needed is three or four sessions of modest intensity, low impact and 30 minutes or so duration each week. Even with poor anatomy and running technique, the gradual development of such a programme is unlikely to cause injury. If, however, one aspires to competitive success, the frequency, duration and intensity of training required cause a significant risk of injury if anatomy, equipment and technique are less than perfect.

Correct Running Technique

What constitutes balanced muscles and good training, however? Despite the fundamental importance of the correct execution of an activity which is repeated 400 times per kilometre or 90 times a minute there is an alarming lack of description in the coaching literature of what constitutes good running technique. Here is my attempt to encourage further consideration of this subject.

Running is a series of jumps in which coordinated rotary movements of the joints cause horizontal translation of the torso. The movements are powered by muscle contraction aided by gravity and elastic recoil.

Speed is the product of stride (double pace) length and frequency. Many good and excellent long distance track and road runners adopt a stride frequency of 90–95 per minute.

The running cycle consists of support phases when each foot is in contact with the ground and swing phases when they are not. For a double pace cycle time of 650 milliseconds, ground contact time would be about 250ms and swing time 400ms for each lower limb. Joint movements should make the lower limb the shortest possible lever when swinging and the longest possible lever when providing propulsive force. Typical ranges of movement for each joint with angular velocities are shown in Table 2 (below).

Of particular note amongst these figures are those for hip extension and ankle dorsiflexion. Stiffness in the hip flexors transmits extra load to the lumbar spine predisposing to backache. Stiffness in the calf muscles transmits abnormal stresses to the whole of the lower limb and lumbar spine. It is important to be able to achieve full knee extension throughout the range of hip flexion.

Hip	10° extension to 80° flexion	450°/sec flexion; 320° sec extension
Knee	0 to 110 flexion	500°/sec flexion; 350°/sec extension
Ankle	30° dorsi– to 30° plantar-flexion	150°/sec dorsiflexion; 240°/sec plantarflexion

Table 2

Action	Main muscles shortening	Main muscles stretching
Hip flexion	Psoas, iliacus, rectus femoris, sartorius	Gluteus maximus, hamstrings
Hip extension	Gluteus maximus, hamstrings	Psoas, iliacus, rectus femoris, sartorius
Knee flexion	Hamstrings, gastrocnemius	Quadriceps
Knee extension	Quadriceps	Gastrocnenius, soleus, tibialis posterior, toe flexors
Ankle dorsiflexion	Tibialis anterior, toe extensors	Gastrocnernius, soleus, tibialis osterior, toe flexors
Ankle plantarflexion	Gastrocnenius, soleus, tibialis posterior, toe flexors	Tibialis anterior, toe extensors

Table 3

The important muscles for these activities are shown in Table 3 (above).

Therefore, to be fit enough to start running one should have sufficient strength and flexibility in the muscles in table 3 to be able to perform the activities in table 2. An accredited coach or chartered physiotherapist should be able to tell you how to achieve these. Strength can be gained by correct, supervised use of sliding weights. There are several good sources of exercises for improving static flexibility.

This is not sufficient, however. There are passive and active (or inert and vital) limits to stretching which behave differently depending on the rate of stretching. The passive limit is because of the property of biological tissues called visco-elasticity. In other words, biological tissues are stiffer if stretched quickly and are able to stretch less before damage occurs. The active limit depends on the stretch reflex and is best summarized by the term co-ordination.

It is no coincidence that the muscles which act across more than one joint (hamstrings and gastrocnemius) are those most commonly strained. During the running cycle parts of these muscles are trying to shorten while others are being lengthened. Momentary mistiming causes a pulled muscle. Improved co-ordination is best achieved by attempting a movement slowly first and then increasing the speed. Slow, sustained stretches are inadequate by themselves to prevent injury. Progressively increasing rates of swing are also needed. This type of exercise also benefits joint lubrication.

The above description is a simplified account of running on firm, flat ground. Soft, hilly, uneven terrain presents additional hazards for orienteers. Soft ground means that less of the energy for propulsion comes from passive elastic recoil and so one either slows down or has to contract muscles more strongly. When running uphill, initial contact with the ground is by the forefoot instead of the heel. This affects the forces transmitted up the whole limb but especially within the ankle plantar flexors, making them work harder. Gravity adds to speed running downhill and so more energy has to be absorbed with each step. Uneven ground tends to increase sideways movement – too much sideways movement diminishes forwards movement and so strong hip and ankle stabilizers are desirable. The important muscles to stretch and strengthen are gluteus medius, tensor fascia latae, the hip adductors, the peroneal muscles and tibialis anterior and posterior.

At this stage one is fit enough to start a regular training programme. However, the frequency, duration and intensity of such training sessions should be tailored to each individual's capabilities. This depends on the concept of elastic strain energy as well as on aerobic fitness. Elastic strain energy is the force which tends to deform tissues as a result of impact with the ground and which is stored for conversion back to kinetic energy for the next step (passive elastic recoil). In moderation, this energy is an important stimulus of a training effect, but too much too quickly causes an acute injury. Repetitive application without allowing for healing in between causes overuse injury. Stiffer tissues, such as bone, are more susceptible to damage by elastic strain energy. Less stiff tissues such as muscle can shield bone from these effects when they absorb shock by acting eccentrically (lengthening as they generate tension). Tired, aching muscles do this badly. Bone absorbs shock by forming micro-fractures. Too many micro-fractures cause a clinically evident stress fracture. Such stress fractures near joints can interfere with joint nutrition, creating a predisposition to degenerative arthritis. This is one reason why warming up is important. Warm tissues are less stiff. Frequent stretching during prolonged repetitive activity may also reduce stiffness. Additional protection for joints is provided by synovial fluid within them. It aids cartilage nutrition. Hips, knees and ankles must be put through a full range of movement before starting a repetitive weight-bearing activity so as to coat the articular cartilage with lubricant and thicken

it by hydrating it. Non-weight-bearing swinging, so-called open kinetic chain, exercise is helpful for this and for improving co-ordination.

In summary, one needs balanced, strong, flexible muscles, balanced, shock-absorbing footwear and a well-balanced, strong but flexible coach. Stiff, tired muscles are a real risk factor. It is important to pay attention to your diet throughout your training programme rather than just immediately before races for the sake of improving performance as well as injury prevention. Sixty-five percent of the energy should be provided by carbohydrate, ideally starchy foods. An outline daily diet is shown in Table 4.

Carbohydrate	350g = 1500 kcal
Protein	70g = 300 kcal
Fat	50g = 450 kcal

Table 4

Each gram of muscle glycogen is stored with 3g water and so 1 litre of water is needed daily for glycogen storage. Furthermore, high complex carbohydrate diets tend to be high in fibre and this requires a high fluid intake to be beneficial. Even in British conditions sweat loss can easily exceed 1 litre per hour and with 1.5 litres of fluid being required daily for other essential processes an orienteer training hard needs a minimum of 4 litres of non-alcoholic fluid daily.

Sarah Brown gives a thoughtful and useful description of daily dietary requirements and nutrient content of foods in her *Vegetarian Cookbook*. However, a vegetarian diet is not essential for athletic success and I believe that a weekly diet that has the main meal of the day based on red meat, poultry, offal and fish for one day each, with the other three days as you wish, is hard to beat. It is important to manage your diet. Hard training athletes need fat, which is energy rich, as well as an adequate amount of nutrients including vitamins, minerals, protein and fibre. Carbohydrate intake should only rise as a response to higher energy needs as training increases, not to replace other nutrients.

My final word on tertiary prevention of overuse injuries relates to balance and posture. In many sports a major factor separating the champion from the also-ran is balance. Orienteering is no exception. Correct trunk posture, such as recommended by the 'Alexander Technique', is important. So too is knee and ankle proprioception or position sense. This forms a useful link to primary prevention of acute injury.

ACUTE MUSCULOSKELETAL INJURIES

Ankle Ligament Sprains

Joints are stabilized by bone shape, ligaments and muscles. Although ligament strength increases slightly with an endurance training programme, the main factors within our control to improve joint safety are muscle strength and proprioception. Proprioception is a combination of spatial awareness and rapid reflex correction when balance is lost.

All muscles acting on the ankle and foot can and should be trained to improve strength and proprioception but as the lateral ligaments are most commonly injured it is particularly important to train the peroneal muscles.

Much has been written about ankle taping for prevention of ankle injuries. In brief its role in primary prevention is doubtful, secondary prevention certain and tertiary prevention likely. To be of any use, though, it must be applied correctly.

A similar rationale applies to the use of braces. They are less desirable than correctly applied taping but more so than poorly applied taping. Beware, though, that running performance can be adversely affected by these devices. A five percent deterioration in running performance has been estimated for one popular brace.

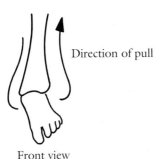

Direction of pull

Front view

Horizontal strips

Correct ankle taping procedure.

Knee Ligament Sprains and Patellofemoral Joint Disorders

For primary and tertiary prevention strong quadriceps and hamstrings and flexible hamstrings are needed. For anterior cruciate ligament injuries hamstring strength should predominate while for anterior knee pain associated with patellofemoral joint disorders, strength in the lowest part of vastus medialis muscle (vastus medialis oblique or VMO) with flexible hamstrings should be greatest.

Muscle Strains

As mentioned in the section on overuse injury, muscle strength, flexibility, proprioception and co-ordination are important in preventing these injuries. Interestingly, muscles tend not to tear in the place where they are moving fastest, in other words the swinging end.

'RICE'

Secondary prevention for all soft tissue injuries means accepting that the injury has occurred! (This is stage four of the natural grief response, following denial, anger and guilt. Go straight to stage four!):

- Rest the injured part.
- Ice the painful area for 20 minutes two to three times daily for 48 hours.
- Compress the affected area with a bandage, ideally with a piece of felt cut to avoid bony prominences.
- Elevate the injured part above the level of the heart.

Seek appropriately qualified assistance to supervise your rehabilitation.

RICE aims to minimize swelling and hence reduce the effects of the injury.

SKIN AND EYE COMPLAINTS

Blisters

Primary Prevention

Wear soft, clean socks and well-fitting shoes which have been gradually broken in. Hot weather and hard ground are particular risk factors when additional benefit can be gained by taping susceptible areas such as the big toe, sole of the forefoot and heel. That may sound obvious but blisters are the commonest injury needing treatment at the Scottish six-day events!

Secondary Prevention

Do not burst the blister! To do so increases the risk of infection. If it is small it can be protected by applying a padded dressing directly over it. If large, a doughnut of moleskin or a corn plaster can be applied around it that should be greater than the height of the bleb. If it is so large that it will inevitably burst then do so under conditions as clean as you can make them and leave the overlying skin as a dressing.

Cuts and grazes

Primary Prevention

Ensure that you are immunized against tetanus! If you are not already covered a course of three doses one to three monthly is needed followed by a booster dose every ten years (although it may be wise to have an additional dose if you suffer a particularly heavily contaminated wound more than five years after your last dose). Whether or not protective gear such as bramble bashers or gaiters are helpful is a tricky question. All such gear adds weight to your legs making it more difficult to avoid brambles and making

133

you more tired at the end of the race when many injuries tend to happen.

Secondary Prevention

Clean the wound thoroughly and cover it! Any dirt left behind increases the risk of infection and can cause tattooing of the skin when the wound has healed. Thorough cleaning is the best way of preventing tetanus. The wound should be covered with a sterile non-stick dressing. If bleeding is brisk, control it by direct local pressure and elevate the limb. Tourniquets are dangerous. Seek medical attention early if in any doubt about your ability to deal with the wound.

Eye Injuries

Primary Prevention

The ideal goggles which do not steam up or obstruct peripheral vision are not yet available. Therefore, wearing goggles may make you more likely to misread the map or fall, thereby increasing your risk of other injuries. As with any protective equipment, the decision to wear it depends on each individual's priorities.

Secondary Prevention

Have the eye examined carefully to determine if it has been penetrated or not! Such an examination may require the use of local anaesthetic drops, fluorescein, a mydriatic (to dilate the pupil) and an ophthalmoscope. Non-penetrating injuries should be washed out and may require antibiotic drops or ointment. Penetrating injuries require immediate referral to hospital. Cover the eye with a thick pad after using local anaesthetic drops if the eyeball has been penetrated.

Insects and ticks

Primary Prevention

Wear full body cover, consider insect repellent and obtain immunization where possible! Ticks are carriers of a variety of unpleasant infections depending on geographical distribution, such as Lyme Disease, Eastern European Encephalitis and Rocky Mountain Spotted Fever. Immunization is available against tick-borne encephalitis – a course of two doses a month apart for a short trip to an endemic area (including parts of Scandinavia), with a further dose 6 to 12 months later if you will be making regular or longer trips. The most reliable information about this may come from a travel agent or your local infectious disease unit. Although available via the National Health Service it is considered a luxury item by some practices where private charges (about £30 per dose) apply. The risks of infection following a tick bite are small but the consequences of infection (up to thirty percent mortality with one virus) are severe. No vaccine exists to protect against Lyme Disease.

Secondary Prevention

Tick bites: remove the tick completely and clean the area and your hands thoroughly with antiseptic! Also remember the event – such information may come in useful if you are troubled by otherwise unexplained malaise, muscular aches, chest pains, headaches, joint swelling and stiffness or muscle weakness during the subsequent few years. To remove the tick, some people swear by a twisting motion, others insist on a straight pull. In any case, ensure that the mouth parts are removed completely and avoid bursting the engorged tick during removal. Matches and whisky are probably unnecessary.

Stings: Remove the sting and cool the area! For persistent irritation topical antihistamines or calamine lotion may be needed. For severe allergic reactions oral or injected antihistamines with adrenaline and oxygen may be needed.

ENVIRONMENTAL PROBLEMS

Heat-Related Collapse

This can occur in any weather conditions. The risk increases above 22°C and there is a strong argument for cancelling events when the temperature is above 30°, especially if the humidity is high (over 80%).

Primary Prevention

Acclimatize, drink plenty, wear light clothing! Acclimatization takes 10 to 14 days of exercise under similar conditions to those expected on race day. Drink before, during and after activity (500ml before and 300ml every 20 minutes during the activity). The ideal fluid depends on personal taste. Science suggests dissolving about ½ teaspoonful of salt in 1 litre of water and adding just enough sugar to disguise the taste of the salt. About 1–3g of sugar per l00ml should be sufficient for exercise in hot weather which will not last for more than about 90 minutes. A higher concentration is counterproductive because it delays gastric emptying but may be useful for more prolonged exercise when carbohydrate replenishment becomes a priority. Monitor fluid replacement by checking body weight and resting heart rate daily. Additional salt replacement may be required if conditions are extreme and exist for a long time. Exercise intensity can be monitored by checking exercise heart

rate. Intensity should be sharply reduced during the initial stages of acclimatization.

Secondary Prevention

Recognize the symptoms of dehydration and heat exhaustion early! Heat stroke is a medical emergency. Tiredness, anxiety, irritability, feeling dizzy or faint, headache, nausea, vomiting and breathlessness are possible symptoms. Pallor, goose flesh with cool, dry skin, lack of co-ordination, and altered conscious level are possible signs. Rectal temperature above 39.5°C confirms the diagnosis of established heat stroke. Treatment should begin immediately by calling for an ambulance, removing the victim to the shade and applying cold packs to neck, groin and armpits. Fully-conscious casualties who are not vomiting should drink. Others should be given intravenous fluids.

Cold-Related Collapse

This can occur under any weather conditions, especially when a competitor is tired and slows down at the end of a race. The main risk factors are cold air temperature, wind speed, immersion in water and inadequate protective clothing.

Primary Prevention

Wear several layers, protect your head, hands and feet and eat a suitable diet! The outer layer should be water-repellent if the weather is likely to be wet. Event organizers should be able to disqualify improperly dressed competitors to prevent rescuers being put at avoidable risk. To avoid 'hitting the wall', for events of 1 to 2 hours duration a diet with two thirds of the calories from carbohydrate for the preceding week is important. For events over 2 hours take carbohydrate regularly during it. How, again, depends on personal taste. Some people are unable to tolerate solids during races. Liquids should provide 50g per litre in divided doses each hour. 50g per litre of simple sugars, such as glucose, is probably too sickly for many people. Maltodextrins (short chains of sugars) allow greater concentrations while maintaining palatability.

Secondary Prevention

Recognize the symptoms of hypothermia early! The symptoms and signs are very similar to those of heat-related collapse but rectal temperature is below 35°C. The casualty should be moved to a sheltered spot and provided with dry clothes and warm drinks if fully conscious. More serious cases should be transported gently to hospital (robust handling can precipitate cardiac arrest).

OTHER PROBLEMS

Overtraining

Overtraining has been divided into three types.

- *Physical* – overuse injuries considered above.
- *Mental* – also known as staleness.
- *Overtraining syndrome* – a serious condition associated with poor resistance to infection and chronic fatigue which usually requires a long lay-off and may end a competitive career altogether.

All of life's stresses are cumulative. An orienteer may be at risk of overtraining without altering training or competition load. An alert and sympathetic coach will take note of domestic, financial and occupational pressures and reduce the training load (intensity, duration or frequency) accordingly. Early warning signs are an elevated resting heart rate, poor sleep, increased muscle soreness, persistent fatigue and loss of desire for the sport. An unexpected deterioration in performance should cause you to *reduce your training!*

Cardiac Arrest

Though cardiac arrest is fortunately rare at orienteering events, the only hope of survival comes from prompt appropriate action from the first person on the scene. Basic life support is a relatively simple skill that should be within everybody's capability. It can only be learned by practice, though. All of the voluntary first aid organizations hold frequent courses and there should be one in your area.

Do not train or compete if you have a high temperature! Even a cold requires rest and reduction in training levels. An infection can cause swelling in the muscles and valves of the heart and the stress of hard exercise can cause serious damage. With all training listen to your body and make sure especially that you get the amount of sleep which the exercise, recovery and adaptation processes demand.

SPECIAL TOPICS

First Aid Requirements

BOF Rules and Guidelines stipulate first aid requirements for event organizers. BOF National Office produces safety guidelines for schools, outdoor centres and squads and details of relevant courses. All participants in the BOF Coaching Award Scheme must have a recognized first aid qualification.

Doping

Drug-taking is dangerous, has no benefits and is against the rules. Ignorance of drug-testing procedures is no defence against a positive test. All registered orienteers are liable to be tested at any time. Failure to provide a urine sample when requested is equivalent to a positive test. Relying on your GP's knowledge of banned drugs is risky; pharmacists probably know better but the responsibility for avoiding such substances rests with you. Further information can be obtained from:

The Sports Council's Doping Control Unit
3–10 Melton Street
London NWI 2EB
or the Drug Information
Hotline (0171 383 2244).

Psychology

Mental and social factors are important in relation to injury. An injury prone personality is reported to exist, especially affecting someone who is tentative about sport. Such factors are also important for recovery from injury. Athletes who lack adequate social support often recover slowly but coping strategies can be trained. This is a fascinating field which requires specialist advice.

REHABILITATION

I wish to end as I started, by considering tertiary prevention. I have tried to avoid specific treatment and rehabilitation advice where possible. Such areas are the province of the professional, such as a chartered physiotherapist or sports physician. Sports injury treatment is a growth area and it can be difficult to know how experienced the therapist is at your local clinic. The Scottish Sports Council and British Association of Sport and Medicine provide one form of safeguard by their systems of accreditation of sports injury clinics, but there may not be such a clinic near you (and I do not think that either organization would claim that their accreditation is exhaustive).

Here is the *American College of Sports Medicine's Checklist* which you may expect your ideal therapist to follow when helping you to recover from injury:

(1) Establish an accurate diagnosis.
(2) Minimize adverse local effects of the acute injury by taking appropriate secondary prevention (this will probably involve relative rest of the affected part).
(3) Allow proper healing (by such methods as ultrasound, drug therapy or controlled movement).
(4) Maintain other components of fitness (such as swimming or cycling for general cardiovascular fitness and strength and flexibility training for the uninjured parts).
(5) Provide a supervised return to athletic function (in other words continue treatment until you are capable of carrying out the tasks in the section on overuse injuries above). Stage 5 is carried out when the injured part is not painful, stiff or swollen and consists of progressive exercises such as static strengthening, range of movement exercises and then dynamic strengthening exercises as well as sports-related skills which start off simple, slow, short and low resistance and end up complex, fast, long and high resistance.

Because of under-provision for musculoskeletal disorders, a typical general NHS hospital clinic will not take you through Stage 5. Discharge from such a clinic does

137

not mean that you are fit to return to sport. You should ideally seek a sports injury clinic or, if unable to find one, follow the progressive staircase below:

Full Fitness!!

Category A Hills and Boulders

Undergrowth

Hills – category C then B

Gentle slaloming on flat ground

Running straight at race pace

Running straight, slowly on flat ground

Walking on flat, level ground

Injury

(Categories A, B and C relate to the Fell Running Association's classification of hill races.) One must only progress to the next stage when the current one is accomplished comfortably without swelling or stiffness. A final note of caution: if your injury is not healing as expected, be prepared to reconsider the diagnosis. Medical complaints unrelated to sport can mimic sports injury. The greatest requirement for successful treatment is a correct diagnosis, so be prepared to seek appropriate help early.

BIBLIOGRAPHY

General Reading

Alexander, R.M., *The Human Machine*, Natural History Museum Publications (1992).

Brown, M. and Adamson J., *The Flexibility Factor*, Pelham Books, London (1995).

Brown, S., *Vegetarian Cookbook*, Dorling-Kindersley, London (1984).

Grisogono, V., *Sports Injuries: A Self-help Guide*, John Murray, London (1984).

Peak Performance (fortnightly research digest) Stonehart Leisure Magazines, London.

Voluntary First Aid Organizations, *First Aid Manual* (5th edition), Dorling-Kindersley, London (1987).

Specialist Interest

Cantu, R.C., and Micheli, L.J., *ACSM's Guidelines for the Team Physician*, Lea & Febiger, Philadelphia (1991).

Lutter, L.D., Mizel M.S., and Pfiffer, G.B. *OKU Foot and Ankle*, AAOS, Rosemont, Illinois (1994).

Macleod, D.A.D., Maughan, R.J., Williams, C., Madeley, C.R., Sharp, J.C.M., and Nutton, R.W., *Intermittent High Intensity Exercise*, E & FN Spon, London (1993).

Steele, P., *Medical Handbook for Mountaineers*, Constable, London (1988).

Tippett, S.R., and Voight, M.L., *Functional Progressions for Sport Rehabilitation*, Human Kinetics, Champaign, Illinois (1995).

Straffin, P.D., *Game Theory and Strategy*, Mathematical Association of America New Mathematics Library, No 36 (1993).

7(i) Coaching Adults

DEREK ALLISON

This book has now taken the reader through the evolution, resources and skills of orienteering. We now know about techniques, fitness training, medical concerns and psychological areas. It is time therefore to deal with the coaching issues and to look at the most effective ways of improving performance for the variety of people who take up orienteering and want to get the maximum enjoyment from it.

For convenience, this Chapter has been split into separate sections dealing with adults and children. In the following Chapter Tom Renfrew looks at various adaptations of the sport for those with disabilities. In a sense, all these categories are arbitrary There is considerable overlap between them and the same coaching considerations apply equally to all three. Just as the term 'child' covers a spectrum from the acquisitive five year old to the fractious teenager, so 'adult' covers young competitive men and women, the recreational veteran and the early retired 50 year old who still wants to train for competitive success, but is worried about following the heavy training regimes of the elite.

Also, because orienteering is such a popular sport, mother, father, children and even grandparents like to share competitive experiences and ideas on how to get better at it. Nevertheless, there are clear differences between each category for which coaching styles have to be flexible. Children are used to teacher–pupil relationships and learning new skills, whereas adults can be suspicious of too much instruction or direction. A sport which involves direct running over rough ground and through dense forest obviously has to be adapted radically for those with serious physical disabilities. Many of the coaching issues have been covered in other chapters and where this is the case I will make my point and refer to the relevant section where it is dealt with in greater detail.

Adult covers a wide field.

Learning from the elite.

Let us now focus on our adult clientele and look at some coaching strategies which I have found popular and effective on training courses and in club personal performance sessions. Basically, I shall be concentrating on the grass roots orienteer and leaving men and women with elite pretensions to follow Steve Hale's prescriptions for success.

People take up orienteering for a variety of reasons – competition, recreation in pleasant natural environments, challenge, social interaction or self-fulfilment. Before looking at ways to improve personal performance the coach needs to know what people are looking for from orienteering; what are their personal strengths and weaknesses; what are the demands of their favourite form of orienteering and how much time they can devote to training for improvement.

Competitive orienteering demands moderate levels of physical fitness, strength, map reading skills and a range of technical, psychological and navigational strategies in which physical and technical competencies have to be matched and knitted together. The recreational orienteer can get satisfaction and enjoyment from a lower level of physical fitness and slower navigation while the disabled competitor tackling Trail 'O' control choice courses needs precise map visualization skills and physical fitness factors do not apply. Nevertheless, whatever people's motives or expectations, they will enjoy orienteering more if they can do it better and the process of trying to improve means sharing that experience with other like-minded people, which can be satisfying in itself. Even if winning is not important to you, the enjoyment of moving through unknown terrain with skilful, confident map and compass work is infinitely more enjoyable than continually getting lost.

The other 'good news' is that the same basic techniques work for every age and level of ability. The Skills Step System works for men, women, children and veterans and is equally effective in every type of terrain. Veterans may be affected by failing physical strength and flexibility, deteriorating eyesight and poorer short-term memory, but within limits every orienteer can improve by working at the same basic skills progression. Once the orienteer learns to analyze their own personal strengths and weaknesses in an effective, honest manner and to share these with a coach or friend, then it is only a question of practice, working with fellow competitors and making weaknesses into strengths. As stated in the Foreword, the orienteering coach is constantly seeking to make themselves redundant by placing more responsibility for self-analysis, accurate feedback and personal training planning on the individual athlete.

'Where' to practise and 'how long' will depend on individual circumstances. The 'what' I will share with you now is experience gained from a variety of scenes and venues both in Britain and abroad. Most Scandinavian clubs provide a regular training programme for members throughout the year. In Britain there are regular National and Regional weekend personal performance courses for adults at centres like YMCA Lakeside on Lake Windermere including an annual Women Only Course and many clubs provide training opportunities, especially in the summer months. There are also 150 permanent courses in the UK where individual orienteers can permutate permanent marker posts to provide their own training exercises.

First, I will touch on general areas where an orienteering coach can advise and encourage, then I will describe some exercises and strategies which I have found particularly helpful with club orienteers. It is important at this stage to understand the difference between training and coaching, and between teaching and coaching. Training involves specific practical work whether physical, technical or psychological. Teaching is direct instruction to a group. Coaching is the personal guidance given on improvement strategies which may or may not include specific technical exercises or instruction. In many cases, orienteers are forced to use local or low-key events for technical training because their home environment has no suitable terrain forests or parks. This is the sort of area where a sensitive, knowledgeable coach can give positive help and encouragement.

PHYSICAL TRAINING

This area has been fully covered by Andrew Kitchin in Chapter 4 and Ian McLean in Chapter 6. I would only stress the importance of the warm up and down for injury prevention and repeat that *all* muscle groups need to be covered.

Other Points

- If orienteering demands the ability to run in terrain, then that is the most appropriate type of training for improvement. If you run around a track for 20 minutes a day, that is what you get good at.
- The importance of sufficient rest and the right food and drink.
- Training effect is reversible – if you stop training, you will lose fitness relatively rapidly.

- The physical and technical areas often merge together, for example oxygen debt generates navigational mistakes.
- It is a good idea for veterans to have clearance from a doctor prior to starting on a structured physical training programme. Having said this, orienteering is an excellent sport for competitive 'oldies' of both sexes. They can compete on equal terms in their own five-year-age band throughout life and orienteering training can take place in pleasant surroundings and on soft surfaces which cushion shock to bone, muscle and sinew. Even the competition is mostly unseen in forest so adrenaline levels stay relatively low.
- Anyone orienteering regularly at weekends should be at least jogging fit, that is, capable of jogging for 2 to 3km without stopping. Running training of 1 to 2 hours in two sessions during the week should achieve this comfortably.

The table below suggests some general idea of training programmes but these are only a guide. As Andrew Kitchin stresses in Chapter 4 all training schedules must be specific to the individual.

Technical Training gets comprehensive treatment in Chapter 3(i) and (ii). It is more difficult to organize than physical training so many orienteers neglect it, which is unfortunate as orienteering is a very technical sport. In fact, improved navigation can bring dramatic improvement, while improved running fitness 'buys' only a few minutes on an average course. It is also vital to keep tech-

1	Relatively Unfit	
	Men	Women
Monday	Rest	Rest
Tuesday	20 mins run/walk 'O' club night	20 mins run/walk 'O' club night
Wednesday	Rest or other sport	Rest or other sport
Thursday	20 mins run/walk	20 mins run/walk
Friday	Rest	Rest
Saturday	'O' technical training if available	'O' technical training if available
Sunday	Orienteering event	Orienteering event
2	Semifit	
	Men	Women
Monday	Rest-or other sport	Rest or other sport
Tuesday	20–30 mins easy run 'O' club night	20 mins easy run/ 'O' club night
Wednesday	Rest	Rest
Thursday	20–30 mins fartlek run	15–20 mins fartlek run
Friday	20–25 mins jog	15–20 mins jog
Saturday	Other sport or 'O' technical training if available	Other sport or 'O' technical training if available
Sunday	Orienteering event	Orienteering event
3	Basically fit	
	Men	Women
Monday	20 mins jog	15 mins jog
Tuesday	35 mins steady run with map 'O' club night	25 mins steady run/ with map 'O' club night
Wednesday	Rest	Rest
Thursday	35 mins fartlek run	25 mins fartlek run
Friday	Rest	Rest
Saturday	Other sport or 'O' technical training if available	Other sport or 'O' technical training if available
Sunday	Orienteering event	Orienteering event

Suggested Training Programme

nique in line with faster running speed brought about by increased training.

It does not demand fancy exercises like 'window corridor' or first-class terrain. In Britain, many overgrown industrial sites like those in the West Midlands make excellent training areas for 'urban orienteers' if accurate maps are available and club coaches use some creative imagination in suggesting 'line runs' and 'map exercises'. Local Competitions too can be used for technical training, as mentioned earlier, particularly if sports watches are used to provide split times for comparison with a partner in judging route choice or speed between controls on direct legs.

Good *quality* technical training is more important than large quantity and it is useless to expect one high-powered course per year to provide instant improvement. It is what comes between courses which is important and this requires some personal analysis and planning, plus determination and regular commitment. This applies for all abilities of orienteers. In the final analysis, the effectiveness of any training must be judged by outputs rather than inputs – improved results in events rather than hours spent running.

There is a lot of psychology in orienteering, but in my opinion the two most important aspects upon which to concentrate are confidence and concentration. Success breeds success. If an orienteer is following a systematic physical and technical programme and is preparing methodically for each competition then they will feel more confident and perform more consistently. If the competitor has confidence in their own ability then they are less likely to be distracted by others in the forest and more likely to produce their own optimum performance. This applies particularly to women, who generally prefer to keep map to ground contact and

not to take chances with the rough run and relocate technique favoured by some men. Improvement often takes time. Those new to the sport should not expect instant success once they start training. It may take months or years, and there could be a lot of mistakes and disappointments on the way. It took Jörgen Mårtensson 14 years as an adult orienteer before he won the first of his many World Championship medals. Resilience and determination are two vital orienteering qualities.

In all this, goal setting can be a vital mechanism for motivation and achievement. Where are you? Where do you want to be? How do you get there? How do you know when you have arrived? Goals can deal with *outcome* (for example position in a competition – though this is outside your control); *performance* (for example less than 10 mins per kilometre – which is controllable and measurable); *process* (for example keeping running up a hill). Sue Walsh deals with goal setting from a psychological viewpoint in fascinating detail (Chapter 5). I would only add that I have found the use of goals which have been negotiated between coach and orienteer in a realistic, measurable form to be particularly effective in raising expectations and achievement.

SOME KEY COACHING POINTS

(1) Orienteering is all about map reading but 'back-up' technique is essential in avoiding bad mistakes and keeping navigation consistent. The two most important back-up techniques are the compass whether used as an orientating instrument or for bearings and distance judgement by pacing, in which a personal scale either in metres or double paces per 100 metres (calculated by

counting every time a single foot hits the ground over a measured distance) is fixed to the end or side of the compass base plate.

The compass is often neglected in continental terrain where there are a lot of paths and line features. It is vital in Scandinavian terrain and where visibility is low. The important thing about the compass is not what kind it is but whether it is used properly and frequently. It should be held steady and sighting points should be used as far ahead in the terrain as possible. It should be checked every time a crest is crossed or you emerge from thick trees.

Distance judgement is obviously affected by hills and rough terrain. It can only be a guide and with experience 'eye' may take over from methodical pacing. Compass and pacing can be vital in finding difficult controls on short hauls through featureless forest. Both can be improved dramatically with regular practice.

(2) Good orienteering technique means being positive. Always decide your leg route before you set off, using map evidence and confirming your progress by observing terrain features as you proceed (map to ground technique). You need to simplify the map and create a mental picture of the terrain (map visualization). Look, too, to see what you would see if you strayed left or right or overshoot your chosen line. *Never* run in hope and rely on picking evidence from the ground to tell where you are on the map – though this can be a useful relocation strategy if you do get lost.

(3) Route choice. For the best results in competition, orienteers should be encouraged to play to their personal strengths. This may mean a good runner with technical shortcomings diverting from the straight line on a leg to run round paths, while an orienteer who is good at compass and pacing could follow a more direct route. Knowing your strengths and weaknesses is critical. When drawing your route on a map (after the event) use arrows when following a line and draw a solid line when running through the forest. This helps in analyzing technique requirements in different types of terrain. You can then practise your weaker areas in unimportant events and use your strengths in major competitions.

(4) Rough 'O' does not mean careless 'O'. It means running as fast as possible using the minimum amount of information to keep in control.

(5) Contour interpretation is the supreme orienteering skill. Ground shape never changes; man-made features (including planted forest) can change frequently. Working at contour interpretation and ground shape visualization from the map is vital if people want to become 'gold standard' orienteers. One of the best ways of improving this technique is to try some mapping yourself. Getting into the mind of the mapper is important for all orienteers.

IMPROVEMENT STRATEGIES

I'll conclude this Chapter by listing a series of strategies that I have successfully used with adult orienteers.

Shadowing

Most orienteering performance takes place out of sight of the coach and getting feedback can be difficult. Shadowing is one way of doing this, although because some adults dislike being followed and watched, it may be better to work as a pair with a friend.

Shadowing Checklists for Training in Matched Pairs

Between Controls

- Is the map being read on the run?
- Is the compass being read on the run?
- How often is the compass used?
- Is the speed appropriate?
- Is simplification used? (Concentrating on important map and ground features and ignoring unnecessary detail.)
- Is the choice of line good?
- How good is their running in terrain?

Standing at the control – has she planned ahead?

Into Controls

- Is an attack point used?
- Do they know the code and description before arriving? Is there hesitancy in the circle?
- Is their speed appropriate?

From the Control

- Do they stand at the control? Have they planned ahead?
- Do they flow through the control?

Missed Controls

- Do they stop and look around?
- Do they relocate rapidly?
- Do they find a new attack point?
- Is their handling of mistakes systematic?

General

- How many stops and how long is spent to read the compass; to read the map; to select a route?
- How much are they distracted by other competitors?
- Is route choice biased towards easy path routes?
- Is full use made of available contour detail?
- Is their general level of fitness able to cope with the demands of the terrain?

Shadowing often results in a change in style of the person being shadowed. To minimize this, keep 20m back where possible and do not stop the participant in mid-course more than once. Talk as little as possible. Make brief notes under the above headings at the end and use it as the basis for a discussion and setting of goals for future exercises.

Relocation Strategy

- Stop
- Think! When did you last know definitely where you where?
- What have you done since then?
- What can you see around you?
- How would it be shown on the map?
- Using all the above information, look at the map and make an estimate of your current location.
- Check by either going to the control or an obvious nearby feature. (Relocation is covered in detail in Chapter 3.)

Preparation for a Major Event

- Everyone is an individual – what works for me may not work for you. Read, assess, adapt and adopt.
- The best preparation is to plan and execute an effective training programme in the years before the event, with year plans indicating important races and 'peak periods'. The next best is to have a training programme for the months up to the event.
- Find out as much as possible about the event, terrain and the organization beforehand. Look at a road map/atlas and find out where it is. Look at copies of old versions of the map.
- Run in similar terrain, aggressively through rough/green areas; run with similar maps; run at the same time of day as the races; run in the heat and enjoy it.
- If it is to be hot, plan to saturate yourself with liquid before you race. You can continue sipping a small amount right up until you start. Try this out beforehand. It is not a good idea to try new things out in an important race. Resolve to use the refreshment points during the race.

Race Day

- Write down your training plan for the week up to the race, taking into account the time you will need to spend travelling to the event.
- Check all your clothing and equipment is up to standard, and have spares.
- Clean your compass and look after it well.
- Write down your timetable for the day before the race.
- Write down your timetable for the race day once you know your start time.
- Consider what and how much food you will eat before you race.
- Are you happy about the travel arrangements; do you need to set off earlier?
- If you are flying to a competition, always carry your racing kit with your passport in your hand luggage.

Before the Start

- Read the race details again.
- Collect your number/bib.
- Start method? How far to the start from the car park?
- Prepare your control card and description sheet. It is not the time to try a new method.
- Warm up.
- Observe the terrain on the way to and near the start.
- Think about control procedure and flow.
- How far is it from the last control to the finish? Can you see it from the finish area?
- Where are the refreshment points?

- Be ready for the unexpected: manned controls, television, spectators, sunshine, rain, hail, snow.
- Do not worry about the opposition. You cannot control what they are doing. Think about them when you look at the results at the finish.

Examples of Personal Competition Strategies

The following examples of personal competition strategies take into account personal strengths and weaknesses.

Mechanics of Flow Through a Control

(1) Well before the control;
    (a) select the route to the following control.
(2) Before the attack point:
    (a) check the description and code;
    (b) have a mental picture of the area around the control;
    (c) prepare your compass bearing and measure the distance from attack point to control;
    (d) know the cardinal point of leaving the control.
(3) At the attack point:
    (a) pause, check what feature the control is on;
    (b) think, slow down/walk;
    (c) go through (b) again, have your control card ready;
    (d) walk, jog into control with eyes *open*.
(4) At the control:
    (a) check the code and then punch;
    (b) check your compass for direction of leaving;
    (c) walk, jog away, recheck the compass;
    (d) look at the map;

    (e) get into appropriate running rhythm for the next leg.

Mechanics for Choosing a Route

(1) Judge difficulties of legs well in advance to allow choice of appropriate speed and strategy. What is the penalty if I miss the control? Does it look easy? For example, if it's in 'green' or difficult will it pay to walk with careful map reading, compass and pacing?
(2) Pick an appropriate attack point for the difficulty (< 200m use the previous control):
    (a) Is the attack point an attack point or an additional control?

        Yes   No

    (b) Is the direct route to the attack point feasible?

        Yes   No

    (c) Is any route to the control better than (b)?

        Yes   No

(3) Take route to attack point for the control

Seven Ages of Orienteering – An Ideal Adult Development Plan

(1) *Can I find all the controls?* Newcomers often choose a course which is too difficult and hope to survive.
(2) *Acquisition of some basic skills.* Orientate the map, use line features all the way and make few mistakes.
(3) *More skills.* Back-up techniques to give consistency and allow more speed, compass, pacing, using of contours, thumbed route relocation.

(4) Speeding-up. With more physical and technical training:
  - (a) coarse 'O', fine 'O' from attack point;
  - (b) fitness to do coarse 'O' faster and avoid oxygen debt mistakes;
  - (c) map perception.

(5) Choosing the fastest method:
  - (a) route choice;
  - (b) compass and pacing;
  - (c) checkpoints on the line – read into the control.

(6) Speed strategy – the right speed and technique at the right time to avoid getting lost.

(7) Refining techniques and fitness in a year plan and long-term strategy. Psychology.

CONCLUSION

I like to think that any orienteer of whatever age who develops through the 'Seven Ages' not only becomes a consummate orienteer but also gets far more satisfaction from their sport than a 'Hit or Miss' anti-coaching friend. However, life is never perfect. There are orienteers – the romantics – who get a 'buzz' from battling with their own short-comings and get a great thrill from finding the magic marker in the forest by chance rather than skill.

I conclude by sticking to my basic argument as a justification for the advice and comment given in this Chapter. Both logic and experience tell me that people enjoy any human activity much more if they have a basic competence in it. I hope you will take my words in this spirit and enjoy running in sunlit forests just that bit more in the future.

Enjoy running in sunlit forests.

7(ii) Coaching Children

PETER PALMER

The basic skills of orienteering are the same for all ages and both sexes but there are a variety of methods for teaching and developing them. Children especially need to be taught and coached in ways which strengthen motivation rather than stifle enthusiasm under a blanket of repetitive instructions and drills.

Orienteering certainly has a lot to offer children and more than most sports it pos-

You are never too young.

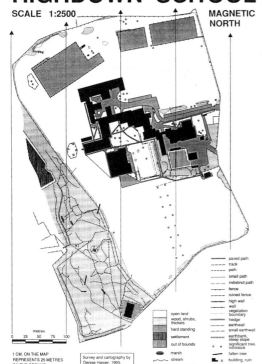

School site orienteering.

sesses the capacity to adapt its formats to different environments, ages and abilities. It offers competition against self as well as other people. The challenges it provides take place in forests away from the critical eyes of peers. Its venues are usually attractive natural ones, and for the inner-city child it can offer countryside adventure on the doorstep. It can cater for the whole spectrum from the competitive athletic child to those with physical or mental disabilities and it can easily be adapted to offer different balances of exploration, problem solving or running activity according to situation or group.

For schools, orienteering provides many educational dimensions. As an Outdoor Adventurous Activity within the English

Physical Education National Curriculum and Scottish 5–14 Curriculum it offers an attractive option which can be taught on the school site and is relatively cheap. It can also be used as a practical vehicle for delivering attainment targets in Geography and Mathematics as well as providing cross curricula links between these subjects and with others like English, Technology and Community Studies. However, even with the most skilful teaching and imaginative progressions from classroom to campus, 'educational orienteering' can be less than inspiring for many children unless it involves forest fun, challenge and progression to more adventurous environments outside school like a local park or common.

Even in a competition context adults should be careful not to burden children with their own expectations for success. It is only too easy to constrict children's orienteering in a straitjacket of adult competitive structures, rules and procedures which can turn children away from the mainstream sport. These considerations all have a direct bearing on teaching and coaching styles, but before tackling specific issues it is important to set orienteering in the wider perspective of sport as a whole – what it can offer and how it can fulfil the expectations which children have for it.

Children are not miniature adults. They are young human beings developing at different rates and sometimes in unexpected ways into mature people. They often have their own ideas on orienteering as on any other sport and these should be listened to by teachers and coaches. Nor should children be treated as one homogeneous group. A six year old has a very different attitude from an eleven year old to sport and to life and a fifteen year old adolescent is a 'different animal' altogether.

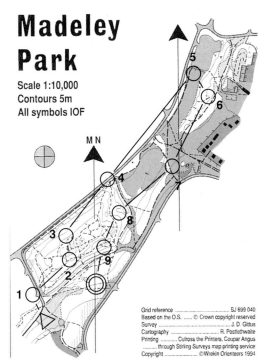

Madeley Park

Scale 1:10,000
Contours 5m
All symbols IOF

M N

Grid reference	SJ 699 040
Based on the O.S.	© Crown copyright reserved
Survey	J. D. Gittus
Cartography	R. Postlethwaite
Printing	Culross the Printers, Coupar Angus
	through Stirling Surveys map printing service
Copyright	©Wrekin Orienteers 1994

Simple children's course.

Very young children can use maps.

Learning the basic skills of orienteering is easiest for young children who are busy assimilating so much other knowledge about the world and their place within it. Very young children of six and seven can use maps and compasses to navigate around simple courses. They can appreciate the relationships between ground and map features and they can quickly learn to use line features as navigational handrails. All the basic skills can be acquired and used consistently by the age of fourteen.

As in other sports such as gymnastics and swimming, an early start can raise important questions. What are the most appropriate competitive structures for very young children? How can their interest and involvement be encouraged without introducing the competitive pressures of adult sport? How can newcomers be introduced – both very young and adolescents – without their confidence being destroyed by getting lost on courses which are too difficult? What about early developers whose confidence withers when they are overtaken by those who mature later? What about girls who before puberty can match the performance of boys but undergo difficult physical changes which set them back during adolescence and can cause them to leave the sport when planners and coaches are not sensitive to their needs?

Finally, there is the nature of orienteering itself. Few other sports tread such a delicate line between bliss and misery. Several hours lost in a dark, wet forest can be a trauma which turns children off orienteering for ever. On the positive side, orienteering can offer adventure, a mixture of mental and physical activity in a countryside setting, excitement, success, competition, an active healthy lifestyle, mastery of map and compass skills, self-confidence, social interaction, creative expression, familiarity with the nat-

Very young children can be energtic.

ural world and respect for the environment. Whether these experiences are enhanced or distorted depends crucially on the sensitivity of teaching, coaching and planning.

In the words of the IOF *Guidelines on Orienteering for the Young* 'Children take up sport for a variety of reasons. If their experiences are to be fulfilled and the sport of orienteering is to develop its potential as an enjoyable challenging activity for the young, it is vital that everyone concerned in the organization, planning and coaching of orienteering should see their work in terms of meeting the needs and aspirations within the sport of young people themselves.'

The advice which follows is offered within this coaching context. The perspective is a long-term one in which childhood is seen as an important stage in the human progression from cradle to the grave. The three age categories within which suggestions are set should be seen as flexible guidelines.

Children obviously grow up and develop within different timescales. Here then are a series of recommendations for teaching and coaching orienteering at different stages in a child's development.

CHILDREN OF TEN AND UNDER

Teaching, coaching and competition for these very young children must be closely related to their level of maturity. Children at this age tend to be egocentric, energetic and socially immature. They crave success and encouragement.

(a) *Teaching emphasis* should be on practical games and exercises in familiar environments of classroom and playground. Skills learnt in this context will build up confidence and translate to unfamiliar environments at later stages. Starting

Confidence in familiar environments.

with map literacy, orientation, thumbing and handrail techniques, each skill can be made a platform for the next. Constant practice through fun activities will reinforce new knowledge. The illustrations included show examples of this approach. Publications like *Teaching Orienteering* and *Start Orienteering* describe methods and lesson plans in detail.

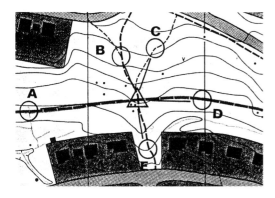

School star event.

(b) *Teaching and low-key competitive activity* must be seen as a whole. Very young children should never be put in competition situations which demand skills they have not yet mastered. Similarly, adults should be careful in teaching more advanced skills which take children well beyond the skill levels of their competitive courses. There will always be the 'Yvette Hagues' who can move up skill ladders quickly and bright children are quite capable of absorbing and mastering new ideas quickly. The problem arises when they find themselves on courses which they have the technical skills to master but not the physique. This is a delicate area for teacher and coach.

(c) *Clover loop courses, star exercises, mini relays* and the like all provide fun competition but these should always be put in a learning context. If young children are pressured to perform well in age group competitions before they are confident in map and compass skills, this will have a negative effect on attitude and progress. At this age if children are taken to BOF competitions, string courses and the colour-coded system (which is skill- rather than age-based) offer a much more appropriate context for competition than age-based systems.

Drawing maps improves other skills.

(d) *The mapping dimension* should never be neglected as a teaching tool. Even young children enjoy drawing plans and maps, whether of desk top models, the classroom, garden or school field. They can be used for mini competitions or treasure hunts – or simply to adorn a bedroom wall. Familiarity with maps and simply surveying and drawing will reinforce distance judgement, orientation, compass skills and spatial awareness.

It is an important part of the responsibility of teachers and coaches to protect young children from high pressure competitions like National Championships, Relay Races and Chasing Starts which are not appropriate for young children. Gifted youngsters may wish to make up teams with their older peers, but it is only too easy for a 5-minute mistake to ruin a team's progress and for hard-won confidence to drain away when the finger of blame is pointed at the youngest in the team.

CHILDREN OF ELEVEN TO FOURTEEN YEARS

This is a key stage in skill development but one of the most difficult for which to plan courses and coach. Most youngsters of this age are receptive, motivated and hungry to learn new skills. The social group is more important than with younger children and they like to compare performances with their peers. At this age girls are more mature than boys but both sexes can be coached together. With sound teaching methods they can both make very rapid progress. Children can be led up to the Step System through the complete range of basic skills (*see* illustration on page 34) from handrails to attack point strategies, compass techniques, route choice and contour interpretation. They can be best kept motivated with a series of short exercises interspersed with plenty of route marking on maps and discussion. The fun element can be used to give everyone the feeling of success and progress, as well as practising and reinforcing new skills. Formal physical training is not necessary at this age. Plenty of group games and running activity will build up cardio-vascular fitness naturally. Participation in other sports should be encouraged which will also build up strength without blunting enjoyment. Children at this stage like variety and enthusiasms can change quickly.

The difficulties arise from differing rates of maturation. Children can grow very rapidly during these years and a four-foot boy may well find himself competing against a six-footer in the same age class. Girls who develop early can find it difficult to cope with extra weight on hips and thighs and changes in centre of gravity – and may resent being beaten by their pre-pubescent contemporaries. Quick bone growth can also bring tendon and ligament problems in knees and ankles.

In many ways age group competition brings the worst of all worlds to this age group and both early and late developers can suffer. Boys who develop early can get undue success and then be demotivated as late developers overtake them later. With girls, for reasons given earlier, the reverse is also often true. With all children at this stage performance is often erratic. Even with the most gifted, fluctuation in performance from week to week should be accepted as normal.

Taking all these considerations into account, here are some recommendations for teacher or coach working with the eleven to fourteen year olds.

(a) *The colour-coded competition system* is more suitable for these children than an age band structure. Because colour-coded courses are based on skill levels rather than chronological age the system can cater for differences in maturation rates and motivate children to move up the skills ladder without worries about being beaten by contemporaries.

(b) *Coaches should not put too much emphasis on high pressure competition,* particularly in a representative sense. School and District Team Competitions may be appropriate with the right guidance. International competition is not appropriate. Relays should be treated as fun. The nature of orienteering combined with the natural inconsistency of this age group make it extremely likely that one bad error or an erratic run can let down the team. This can be very stressful for immature competitors. If selection procedures are necessary they should not be based on one or two major events. It is much better from all points of view to look at performance over a given period and to match this against skill level and experience.

(c) *'Goals'* can be important motivators in improving performance and encouraging skills practice but they should be 'internal' ones, by which success is measured by self-improvement rather than by comparison with peers. A goal of finishing in the first three is too dependent on others.

(d) *Indoor activities* can also be very popular, particularly if a gym is available. Forest circuits, map shuttle relays and team 'punching' competitions can provide plenty of running activity as well as encouraging skills development. Other sedentary activities like 'O' Bingo, 'O' Beetles and 'O' Snakes and Ladders can provide fun in winter months as well as helping to cement social loyalties which become more important to youngsters with the approach of adolescence. Youngsters also enjoy post-competition analyzes and discussions which involve marking routes on maps, noting time loss and keeping files and diaries. Coloured graphs plotting improvement or training activity can also be popular. Map collecting can encourage swapping contacts with children from other regions and other countries.

(e) *Training* should always be treated in a fun context at this age, but children should be encouraged to work with and to learn from each other. Placing and Retrieving exercises in pairs, Sprint 'O' Loops, Route Choice in twos and threes and 'Triangle' training can all be used to give skills practice a social element as well as low-key 'fun' competition on a 'hang and retrieve' principle. The important thing is to keep exercises simple. Orienteering activities should never

Post event discussion.

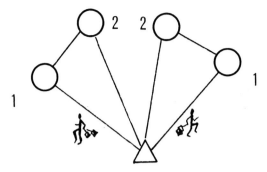

Placing and retreiving in pairs.

become intellectual puzzles, nor should coaches need to resort to window or corridor exercises. At this stage extracting relevant information from a coloured map is important in building up map literacy.

(f) *Safety* is always important in the planning of children's orienteering events, but it should be a special priority with the age group. Children of this age have little awareness of their own physical limitations and have difficulty in assessing the danger of hazards like steep crags or wide streams. They are also extremely susceptible to extremes of temperature. More important than emergency procedures like whistle blowing, first aid and safety bearings are preparation and pre-planning with safety in mind. Courses should be planned to avoid hazards and to offer obvious catching and collecting features at key points depending on terrain and the experience of the children. If necessary, extra control points or taped sections should be included to lead competitors round a potential hazard. A teacher/coach should always be at Start/Finish throughout the activity to monitor progress and act on any reports of problems. Everyone involved must be aware of event procedures and understand

them, and for this age group they should be kept as simple as possible. Whatever the children say, ensure they wear cagoules, gloves and hats on cold days. If they still look very cold, stop the activity, put on more warm clothes if possible, get warm liquid and/or food into them and if a journey is involved get them into the minibus and back home as soon as possible. Change all wet clothing for dry. A change of clothes after an event is essential. In hot weather, watch out for overheating symptoms and treat accordingly. Most twelve year olds are like young puppies – scampering around and playing energetically, or sleeping. Limits don't enter into their comprehension.

(g) *Map scale* is not critical. Most children have no trouble with their eyesight. As long as relevant detail is clear and the exercises planned are within the correct skill range, and so long as the size of the map allows for convenient folding and thumbing, the scale can be that which most easily translates onto an A4 sheet. Orientation of the map is important and children should be constantly practising this with or without a compass. For this reason maps with diagonal magnetic lines should be avoided. All conventional orienteering maps have North lines converted to Magnetic North.

(h) *Pre-adolescent children* normally show great respect for rules and regulations and will often be highly critical of those who break them. However, this will not stop them bending rules if the opportunity presents itself. For this reason it is important to use punches or other means to verify correct identification of controls. On the other hand, it is a mistake to put too much emphasis on timing. Losing face after a mistake easily encourages negative coping strategies like feigned injury or illness. Teaching this age group can be immensely satisfying but there is always the temptation to look for short-term success. Good performances can be produced by an early developer performing at a skill level below his or her potential – and the youngster be put on a pedestal from which a fall later is inevitable. All children's coaching should be seen in a perspective of years rather than months and mature success in mid to late twenties requires sensitivity and protection in the formative years.

The coaching objective for all young children should not be international achievement in adulthood but getting the maximum enjoyment at their own level while young and creating a platform of skills upon which a variety of navigational experience may be built in later life. For some, satisfaction may come in trying to climb the ladder to elite success, for others it may be club competition, coaching, mapping or simply healthy outdoor recreation. All are valid orienteering experiences and teachers, coaches and parents should beware of being prescriptive or overambitious for their charges. Unreasonable pressures based on adult expectations can inadvertently damage children's long-term interests. Any child turned away from orienteering by a badly planned or overtaxing course – or over-ambitious training activity – is one too many.

Orienteering, as well as introducing and developing the valuable life skills of map and compasss has a wealth of challenging experiences to offer children in this age group. Even if they do not remain in the sport as adults, exposure to the philosophy and values of orienteering can be of immense benefit both to children and our sport

YOUNG PEOPLE OF FIFTEEN TO EIGHTEEN

The adolescent years are as difficult for young people to cope with as for adults to cope with the young people. As one parent put it to me, 'It is as if they are careering down rapids in a canoe from fourteen to seventeen. You just hope it is the right way up and pointing in the right direction when they float into adulthood at the end.'

Not only is the body chemistry reacting at furious levels during adolescence, but physical changes are affecting centre of gravity, balance, weight and strength. Pressures of school work and examinations often conflict with the demands of sport and parental expectations can lead to conflict as young people seek to assert their own personal identities. The rules of sport, like teachers and coaches, are seen as representing authority and teenage rebellion can involve a rejection of sport. Personal relationships – especially with the other sex – and respect from the peer group are of much more importance to this age group.

Widening sex differences in physique during adolescence not only affect the execution of orienteering skills but also influence the facility with which any new skill is acquired. Physiological changes cause significant differences between the sexes in such things as systolic blood pressure, heart rate, haemoglobin concentration and vital capacity. While boys develop more running speed and strength, for girls, if only temporarily, it can seem to be the reverse. Yet girls do not become inferior to boys any more than the typical adolescent is simply a miniature

157

adult. On the positive side, it is a time when increasing maturation and confidence lead youngsters to see excitement and challenge as part of the process of discovering themselves. With sensitive planning and coaching orienteering can be an ideal sport to fulfil these expectations.

The most important considerations for an adolescent therefore are their friends, the opposite sex, testing out their own values against what they perceive as the adult world, music, hero worship and day dreaming. The first stage in adolescence is to observe adult behaviour, the second is to copy it and the third is to become young adults with their newly established identity. Girls go through these stages earlier and faster than boys, sometimes helped by a relationship with an older boyfriend. Some boys never really do grow up! Middle-class children tend to tolerate adult structures longer than those from a working-class background.

Young people take up sport partly for social reasons, partly looking for excitement, and partly because it offers an opportunity of belonging to an identifiable group and wearing its uniform and badges. Sport can offer new skills, success, fitness, aesthetic experience, friends and social opportunities in exciting settings. Sometimes the social structures surrounding a sport can be more important than the sport itself. Sports like orienteering which are individual and performance-based have a powerful appeal because they offer personal challenges and tests respected by the outside world. Achievements in sport can act like tribal initiation ceremonies. My own research with 300 adolescent orienteers identified social appeal, challenge, the countryside and exploration as the major attractions of orienteering. Bad weather, lack of social opportunities and poorly planned courses were

described as the biggest 'turn-offs'. This last criticism illustrates an interesting point with all sport for young people: activities have to be planned to slot into a flow between the two extremes of anxiety and boredom. Orienteering has a particular difficulty in this respect in that a delicate balance has to be maintained between under and over extension of navigational skills. This obviously has direct reference to coaching methods.

On the other hand, orienteering can offer many coaching opportunities for the young not available to other sports. It can provide training weekends in beautiful and challenging environments, squad camps and courses away from parental constrictions, colourful

Finding forest markers is exciting.

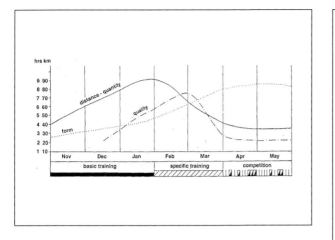

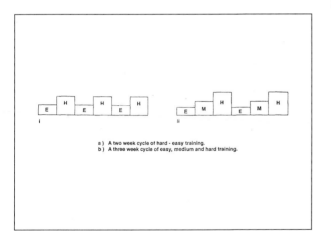

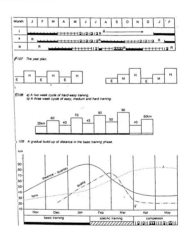

Examples of training programmes.

inexpensive kit (unlike swimming), incentive badges, collecting chains for maps, pen-friends in other regions or countries and opportunities for team competition. Above all, finding markers in exotic forests is exciting and adventurous and orienteering can be infinitely adaptable in providing such challenges.

The coach then has to lock into these 'turn-ons' and avoid or underplay the 'turn-offs'. Training activities have to be variable and to offer success. While boys and girls like to train together, girls' exercises should be devised so as not just to be shorter or inferior versions of boys. They must offer navigational rather than physical challenges and provide the experiences and challenges which young women seek from orienteering. Typically, girls do not enjoy scrambling through thick trees or brambles but may well like running skilfully through varied forest and hills. Youngsters at this age want to be involved in organizing and planning and are often bursting with energy and ideas which coaches and planners ignore at their peril!

Some Specific Recommendations for Teachers and Coaches Working with these Youngsters:

(a) *While all skills levels can be covered during the adolescent years* and a lot of technical work is possible and desirable, careful attention has to be paid to physical loads, especially during and after periods of rapid growth. As the body settles down after adolescent changes, cardio-vascular fitness levels need more attention than merited by the eleven to fourteen age group and regular training becomes necessary for the first time. Training programmes have to be carefully structured and closely monitored both to build up strength and fitness for longer courses and to provide a platform for adult development. Running training obviously involves a degree of overload and strength training may mean an introduction to weights and tough gym circuits.

All this places a heavy responsibility on the teacher or coach who has to strike a delicate balance

between restraining youthful enthusiasm and encouraging youngsters to take part in fashioning and carrying out training programmes structured to themselves as individuals. As well as stress and demotivation resulting from overload, knees and ankles cause perennial problems for adolescents who may have grown several centimetres in a year and whose tendons and ligaments are struggling to catch up with bone growth. The demands of sport also have to be balanced against school work or a

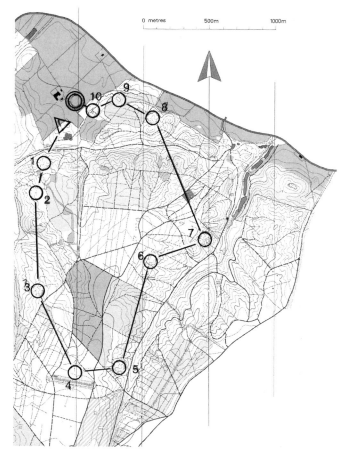

Under 16 girls course with catching features to 'contain' mistakes.

hectic lifestyle and in addition to this, traumas within personal relationships can cause illness and overload. All these considerations become more important to youngsters with elite ambitions. As for most other sports, it is effective training and coaching in the years from seventeen to twenty-one which lay the foundations for future international success in orienteering.

All these issues have to be related to the individual orienteer and no two athletes are the same. As a general rule, training levels for this age group should be raised carefully – perhaps by not more than twenty percent per year. All programmes should be devised after close collaboration between young athlete and coach and training content and amount should be carefully monitored against competitive performance and levels of satisfaction and enjoyment. It is quite normal for improvement to take place in a series of rises and plateaux. Careful coaching and counselling are needed to motivate youngsters when performance level flattens out or even seems to decline. As in all coaching and teaching, youngsters have to be persuaded to co-operate in a long-term strategy and to see progress from a wide perspective – one of the most difficult 'tricks' in coaching.

(b) *For both competition and training,* courses should be planned to be technically challenging and interesting while trying to minimize loss of face caused by mistakes. Collecting and Catching Features should be used to 'contain' mistakes on difficult legs.

(c) *Involve the young people themselves* in deciding upon goals and training programmes. Encourage them to organize events for others and to help younger

Post-event analysis can be important.

children. To ease pressure in timed training exercises, let them take their own times.

(d) *Pay special attention to newcomers to the sport.* In orienteering terms, it is much easier for an eleven year old to take up the sport from scratch than a sixteen year old. Youngsters are much better starting off within the colour-coded system with an orange or red course and then, when they are confident at this basic skill level, to progress to the relevant age class competition. Adolescents normally resent being 'B' class, but often flounder and drop out of the sport when 'thrown in the deep end' on 'A' courses.

(e) *Young people enjoy team competitions, relay races and chasing starts.* Coaches can play to this with training exercises which involve a team element and allow skills to be learnt and practised in a low-key competitive context. 'Sprint O's, Loops, Clover Leaf Relays and Pair-Hanging and Collecting Exercises are especially popular. They also enjoy making up teams with friends, which can be a useful method of recruiting newcomers into the sport.

(f) *Youngsters enjoy minibus trips, camping weekends and other outdoor activities* like canoeing, abseiling or fell walking mixed in with the orienteering element (as long as instructors with relevant qualifications are organizing them). 'Hide and seek' often proves a popular evening activity even with seventeen and eighteen year olds! In a middle-class, middle-aged, family-dominated sport like orienteering it is important to give young people opportunities to 'breathe' outside the adult versions of the sport.

Girls enjoy running.

(g) *Role models are important.* Encourage youngsters to help with the younger ones. Invite 'stars' along to present prizes and to help on training courses. Incentive schemes like the National Badge and Colour-Coded Schemes can be important motivators. Plotting personal improvement by moving up an achievement ladder and collecting badges at the same time can be fulfilling routes to success at a personal level. Coaching adolescents is all about narrowing the gap between potential and achievement by using a mixture of whip and carrot.

(h) *All young people are different* and may be attracted to different aspects of a multi-discipline sport like orienteering. Some may like running competition, some maps, some relaxed recreation, some treasure hunts and others fundraising or simply helping to organize events. The coach's job is to lock into the individual's interests and to provide something positive to develop them – perhaps a recipe for all successful coaching.

Young boys enjoy a challenge.

(i) *Not all youngsters have orienteering parents.* It is particularly important for those without knowledgeable family support that coaches help with event entries, transport, preparation before events and advice on kit (particularly footwear). There is no good reason why clubs, like those in Scandinavia, should not look after and encourage their juniors in this way. They may 'fly the nest' as they grow up and move to university or employment in another area, but the sport will be richer for the experience they have gained from your club and these things have a habit of turning full circle as other clubs follow your example.

(j) *Young people like to talk about their performances in competition.* Post-event analysis can be important in identifying specific weaknesses in technique and devising strategies to eliminate them. Listen, encourage and advise, but unless you are an elite competitor, don't bore them with tales of your own success, or lack of it!

(k) *Hard training for orienteering does not automatically win competitive rewards.* Orienteering, by its very nature, can punish cruelly the fast running of a newly fit eighteen year old with a ten-minute mistake when speed outruns technique. In cases like this, the coach should always look for and accentuate the positive, as well as providing a shoulder to cry on. Stress that ninety percent of the race which went well, identify the particular problems and suggest training ideas to put them right.

(l) *Encourage young people to get involved in other outdoor activities related to orienteering.* Orienteering skills transfer readily to navigation in the wider outdoors. Fell running, Duke of Edinburgh Award Schemes and expeditions and National Navigation Award Badges all broaden and reinforce orienteering experience and help to build up navigational confidence in a variety of terrains.

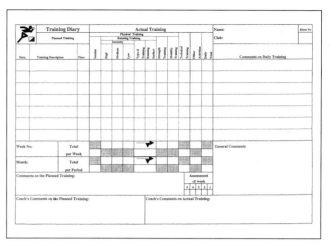

Juniors enjoy filling in training diaries.

(m) *Be careful about the educational dimensions of orienteering for older pupils.* Many adolescents are under great pressure from schoolwork and examinations. It is important that orienteering should be viewed as an enjoyable release from the academic treadmill rather than an addition to it. Close links between clubs and schools not only ease the passage for enthusiastic young orienteers into the mainstream sport but can help make school orienteering more progressive and interesting particularily if clubs help in providing mapping and introductory coaching.

(n) *The world of young people is more spontaneous and immediate than that of adults.* Delayed results, long walks to start and finish areas and complicated entry procedures can easily turn youngsters off orienteering. If local competition systems are slow or cumbersome, involve those juniors who are critical either by supplying manpower for results, calculations and display or listening to youthful suggestions and involving them in decision-making processes.

	The Ladder	Coaching Structure
Stage 4	Getting to the top	National Squads; Senior Coaches; Coaches.
Stage 3	Getting higher	Club and Regional Squads; Coaches/Club Coaches.
Stage 2	Getting it right	Club/school; Clubcoaches.
	(Colour Coded Badge Events)	
Stage 1	Getting Started (Introductory Events/ Exercises)	Club, School and Outdoor Centres; Instructors, Club Coaches.

The progression ladder.

(o) *In coaching terms, empathy with young people and sensitivity to their expectations* are more significant than deep technical knowledge of the sport. Some appropriate activities for teaching, motivating and developing skills with this age group follow at the end of this Chapter. Others are dealt with in Chapter 3.

Coaching adolescents involves challenges and problems, and outcomes are often unpredictable. On the other hand, it can give immense fun and satisfaction as well as surprises. Young people ensure life is never dull and, as they tread on the threshold of the adult world, a helping hand can be significant for their future sporting achievement, particularly for those at excellence levels. Hard training and effective coaching between fifteen and eighteen years can reap rich rewards later.

TRAINING AND SQUAD STRUCTURES

We will conclude this section with recommendations on training and squad structures for all three age categories. All children enjoy working together for improvement as part of school, club or squad groups. Some clubs and all BOF Regions organize squad training for boys and girls. A national squad prepares elite competitors for international competition from the age of seventeen plus.

As I have repeatedly indicated in this survey, children have different expectations from orienteering and different attitudes to it at the various stages in their development. Often these stages are not chronological. How does a coach who wishes to encourage junior development and involvement go about things? I will assume that the coach is working within a club rather than in an educational context and that he or she is dealing with a wide age and ability range. Most teachers are forced to work in an age structure both within and outside the curriculum and in practice, and most schools do not possess the human or terrain resources to progress children's skills beyond introductory levels.

(a) *For the under ten category* squad training is not appropriate. Children of this age are self-centred and orienteering should be treated as one of many exciting new interests. Orienteering is best taught and developed within a family or school multi-activity context.

(b) *For the eleven to fourteen year olds,* skills and performance improvement are best tackled at a club level. Outstanding youngsters may be introduced to regional squads, though with all the provisos already detailed on guarding against the risks of early or late development.

(c) *The fifteen to eighteen years age group* offers great opportunities for club, regional and national squad training. While coaches and leaders should treat training and coaching within the context of schoolwork and other adolescent pressures, development of performance levels can be dramatic with the right balance of structured courses and coaching guidance. Coaches should always be on their guard, however, against seeking short-term glory for region or coach at the expense of the junior's long-term progress. Squad weekends offer opportunities to get away from parents, to socialize and to enjoy non 'O' activities. These can also fulfil youngsters yearning for self-esteem and personal development.

Training programmes should include short practical sessions interspersed with periods of analysis and discussion in which youngsters are encouraged to express their own reactions and ideas. There should be a minimum of waiting around and however much the competitive element is included, a course should always conclude with some sort of competition in which skills elements are put together in something approaching real orienteering. Mass start loop relays are preferable to conventional relays which involve waiting for other competitors to finish. With all junior coaching, the closer the exercises come to real orienteering the more effective they will be. This includes using punches and control cards for most exercises. A comfortable venue is important. Effective feedback is difficult in a dripping tent or a steamed-up car.

What happens between squad weekends is equally important. The squad weekend should not become the sole training message. Filling in and monitoring of training logs, event analysis and induction into good training practice should also be vital coaching priorities with young, immature orienteers. Similarly, where opportunities exist, overseas and regional exchanges should be encouraged, as well as training and competition courses in other regions and countries.

Excellence at National Level

Gifted youngsters need and deserve special coaching, guidance and protection if their potential is to be fulfilled in adulthood. Orienteering, like most sports, has to deal with the dilemma of developing skills and good training practice with vulnerable youngsters who already have to deal with the pressures of a new adult world. Yet success at international level depends usually on work done in the teens. The coach has to motivate and develop good practice at this receptive age, while being careful not to blow too hard on the spark of talent, thereby extin-

Role models are important.

guishing rather than bringing it to smouldering heat.

My personal view is that there is a case for identifying and giving advanced coaching to outstanding young orienteers in the fifteen to eighteen age group. Careful monitoring of performance by experienced coaches through two or three courses a year and written feedback can be vital in nurturing talent through the difficult adolescent years and providing a platform of experience upon which the national squad can build securely later on.

Finally, I repeat my earlier assertion that with all school, club and squad coaching, the personal and sporting interests of individual youngsters must come first. In narrowing that tantalizing gap between potential and achievement while contriving to encourage self-awareness and wider loyalties, the responsibility for those coaching juniors is an awesome one. Coaching attitudes and philosophies for children's orienteering today will define the shape of our sport for the future.

8 Orienteering for People with Disabilities

TOM RENFREW

Orienteers throughout the world are well aware of how fortunate they are to take part in their sport. They enjoy the mental and physical challenges on offer, the challenge of navigating through wooded terrain, the opportunity to socialize as well as compete with fellow enthusiasts of the outdoors. The same experiences are increasingly being made available to a substantial number of men, women and children who have a disability.

The British Orienteering Federation is committed to integrating people with a disability into the mainstream of the sport in order that they can share the fulfilling experiences the sport provides.

Everyone can enjoy the forest experience.

This chapter is intended to :

- Explain the opportunities currently available for disabled people who wish to participate in the sport.
- Suggest approaches that coaches/instructors working with disabled competitors may use which will enhance the learning experience.
- Alert able-bodied orienteers who may like to act as carers, organizers or coaches of disabled people of their acquaintance.

THE CONCEPT AND NATURE OF DISABILITY

Disabled people should not be considered en masse, because firstly their interests are as diverse as the able-bodied population and secondly the range of disabilities and the different problems created by them affect each person in a quite specific and individual way. Disability has been defined as any restriction or lack (resulting from an impairment of ability) in the performance of an activity in the manner or within the range considered normal for a human being. A more positive social definition could be: 'An individual is disabled when society does not meet the particular needs generated by their particular condition.'

Such a definition is less restrictive and whilst recognizing a person's particular condition it shifts the emphasis from the individual to the social context they are in. It does not define the individual as the problem, but rather the disabling characteristics of our culture.

Historically, sport for people with disabilities has been organized according to seven categories: Visual Impairment; Auditory Impairment; Paraplegia/Tetraplegia; Cerebral Palsy; Limb Amputation; 'Les Autres'; and Learning Difficulties.

Visual Impairment

Persons with visual disabilities have impairment that ranges from total blindness to distorted vision. The majority of persons who are registered as blind do have some form of residual vision and the partial sight may include short-sightedness, age-related failing sight and a variety of field restrictions such as tunnel vision, which allows map-reading but makes moving through forest very difficult. For people with severe visual impairment mainstream orienteering is likely to be inappropriate. For others, however, the development of Braille maps or large-scale maps with wider line widths and the use of magnifiers could provide opportunities for the

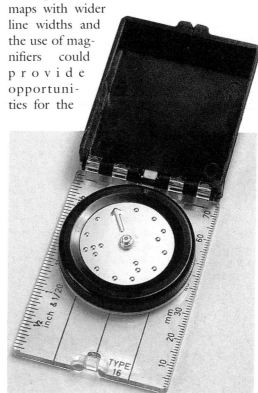

Braille compass.

development of map skills. Large-scale, uncluttered maps enlarged from the conventional 1:15,000 scale maps are also beneficial. Braille compasses are commercially available and frequently used by partially sighted people who go hillwalking or rambling. It is technically possible to manufacture a compass that can be strapped around the waist and will vibrate and emit an audible signal when facing North. Arne Yngström, a Swedish orienteering coach and educator (the co-designer of the thumb compass), has pioneered map skills for persons with visual impairment and speaks highly of the social advantages for previously housebound people being able to make their way to work using map and compass.

At present, the nature of orienteering and the possible dangers of collision, falling and generally fear of what cannot be clearly seen in the forest are likely to keep people with visual impairment in the safe environment of the school, playground and perhaps the open park when developing their map skills.

Visually impaired people often have an increased awareness of their environment and may be able to use other senses to compensate for their lack of vision. It is necessary, however, when taking a group into orienteering terrain to explain carefully the nature of the terrain. When talking to a group that contains anyone who is visually impaired always use names when giving instructions. Safety is of paramount importance and people should not be led into a situation where they may be put in physical danger.

Auditory Impairment

This includes total deafness and a broad range of levels of partial hearing, including those born deaf. The latter are likely also to have a communication problem. Hearing impairment is not usually a problem to orienteers, although start officials should be prepared to signal to deaf competitors where a whistle or 'silent' start is in use. Coaches who find themselves working with a deaf orienteer should be aware that damage to the inner ear may result in a person's balance being affected.

Good communication skills are vital in any coaching situation and communication should not be a problem if coaches provide information in a format suited to the individual's needs:

- determine which ear, if either, has the better hearing;
- do not distort sound by shouting;
- try to eliminate as much background noise as possible;
- if the deaf person is lip-reading keep the light behind them and make sure they can see your mouth;
- speak clearly and as normally as possible and not too slowly. Lip-reading relies on pace and intonation;
- use hand movements and facial expressions;
- use demonstrations;
- establish what you want to say and give all your instructions before the deaf person moves away from you, as it may be difficult to recall them;
- learn the deaf–blind manual alphabet if you work a lot with those with hearing impairments.

Paraplegia/Tetraplegia

Paraplegia refers to paralysis of both lower extremities and may be caused by injury to the spinal cord or by disease. The degree of paralysis depends upon the site of the lesion. If it is in the lower back then the person may be able to walk with the aid of calipers and crutches. If it is in the chest or thoracic section then they are likely to be wheelchair-bound. If the lesion is in the neck region there may also be loss of movement in hands and arms, a condition known as tetraplegia. It is very unlikely that these people will be able to participate in mainstream orienteering. A relatively new form of the sport, Trail Orienteering, is likely to be the most suitable orienteering experience for them (*see* later in this Chapter). Coaches who find themselves working with persons who are wheelchair users or who can only move slowly should ensure that the participants are warmly dressed and well protected from wind, rain and in particular cold.

Trail orienteering.

Cerebral Palsy

This is a condition, not a disease or illness. It is a movement disorder arising in the early years of life as a result of some interference with the normal development of the brain. It is not a single disorder but a variety of conditions with many causes and is often as individual as the people themselves. The three major forms are Spastic CP, Arthetoid CP and Atoxic CP. It is important that coaches and officials are aware that an inability to control facial expressions, speech difficulties and poor balance, whilst initially appearing to present problems for the individual, do not necesssarily indicate an impairment of intelligence or affect the ability to read maps. Some with these conditions are so lightly affected that a disability is not noticed, and others are so seriously affected that they may need constant care. As many as 1:400 births have some form of Cerebral Palsy and it is likely that some of those affected will attempt orienteering. Trail Orienteering may well have a lot to offer these people.

Limb Amputation

Clearly, amputees, particularly if they have lost a lower limb, would be at a disadvantage on timed orienteering courses and may also prefer to take part in Trail Orienteering. Prosthetic devices can be customized to fit closely to an able-bodied foot or leg, but they are expensive and athletes would be unlikely to risk them on an uneven forest floor.

'Les Autres'

This term covers a range of other disabilities, including relatively common conditions like rheumatoid arthritis and osteoarthritis. Advice may be obtained from specialist disabled organizations, such as Physically Handicapped– Able Bodied (PHAB) or the British Sports Association for the Disabled (BSAD), on helping these groups to orienteer.

Learning Difficulties

A learning difficulty (sometimes still referred to as a mental handicap) is not a single disorder but a variety of conditions with many causes. Any condition, illness or injury that interferes with intellectual development before, during or after birth can cause a learning difficulty. It should not be confused with mental illness. Approximately one million people in the United Kingdom have some form of intellectual impairment and very many of these are able to lead normal independent lives with only minimal assistance. A further 160,000 are severely impaired, many of whom need special care. Some of this group have multiple impairments. Educationalists usually classify persons with learning difficulties as mild, moderate or severe, but however the impairment is categorized, persons with a learning difficulty obviously learn more slowly in some areas than others. It is now clear, however, that given the opportunity persons with learning difficulties are more capable of learning new skills and techniques than previously thought. Nevertheless, although many outdoor education centres and schools offer outdoor pursuits for those with learning difficulties, orienteering, because of the thought processes involved in map reading and decision-making, is sometimes considered an inappropriate activity. Research by the author at the University of Strathclyde indicates, however, that if care is taken with the introduction and development of map skills and techniques those with mild or moderate learning difficulties can successfully complete a white, yellow or even an orange colour-coded course with minimal help and much pleasure. Most will work with a partner, but as confidence grows they may also be able to work alone.

The key to success with all people when introducing map skills is to follow a well structured learning and teaching system. The approach suggested by McNeill and Renfrew, in the Start Orienteering series, although designed for children without learning difficulties, has been found to be suitable, provided that sufficient time is spent in a warm, comfortable and familiar environment introducing and developing map skills, through games and movement activities in a measured, systematic manner. The recommended progression involves creating a 'forest' in the classroom, gymnasium and school playground. Through map making in these small, simple and familiar areas,

Indoor map skills for persons with learning difficulties.

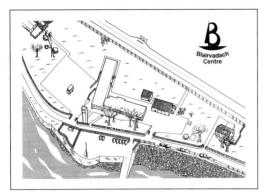

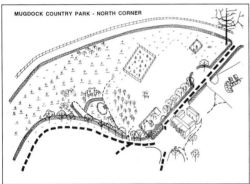

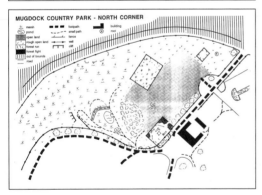

Black and white maps – persons with learning difficulties.

map symbols, map setting and decision-making can be introduced and developed.

Work undertaken outdoors should use large-scale maps which may initially be black and white, and locations should move from the simple on-the-school site to the more complex in parks and forests. A recommended sequence of outside activities includes:

- map walks *(every participant must have their own map)*;
- following streamers to find controls;
- string courses;
- off-string courses;
- star exercises;
- white colour-coded course in pairs;
- white colour-coded course solo.

Teachers/coaches should gather a range of map games, charts and audio-visual resources (available from Harvey's) in order to stimulate the learner through interest and enjoyment.

A minimum of fifty ten-minute sessions are recommended before taking a group with learning difficulties to orienteering terrain with the objective of completing a white colour-coded course. A successful coaching programme should include the following principles:

- the group should be kept small with a coach/pupil ratio of 1:3 or 1:4;
- sessions should be slow-paced with much repetition;
- activities should develop from simple to more complex;
- emphasis should be on practical work;
- key points of the previous session should be reintroduced and reinforced;
- individuals should be progressing at their own pace rather than that of the group;
- there should be positive feedback and encouragement;
- there should be an atmosphere of interest and enjoyment;
- a sense of failure should be avoided;
- the whole group should be aware of the eventual goal.

173

There should be little need to stress the competitive element of the sport. In the early stages the emphasis should be on the personal satisfaction of achieving objectives. The recommendations of the National Coaching Foundation and the Australian Coaching Council have been found to be appropriate when working with persons with learning difficulties:

- break down each skill into precise, simple and short instructions;
- avoid using jargon or uncommon words;
- avoid using patronizing language;
- learn to perform with your voice, as tone and intonation can play a big part in getting your message across;
- make coaching sessions progressive;
- use repetition to help make skill acquisition permanent;
- encourage joint decision-making by providing accurate, reliable and consistent feedback;
- if in doubt, ask the learner to repeat or explain the instructions you have given;
- remember communication is a two-way process – the learner's comments should be valued and the teacher or coach be patient, approachable and concerned;
- assist when and where requested, anticipate when assistance is required but do not offer sympathy and do not direct or lead; educate rather than instruct.

It could, of course, be argued that all this advice applies to the coaching of all orienteers of every age and ability.

There is no reason why people with learning difficulties should not join orienteering clubs and become involved in club life. Indeed, it is desirable that they should be encouraged to do so. Where they are in residential centres or attend centres on a daily basis, it would be ideal if orienteering clubs made contact and assisted in the implementation of recommended teaching programmes. Local Authority Sports Development Officers with a special needs remit can be an ideal first contact for a club wishing to open up opportunities to a wider spectrum of abilities.

TRAIL ORIENTEERING

Orienteering, as can be seen from our analysis so far, can be a difficult sport for those with physical or mental disabilities, but dedicated orienteers with imagination have worked hard in a global setting to develop adaptations which can give the same navigational, recreational and environmental experiences as conventional orienteering but without the pressures of timed competition in rough forest terrain. Because of necessity, orienteering for disabled people takes place on paths and tracks, and all its variations have been given the generic title of Trail Orienteering. This is now an internationally recognized title and the IOF, as well as national orienteering bodies, have their own Trail 'O' Committees. The BOF publication *Trail Orienteering* and complementary video give comprehensive information on organizing events. Trail Orienteering offers a variety of trail variations but the *control choice form* devised for those with physical disabilities attempts to give mental challenge by testing precise map reading skills.

IOF Rules for Control Choice Trail Orienteering

- The competition is based on map interpretation skill. The choice of which of a number of markers represents the one in the centre of a printed circle must be

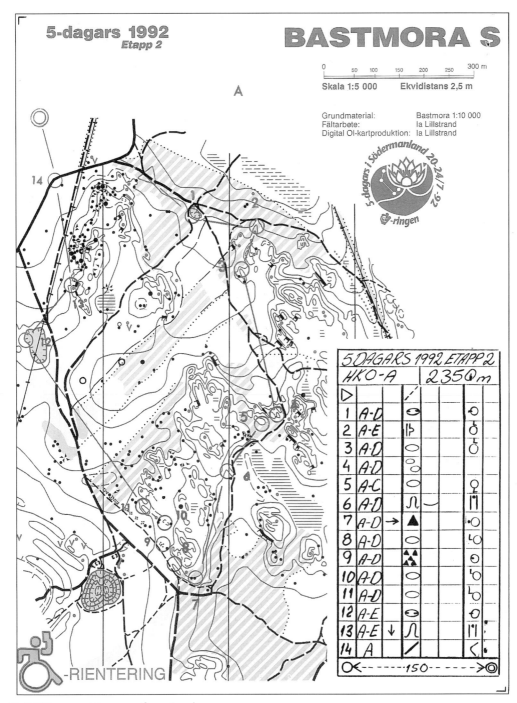

Trail 'O' competition map from Sweden.

recorded on a multiple-choice control card. Competitors must stay on their path to identify the control point.

- The competitor with the highest points score is the winner. In the event of a tie, the competitor recording the shortest time to make decisions at designated timed controls wins. Timing starts as an orientated map with circled control points and descriptions is handed out and stops when the site is named.
- The time of travel between start and finish, within a defined maximum, is irrelevant to the competition result.
- There is no classification by disability or gender.
- Requested physical assistance is permitted. Any recognized mobility aides, apart from a combustion engine vehicle, are permitted.

- The course must be accessible to the least mobile. Competitors must follow the tracks, paths and so on defined on the map, or indicated in the terrain by streamers. All other areas are out of bounds. Information on obstacles or path visibility can be overprinted on maps in red or purple.
- No assistance with navigation or problem-solving is permitted.
- No competitor should do anything that they would deem cheating if it applied to another competitor.

Control Choice Courses are graded as follows:

N. (Novice) A maximum of two controls at each site. It can include tactile map work for the visually impaired. Very Easy.

Control choice competition.

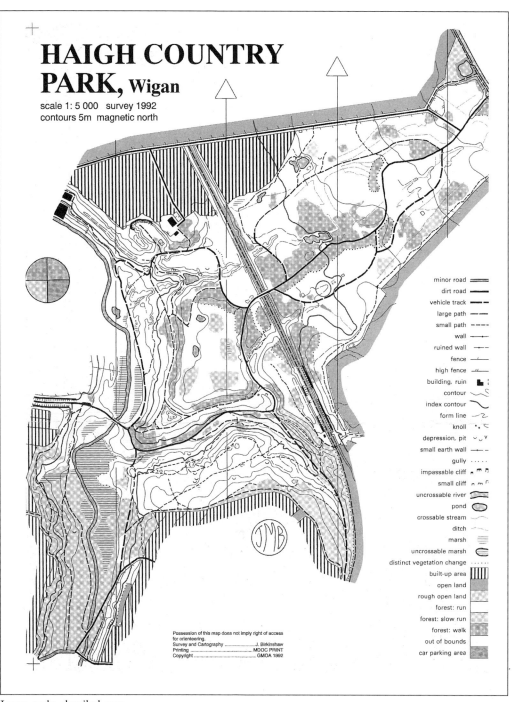

HAIGH COUNTRY PARK, Wigan

scale 1: 5 000   survey 1992
contours 5m   magnetic north

minor road
dirt road
vehicle track
large path
small path
wall
ruined wall
fence
high fence
building, ruin
contour
index contour
form line
knoll
depression, pit
small earth wall
gully
impassable cliff
small cliff
uncrossable river
pond
crossable stream
ditch
marsh
uncrossable marsh
distinct vegetation change
built-up area
open land
rough open land
forest: run
forest: slow run
forest: walk
out of bounds
car parking area

Possession of this map does not imply right of access
for orienteering.
Survey and Cartography ....J. Birkinshaw
Printing ....MDOC PRINT
Copyright ....GMOA 1992

Large-scale, detailed map.

177

C. No descriptions. Two controls on major features, of which one is correct. Easy.

B. With descriptions. Three controls on major features, of which one is correct. Moderately Easy.

A. With descriptions. Up to five controls on difficult point and contour features. Marked viewing point. For experienced competitors. Hard.

E. (Elite) Up to five controls on difficult features. Viewing points may or may not be indicated. An option available is that none of the markers are in the centre of the circle.

Control Choice 'O'

This is the classic form of Trail 'O'. Success relies on precise map visualization skills and practice in using large, detailed orienteering maps. These present a difficult challenge even to experienced competitors. The IOF publishes more detailed guidelines to 'flesh out' these general rules.

Coaching experience in Control Choice 'O' is limited although, as with other forms of Trail 'O', conventional methods described in the technique sections for mainstream orienteers are often relevant or can be adapted. Anne Braggins and Bernard Legrand give some suggestions on Coaching Trail 'O' which conclude this section.

Trail 'O' – Route Choice on Paths

As for conventional Route Choice this involves following a course with control points in sequence between which there is choice of paths or track routes. The area needs to be a suitable one and in most cases the negotiability of alternative paths needs to be shown as on maps for Ski 'O' and Mountain Bike 'O'. To eliminate timing, a task can be offered at each control point or

the result can be decided by the number of controls visited.

If desired, Trail Route Choice 'O' can be used for wheelchair races which can be very competitive and in which timing does decide the result.

Trail 'O' Score 'O'

This involves visiting a scatter of controls with or without tasks at each point. As for Route Choice, Score 'O' can be timed for wheelchairs and given a competitive element by setting a time limit and the counting of control points within the allocated time.

Trail 'O' Treasure Hunt

This involves finding treasure or information at a variety of points on the car rally principle. Controls can be visited in sequence or the route decided between a scatter of controls

As already described, many orienteering activities designed for schools can be easily adapted for different forms of disability. String events and white courses can be very popular for those with learning difficulties, especially if given a 'team' flavour. Anne Braggins' book on Trail 'O' and follow-up video give more detail on all forms of Trail 'O'.

General Coaching Points

• Orienteering can be an excellent vehicle for introducing people with a variety of disabilities to the countryside in a positive way, but the form of Trail 'O' often has to be adapted to particular disabilities if competitors are to share with their able-bodied 'fellows' the joys of success and the sights and sounds of the forest. For example, an imaginative

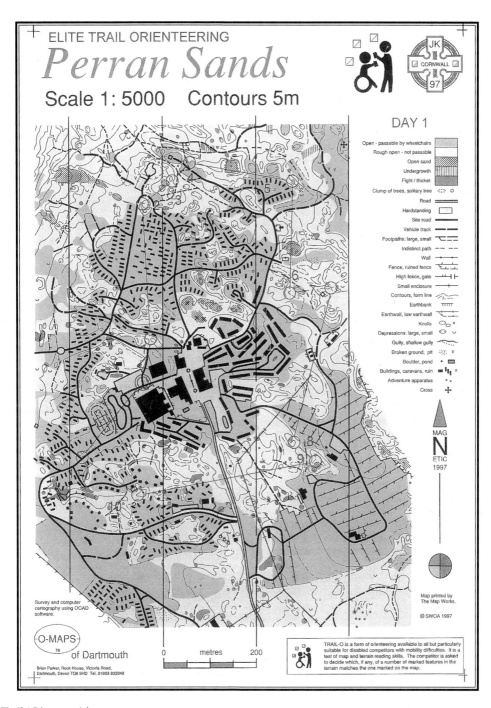

Trail 'O' map with course.

Birmingham teacher used a blind boy to push a wheelchair competitor around a 'white course' with the wheelchair competitor doing the navigation and 'steering'.

- Coaching style and sensitivity to different forms of disability are more important than technical knowledge. It is vital not to appear to be patronizing in any way.
- Setting up Trail 'O' courses and coaching activities can be heavy on manpower and time when set against the numbers involved. However, some forms of Trail 'O' can be equally suitable for very young children, walkers not wanting to be timed or pram pushers, particularly at club events. A little imagination can cater for the needs of several groups as well as helping to integrate disabled competitors into the mainstream sport. Trail 'O' is not just for wheelchair competitors.
- Because Control Choice Trail 'O' demands accurate map visualization and interpretation skills, attendance on mapping courses can help disabled competitors to understand better the thought processes of mappers and surveyors.
- Disabled orienteers at every level should be introduced to IOF Control Descriptions and, where possible, become familiar with them. Disabilities do not recognize national boundaries and even more than conventional orienteers keen Trail 'O' enthusiasts often enjoy travelling and meeting new friends from other countries.

METHOD FOR THE DECISION PROCESS ON CONTROL CHOICE COURSE

Choice of the Route

This is dependent on:

- the position of the next control number (decision point);
- the prohibited paths or roads (marked with series of red crosses);
- the kind of available paths (width, slope, and so on);
- choice of the right marker;
- verification of the control number and the colour of the decision point pole;

Choice of Control

- orientate the map: NORTH to NORTH;
- observe the correct number of markers as mentioned on the control description (A to E);
- do not cross tapes and observe indicated out of bounds areas;
- carefully check the location of all the markers (move along the path);
- what's the question? On the map check the feature(s) included in the control circle and the control description;
- identify the correct marker checking that it is accurately located on the right feature;
- check distance, and any other information available from the map;
- punch carefully.

Timed Control

Do not take any risks. For a wrong answer the penalty is too heavy (0 points +60 seconds). If the map is presented well orientated, read the control description first. Decide which feature(s). If there is only one feature to watch, make a quick decision; if many, make a systematic choice.

The Planners Traps

- Location of markers around a feature such as a small hill. The competitor has to imagine a compass on the centre of the feature.
- Tempting the competitor to make decisions from a point off the feature decision point axis. Differing viewing points can seem to change the position of markers.
- Producing confusion due to similar ground (in and outside the circle).
- Forcing competitors to distinguish between obvious and less visible features.
- Putting markers very close to each other but not on any particular feature.

COACHING SUGGESTIONS

(by Bernard Legrand of the IOF Disability Group)

Possible Training Exercises

(1) Map Reading

- Exercise for a group (discussion). At each control, four markers are placed, all in a bigger circle on the map and on a very accurate location. The aim of the exercise is to find the exact position of all four markers.

(2) Importance of Moving Up and Down

- Course with two poles at each viewing point site (with different control descriptions and choices).

(3) Course Increasing in Difficulty Working in a Group

- Start with easy course 'C', with no control choice and finish with multiple-control choice 'A'.

(4) Timed Controls

- A course planned with all controls timed to speed up decision-making.

(5) Compass

- From a central position, three or four markers are scattered on different features. Competitors have to give the bearing for each one and say which feature each is on.

(6) Distance Judgment

- Markers at different distances (5 to 100m viewed up or down). Participants give their own estimates.

(7) Contour Lines Assessment

- Markers are placed on slopes 2 to 30m viewed up or down. Participants estimate height difference between markers.

CONCLUSION

It takes time, patience and commitment to work intensively with persons who have disabilities. Often progress appears slow and setbacks can occur, especially in periods of ill health or injury. The decision to contribute to disabled sport should not be made without thinking through the demands that this will make on time and coaching technique.

It will, however, be a very rewarding and worthwhile experience. Coaches will discover that keen orienteers with disabilities respond to knowledgeable and enthusiastic coaches just as able-bodied orienteers do. Disabled orienteers will soon make it clear that they are not different, special or fragile with a need to be treated separately. Coaches will realize that odd facial expressions do not equate with lack of intelligence.

The disabled are quite capable of looking after their own personal needs and some want to be very independent. If special assistance is required they will invariably bring along an able-bodied assistant. The reasons given by the disabled for wanting to take part in activities can be the same as the able-bodied, for example the need to socialize and to make new friends and to meet the challenges and enjoy the experiences that sport has to offer. They will continue to participate if they find these experiences, but not if orienteering is seen as just a therapy that is good for them. The myth that all recreational activities have to be drastically modified for participants who are disabled is being broken as more opportunities are offered by National Governing Bodies and as coaches with a deep knowledge of all aspects of their sport spend time with disabled athletes.

Trail Orienteering, although different from mainstream orienteering, is open to all and not just the disabled. Integrated events are straightforward for clubs to organize. Persons with a disability often have untapped talent, a steely resolve to succeed and a determination to realize their full potential. The opportunity to compete will provide the same spur and inspiration as it does for the able-bodied. The stimulus of competition, the drive it imports, the inspiration to train and achieve can be seen at all levels in our sporting society and is exemplified in the Para-Olympics.

For persons with a learning difficulty a more cautious approach to competition must be adopted in order not to subject the competitor to excessive strain, but well organized competitions in carefully controlled and prepared conditions can often transform and invigorate the individual. These caveats of course apply equally to juniors and all newcomers to the sport, and good coaches should use competition positively whoever they coach.

Integration or inclusion is an aim of the Sports Council and should be a central objective in every society. There are, however, instances where segregation of a particular disability group is sensible and necessary. It can provide specialist coaching, a natural group of peers with whom problems particular to individuals within the group can be discussed and it can provide an environment in which competitive and non-competitive sport can take place on equal terms. It may be the initial experience in orienteering which later allows the individual to join a club. However, as the *Snowdon Report* comments 'Integration means that disabled people should have the right to choose which activities to pursue and to participate in them in the widest sense as performers, helpers or spectators.'

Providing coaching and competitive opportunities to disabled people offers them choice and the opportunity to find fulfilment and fun each in their own way. Expanding the orienteering community by including persons with a disability will ultimately benefit our communities, our clubs and all those individuals who make a commitment to offer their services. Above all, it will benefit a deserving group of people.

Appendix 1

RESOURCE INFORMATION FOR COACHES AND TEACHERS OF ORIENTEERING

SUPPLIERS OF INFORMATION, SERVICES AND EQUIPMENT

British Orienteering Federation

The BOF has introductory packs for schools, clubs and individuals and will give information on (groups and individuals) membership, fixtures, permanent courses, regional and club contacts, and coaching awards, including the Teacher/Leader Award. A limited number of videos are available on loan. A quarterly *BOF News* is sent to all members and affiliated organizations and a coaching newsletter is issued quarterly to all coaches who qualify through the BOF Coaching Awards Scheme.

BOF Office:
'Riversdale'
Dale Road North
Darley Dale
Matlock
Derbyshire DE4 2HX

Tel: 01629 734042 (24-hour answerphone service); Fax: 01629 733769.

British Schools Orienteering Association

The BSOA exists to promote and develop all forms of schools orienteering. It provides fixture lists of school events nationwide, discounted schools starter packs, a network of regional contacts advice and help on starting and developing orienteering in school, as well as advice on mapping services, resource information and details of BOF teacher training qualifications and courses. A regular newsletter keeps affiliated schools in touch with new ideas, competition and training opportunities and with each other.

BSOA maintains very close links with the British Orienteering Federation and the mainstream sport at club, regional and national level and with the international scene via the International Schools Sport Federation. Affiliation to BSOA gives automatic rights for a school's pupils to enter local BOF events up to and including Badge standard events and provides opportunities to link with local clubs for access to orienteering terrain and maps and support for the entry of promising youngsters into the mainstream sport.

Affliation includes the cost of the Newsletter and access to discounted starter equipment packs, videos and so on.

BSOA Office:
Peter Palmer
2 Greenway Park Lane
Brocton
Stafford ST17 OTS
Tel/Fax: 01785 662915.

International Orienteering Federation

The IOF can provide information on international courses, competitions and publications as well as addresses for all affiliated national governing bodies. An IOF Scientific Group produces a twice yearly research journal.

Radiokatu 20
FL-00093SLU
Finland
Tel: 00358 9 3481 3112
Fax: 00358 9 3481 3113

The National Coaching Foundation

The National Coaching Foundation provides specific and non-specific sports coaching information, resources and courses for coaches and teachers.

4 College Close
Beckett Park
Leeds LS6 3QH
Tel: 01532 744802.

The Royal Institute of Navigation (RIN)

1 Kensington Gore
London SW7 2AT
Tel: 0171 589 5021; Fax: 0171 823 8671.

National Navigational Award Scheme

The NNAS applies the orienteering method of navigation to the Great Outdoors, by means of a three-level incentive scheme for all ages and abilities. Further details and application forms for centres seeking accreditation are available from the Scheme Secretary.

National Secretary
Peter Palmer
2 Greenway Park Lane
Brocton
Stafford ST17 OTS
Tel/Fax: 01785 662915.

Silva UK Ltd

Silva offers a full range of compasses as well as other orienteering equipment. Discounts are available for group orders from clubs and schools.

P.O. Box 53
Egham
Surrey TW20 8SA
Tel: 01784 471721; Fax: 01784 471097.

Harvey Map Services

Worldwide supplier of teaching resources, materials, books, videos and other audio-visual aids, introductory packs and technique training worksheet. Map-making services include surveying and map printing. A free catalogue is available.

12–16 Main Street
Doune
Perthshire FK16 6BJ
Tel: 01786 841201; Fax: 01786 841098.

Ultrasport Ltd

Ultrasport are specialists in every type of orienteering clothing, equipment, shoes and incentives, including badges and trophies. Discounts offered for group orders. Club and school's 'O' suits can be made to your own design.

The Square
Newport
Salop TF10 7AG
Tel: 01952 813918; Fax: 01952 825320.

Peel Land Surveys

Educational map-making services for orienteering. Survey and computer cartography at inexpensive rates. Free advice and quotes available.

10 Nairn Street
Sheffield S10 1UL
Tel: 01142 663169.

Orienteering Services (Martin Bagness)

Map surveying and drawing, artwork, instruction/coaching for orienteering courses at all levels.

2 Gale Crescent
Lower Gale
Ambleside
Cumbria LA22 OBD
Tel: 019394 34184.

PUBLICATIONS

Skills of the Game

Carol McNeill (Crowood Press) – an informative coverage of every aspect of orienteering by Britain's most experienced international orienteer. Particularly good on methods of improving personal performance through training and preparation programmes and goal setting.

Orienteering in the National Curriculum

Carol McNeill, Peter Palmer and Jim Martland (Harvey Map Services).

Vol. 1 Key stages 1 and 2, 1992.

Vol. 2 Key stages 3 and 4, April 1993.

National Curriculum themes are explored and explained and a series of lesson plans show how orienteering activities can be used to deliver attainment targets in PE, maths and geography.

Teaching Orienteering

Carol McNeill, Jean Ramsden and Tom Renfrew (Harvey Map Services). A comprehensive manual with over one hundred lesson plans and ideas for developing the sport with children and young people.

Start Orienteering

Carol McNeill and Tom Renfrew (Harvey Map Services). A series of six separate books of lesson plans and exercises for teachers covering ages six to twelve years.

Pathways to Excellence

Peter Palmer (Harvey Map Services, 1994) – a comprehensive coverage of performance improvement for all ages and abilities built around the experiences of a typical orienteering family.

The DNS Silva Direct Compass

Jim Martland and Sue Walsh (NCF, 1993), with support from Silva UK Limited – a manual on how to use the compass to develop navigational skills.

Orienteering Outward Bound

Martin Bagness (Ward Lock, 1995).

Mountain Navigation for Runners

Martin Bagness (Misty Fell Books, 1993).

Course Planning

Graham Nilson (BOF Publication, 1995).

Trail Orienteering

Anne Braggins (BOF Publication, 1995).

Orienteering for the Young. The IOF Guidlines for Children's Orienteering

Carol McNeill, Peter Palmer and Tom Renfrew (IOF, 1993).

Learning Orienteering Step by Step

G. Hasselstrand (IOF Publications) – how to teach children orienteering skills in a sequential manner.

Orienteering from Start to Finish

B. Norman and A. Yngstrom (IOF, 1991) – an examination of practical ways to develop orienteering technique with map and compass used together.

Orienteering World

The IOF magazine for news, views and technical developments all around the world. Six issues per annum. Subscriptions available via *CompassSport* as below.

Compasssport

Britain's national orienteering magazine covers fixtures, results, news, features, new ideas and equipment. Six issues per annum.

37 Sandycoombe Road
Twickenham
Middlesex TW1 2LR
Tel: 0181 8929429; Fax: 0181 2550762.

Subscriptions:
25 The Hermitage
Eliot Hill
London SE13 7EH
Tel: 0181 8521457.

Videos also available

Orienteering – The First Steps
Orienteering – Going For It

A two-part video on school site and forest orienteering (Mike Pearson, 1995).

Trail Orienteering for the Disabled

(Mike Pearson, 1996).

Appendix 2

THE TRIANGLE SYSTEM – SAFETY, CONTROL AND FUN

One of the basic challenges in teaching and developing navigational skills is to produce learning situations which balance individual decision-making by the participants against the demands for feedback and safety.

The Triangle System achieves all these things and more, and it can be used equally successfully on open hillsides, in forests or even in school grounds. Basically it works on a star principle with loops radiating out from a central base manned by the teacher or instructor. The number of loops will depend on terrain, resources of manpower and maps and the objectives of the teaching session, and the navigational content can either be the same on each loop or geared to a particular sequence of skill.

The technical and physical difficulty will obviously depend on the age, experience and fitness of the participants, but to exercise control and give opportunity of instant feedback and instruction at each return to base, the loops should be designed to take about 10 to 15 minutes, and should ideally include three legs between start/finish and two control points.

Including evaluation and inter-loop coaching, participants can put in a good hour's intensive work on a three-loop exercise with their performance being closely monitored throughout, and without the dangers of overrunning time limits or getting badly lost.

Here are three examples of how the system can work.

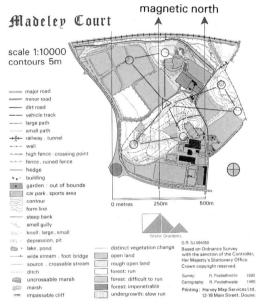

(1)   The Madeley Court School Site

Each triangle is about 700 metres and includes legs which encourage the children to simplify navigation by using attack points and checkpoints. Young children can take part singly or in pairs, and if a competitive edge is needed pairs of children can compete against each other by going clockwise and anti-clockwise, with the first back the winner.

Another idea is to use the loops as a relay, either with each loop run in turn or a mass start in which teams run all three loops in random order.

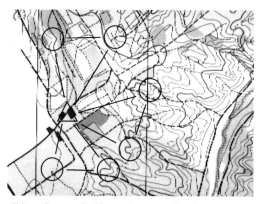

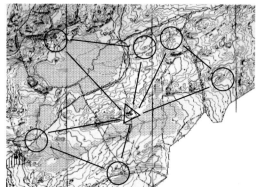

(2)   Cannock Chase Country Park

Once again, the loops concentrate upon simplification and fast running but the control sites are more subtle and the need to adjust speed to navigational difficulty more important.

The Madeley Court variations are still possible but it is probably better in more challenging terrain to concentrate upon mastering the skills and accuracy of navigation rather than competition. Another variation used here with more experienced participants might be to split the group into balanced pairs, allocate to loops and then to ask each one to hang one control carefully and then to pick up the partner's control. This saves the coach having to hang all the control markers before the activity, builds in accuracy in that each participant has to hang a marker on a precise point, and encourages working together and learning from each other. Some mild competitive edge may be introduced by the urge to get back first, but if a marker is wrongly placed, peer group pressure will reinforce the teaching point about accuracy more effectively than any lecture.

(3)   North Wales Mountain Side

The three triangle principle is the same as for models 1 and 2 but the open, exposed nature of the terrain and the difficulty of the control sites means that markers should ideally be hung by the instructor and that attention must be paid to visibility when deciding how to send off participants and how to use the loops. Again, much will depend on age, experience and fitness and whether the exercise is designed for recreational or competitive orienteers.

Each triangle here is designed to teach and test different navigational skills:

(A) The use of line features as handrails in navigating to small control points.
(B) Contour navigation, looking at ground shapes.
(C) Attack points and checkpoints.

All three models give plenty of opportunities for post-activity evaluation upon which future personal improvement programmes can be based. Analysis sheets can easily be designed which ask participants to rate their performance on each leg against a list of relevant skills.

The Triangle System provides control, feedback and safety. It can offer many enjoyable variations for improving navigational skills and another demonstration of how map and compass work together in the orienteering system.

Appendix 3
SAFETY PROCEDURES FOR ORIENTEERING

Orienteering is not especially hazardous. Build safety into course planning whatever the scale of event or activity. Choose a suitable area, with collecting features, handrails, checkpoints and clearly marked out of bounds areas. *Courses should be planned to avoid hazards.* Both participants and organizers must have the right degree of experience and knowledge of maps and basic navigation techniques including *relocation*. Beginners should take part in pairs. *Retirement procedure* – everyone must know it. Print it on the control description sheet with the time limit. The Start and Finish must be manned throughout. Match finishing competitors' control cards with stubs from the start to ensure that everyone is back.

EMERGENCY SYSTEM

Phone numbers and contact procedures for the Emergency Services and base contacts (where necessary) should be available for all the organization team. Participants must carry a whistle and a watch, and know the time limit, safety bearings and procedure if any competitor fails to book in at the finish. If an organized search becomes necessary, bring in the police and appropriate search experts like the Mountain Rescue. *Everyone must know and understand the system.* Ensure adequate equipment for conditions. Protection against cold, wind and rain – stout footwear with grip, waterproofs and sweater, gloves and hat if cold, drinks if hot, map cases etc. In wild country, survival bag or tent and emergency rations should be available at the Start and Finish.

FIRST AID

Minor injuries can often happen in open countryside where expert help will not be immediately available. Coaches and organizers should have available a first aid kit and water bottle so that small cuts and wounds can be temporarily be cleaned, dressed and covered. Blisters can be treated and sprained ankles can be dunked in streams and bandaged to get the injured home. More serious injuries may mean someone in the group going for help. Leaders should be appointed and the group should wait together in safety. Organizers should be aware of the dangers of hypothermia and hyperthermia and know how to treat both. All BOF coaches are required to have an appropriate first aid qualification.

Above all, the difficulty of the activity must be appropriate to the age, skills, fitness and experience of the participants. This principle provides the backbone for all safety in navigational pursuits. Discuss safety with participants and make sure they can relate safety to the type of event. Orienteering in a school or park involves different safety or security considerations from an event in a forest or on an exposed hillside.

Appendix 4
ACTIVITY IDEAS FOR PERMANENT ORIENTEERING COURSES

Permanent orienteering courses are set up and maintained by a variety of bodies – clubs, schools, local authorities, Forestry Enterprise or charities like the National Trust.

Permanent control markers are set on clear, mapped features in a park, wood or section of a forest. Usually they are stout posts with an orange and white orienteering logo, each of which has a code letter or number. Sometimes a *North Arrow* is etched on the top of each post to help people without compasses to orientate their maps.

The position of each marker is shown by a red circle on a detailed large-scale *orienteering map*. The number of control points will depend on the size and steepness of the area but normally there are not more than a relaxed walker can visit in 2 or 3 hours. Twenty is an average number. The control sites may have to be changed every 1 to 3 years to avoid erosion round the posts. The new course has then to be reprinted on to each map. Wooded areas are usually shown as white (though green is used on some Forestry Wayfaring maps), open areas are yellow and dark green indicates thick or impenetrable thickets. The map will have a *legend* giving descriptions of features, symbols and colours used to depict the terrain. *A list of descriptions* for every control will also give the code numbers for each point so that people can check that they are at the right location. Some urban park maps may be simple in the extreme and courses will require participants to weave between buildings, fenced enclosures or flower beds.

Certificates are sometimes offered for participants visiting a given number of control points. Sometimes a *master map* is provided at the Start and Finish point, from which participants have to copy the course circles and descriptions on to their own blank map. Sometimes permutations of points are suggested as courses of given length and difficulty. If this is a first recreational visit with a group of children make sure you pick an *easy course,* linking up the controls the children will visit with either straight lines (to show the sequence) or a line along the recommended path routes. *Make sure, too, that the children take great care to mark the circles in exactly the right position.* The control point should be in the centre of the circle. If the course is to be used as a score event where children choose which controls to visit in a given time, be careful to indicate a scatter which is within the group's skill level. It is sometimes difficult to suggest easy path routes when controls can be taken in any order.

Permanent courses are the orienteering equivalent of *running tracks or sports halls.* They can offer a safe and valuable resource for school, community and club groups wishing to organize competitive training or adventure activities in a convenient but challenging manner. Used imaginatively, permanent courses can offer a variety of orienteering activity including many exercises described in publications like this manual. Because teachers are not required to set out or retrieve markers, more time and attention can be given to instruction and control.

Here are some ideas which can be adapted to the age and experience of participants and difficulty of the area:

(1) Control Points can be permutated into introductory *'handrail courses'*.

(2) Orienteers compete in *'pair challenges'*. Each chooses a control about the same distance from the Start/Finish point. They then hang a marker on their point and then run and pick up their partner's marker. First back is the winner.

(3) *Star exercises* can be used individually or as team relays. Competitors take one control at a time and return to the Start each time before going to another.

(4) *Route choice competitions* can combine navigational and hard physical work. Pairs take alternative routes between a circle of controls. These are best suggested by the coach or teacher. Competitors race each other to each point, rest and then do the same for a series of controls.

(5) *Individual or team score events* can use all or a selection of control points as suggested earlier. A team can be two, three or four – deciding who goes for which controls. The first group all back, having collected all control codes, is the winner.

(6) In *Sprint 'O' competitions* orienteers compete against each other on opposing loops of a short figure of eight course. Each loop should not be more than about 1 kilometre to keep winning times short. A mass start with some doing loop 'A' clockwise, another anticlockwise and a similar allocation for loop 'B' can help break up numbers and generate excitement.

(7) On *Puzzle 'O' courses* competitors are asked a question at each control on a multi-choice card. A correct answer gives the right position of the next control; a wrong answer leads to no control. Because Puzzle 'O' needs more time to set up and complete it is best used on an adventure day rather than in limited curriculum time.

(8) *Compass and distance judgment* exercises can be used to test and improve straight line navigation. Straight lines are drawn between a scatter of controls in a flat, runnable stretch of forest. To make things more difficult in an easy area, sections of the map can be blanked out between controls (corridor 'O') or just a map window left around each control.

(9) *Relocation exercises* are useful in teaching what to do when lost. Competitors set off in pairs with only one having a map. After running towards a selected point, the map is handed over to the second of the pair who has to remember where they have run so far, orientate the map and look carefully around to establish exact location and then to execute a route to the chosen control. The process is then repeated to another point, reversing order of starting with the map – and so on.

(10) Controls can be permutated into *three or four short overlapping or clover leaf loops*. Pupils are allocated an order and then have to run all loops as quickly as possible. Control codes are checked at the end of each loop.

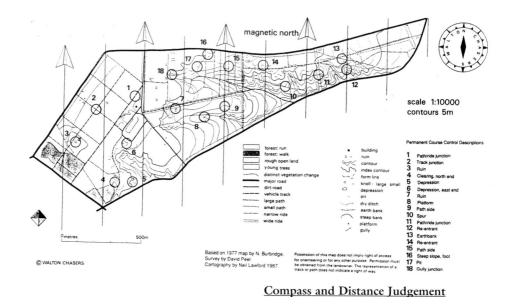

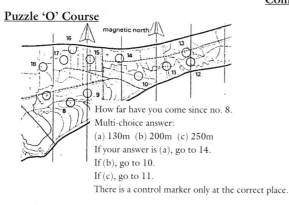

Puzzle 'O' Course

How far have you come since no. 8.
Multi-choice answer:
(a) 130m (b) 200m (c) 250m
If your answer is (a), go to 14.
If (b), go to 10.
If (c), go to 11.
There is a control marker only at the correct place.

Compass and Distance Judgement

For most of these exercises it is advisable that competitors have separate *control cards* on which to enter up the codes – or to punch if the course has needle control punches.

These activities can provide *navigational challenge and physical exercise* even when the area becomes known over a series of visits. A full club or school orienteering programme of six sessions or more can realistically be planned on one permanent course, especially if indoor opportunities are built in to compare routes and discuss problems afterwards.

A *permanent course* can equally well provide the final element in a club training programme which for logistical reasons has to be largely site-based. Once a coach becomes familiar with a permanent course, other ideas and adaptations can easily spring from the basic ideas suggested here.

The British Orienteering Federation National Office can provide a list of permanent courses nationwide. If there is not one locally to suit you, why not follow the example of many other clubs and schools and design your own on or off site?

Appendix 5

GLOSSARY OF COMMON ORIENTEERING TERMINOLOGY

(1) Compass

Bearing A bearing is a horizontal angle fixing a point in relation to North. It can be measured in degrees from North in a clockwise direction.

DNS Silva Direct Compass A starter protractor compass with simplified dial and baseplate for young navigators.

Magnetic Variation or Declination The difference between Magnetic North (indicated by the compass) and Grid North (as shown on most maps – except orienteering maps). Typically it was $5\frac{1}{2}°$ west of Grid North in 1993.

Magnetic Deviation The error of a compass due to local magnetic disturbances.

Map Guide Compass A Silva 'Clip-on Compass' which allows the map to be orientated to North very simply while keeping map and compass together.

Protractor Compass A conventional Silva type compass with a rotational 360° dial swivelling on a transparent baseplate with direction arrow. It allows bearings in degrees to be taken from map or terrain using the Silva 1-2-3 system.

Safety Bearing A bearing given to all participants before a navigational exercise to indicate the most direct 'return strategy' in the event of an emergency (for example 180° Due South to main road).

Thumb Compass A compass which clips to the thumb of the hand allowing easy map orientation and direction finding (but not ideal for taking accurate bearings for beginners).

Parts of the Compass:-(See

(2) Equipment

Control Marker A trapezoid marker (usually orange and white) used to indicate a destination point on an orienteering or navigation course, usually with a clipper attached to punch a control card as proof of a visit.

Description Sheet A list of control feature descriptions with codes for an orienteering course – given to each competitor for identifying the position of control markers.

Pace or Distance Scale A scale bar attached to the leading edge of the compass giving distance in metres or the individual's personal pace count to cover each 100-metre section. It is used to check distance while navigating a course.

Stub Tear-off portion of control card with competitor details and start time given in before the start of an exercise or competition and used as a safety check.

Studs Competition shoes with studded soles to give 'grip' in rough terrain.

Waterproofs Overgarments giving complete body protection from the elements. (A cagoule may be compulsory protection for orienteering in exposed areas.)

(3) Jargon

BOF British Orienteering Association. The governing body for the sport of orienteering in the UK.

Control Feature A clear feature on a map and the ground used as a control point for an orienteering or navigation course.

Cross-Country Orienteering Course A sequence of control points marked on map and ground which have to be visited in a prescribed order.

Leg Section of a course between two control points.

Master Maps Maps with a printed course which competitors use to copy up their course onto their own maps at the start of a navigational competition or exercise.

Mountain Marathon A long distance navigational competition in mountainous terrain, usually over two days.

Parallel Error A location mistake during a navigational exercise in which position is erroneously fixed on a similar parallel feature to the correct one (for example, the wrong ridge).

Permanent Course A 'scatter' of permanent control points set out in a park or forest shown on an over-printed map – usually used for training purposes.

Pre-Marked or Overprinted Map A map with the control points printed upon it, normally given to competitors at the start of an event.

Pre-Start A call-up area usually 3–4 minutes before the actual start of a competition.

Relay An orienteering or navigational competition in teams (for example, three loops).

Score Orienteering A 'scatter' of control points for which competitors are given a time limit for completion. Points are gained for visiting controls and deducted for being over time.

Sprint Orienteering A short distance competition in which pairs or fours compete against one another on opposed loops (for example, a figure of eight for 2x2 loops)

String Course A course for young children marked throughout by string or streamers so that they find controls without getting lost.

(4) Landforms

Col or Saddle Low point between two hills – a 'pass'.

Hill Summit High point from which the ground drops away on all sides.

Knoll Small Hillock.

Pit A depression with steep sides, often man-made.

Re-entrant Small valley or indentation, often in the side of a ridge or between two spurs. A small re-entrant is sometimes termed a 'niche'.

Scree Loose rocks on a steep slope.

Spur A narrow terrace or 'nose' jutting out from the hillside – often between two re-entrants.

Steep Slope A steep hillside which may be uniform, concave or convex denoted on a map by close contour lines. Where these merge a vertical cliff or precipice will be formed, sometimes shown as a crag on the map.

Ride A rough, grassy or uneven break between lines of trees.

Ridge A continuous stretch of high ground between valleys.

Terrace A flat projection on a hillside.

Terrain The general character of a geographical area of forest or moorland. Used as a description (for example, steep rocky terrain; 'bushy' terrain).

Watershed An area of high ground from which water drains away on two sides.

(5) Maps

Cartography The drawing of maps.

Map Contact Keeping careful note of position while navigating with close attention to the detail on the map – using the compass as a 'back-up'.

Contour Only Maps Reprints or photocopies of a map 'contour plate', thereby showing ground shape only and excellent for training purposes.

Grid Reference A uniform method of plotting position with reference to a system of grid squares covering the whole of Great Britain.

Legend or key A list of the symbols represented on the map.

Orientation (Setting or aligning the map). Matching the map to terrain so that North on the map aligns to North on the ground. The basic navigational skill!

Photogrammetry Drawing base maps from aerial photography.

Runnability Screen (walk/fight forest) 'Runnability' of the terrain is indicated on an orienteering map by green colour screens. The darker the green the less runnable or thicker the terrain. 'Fight' would be almost impenetrable.

(6) Navigational skills

Colour-Coded System A competition incentive scheme linked to a navigational skills progression. A series of colours represents levels of technical and physical ability allowing participants to progress up the competition ladder as their skills improve.

Contouring Keeping to the same height by running 'round' a hill rather than 'up and over', thereby avoiding unnecessary climbing.

Fine Orienteering Precision navigation in detailed terrain demanding careful use of map, compass and distance judgement – usually over short sections of a course.

Line Orienteering See Line Event under *Training Ideas*. Following a map line – used for navigational competition or training.

Map to Ground and Ground to Map Navigation 'Map to ground' involves deciding a navigational strategy (for example, route choice) from the evidence of the map and then relating it to the ground to check progress. 'Ground to map' is the reverse, that is, noting ground features en route and referring to the map for confirmation.

Pace Counting A system of counting single or double paces to check off distance covered on the ground. (See Pace Scale under *Equipment*.)

Relocation Finding oneself when lost – using an established strategy of orientated map, route memory and references to obvious features on map and ground.

Route Choice Choosing the most effective route between control points, taking into account difficulty, height loss and gain, the best approach to the control and so on.

Step System A progression of navigation skills starting with map familiarity at Level 1 and progressing to fine navigation at the top level. It can form the basis of coaching, competition and incentive schemes.

Straight Line Orienteering Taking the direct route between control points using accurate map reading, compass and distance judgement.

(7) Navigational Strategies

Aiming Off To aim deliberately to one side of a control point on a line feature so that the navigator knows which way to turn for the control.

Attack Point An obvious feature near a control point from which the control can be safely located by careful navigation with map and compass.

Catching Feature An obvious feature on map and ground beyond a control point which can be used for relocation if the control is missed.

Checkpoint An obvious feature on a chosen route which can be used to check accuracy of progress.

Collecting Feature A feature beside a route which can be used to simplify navigation and 'contain' any diversion from the correct route.

Compass and Pacing The combination of a compass bearing and pace counting in straight line navigation.

Dog Leg Positioning of a control point which allows navigators to approach and leave by the same route, thereby leading in other competitors.

Handrail Orienteering The use of line features on map and ground to simplify navigation (for example, following paths and streams).

Line Feature A longitudinal feature on the map and ground (for example, track, field, earthbank, road).

Map Memory Remembering sections of the legs on a course or control detail to save time studying the map. A useful training exercise if participants have to memorize each leg from a map section to a control point – without carrying a map.

Rough or Course Orienteering Fast navigation on easy sections of a course using rough compass and obvious checkpoints and collecting features to keep on line.

Simplification 'Breaking down' navigation on each leg of a course into easy and difficult sections with the help of checkpoints, collecting features and attack points.

Thumbing The use of the thumb on a folded map to mark location and keep track of progress.

Traffic Lights An extension of simplification by using 'green', 'amber' and 'red' to match speed of foot to the navigational difficulty of the leg.

(8) Training Ideas

Clover Leaf–Triangle Exercises Training loops which enable a teacher or instructor to monitor participant progress and to test a different skill on each triangle–loop as required.

Control Picking A navigational exercise in which each control point forms the attack point for the next, that is, frequent control points in a relatively short distance demanding care and skill.

Corridor Exercise A training course for which participants are only provided with 'map corridors' between controls (the rest of the map is blanked out) to encourage straight line navigation.

Fartlek A Swedish word meaning speed play. Enjoyable running in which runners alternate fast and slow sections – often used for physical training which aims to build strength and speed for navigational competitions.

Line Event A training course or competition to test map contact. Competitors follow a line marked on the map, marking on it the exact points at which controls are encountered on the ground.

Pair Exercises Training in twos whereby navigators learn from one another (for example, hanging and retrieving control markers, shadowing or relocation training).

Shadowing A training method whereby the coach or instructor follows a navigator on an exercise to check skills and to analyze techniques. It can be done by 'pairs' changing roles at intervals.

Star Exercise A training activity operating from a central start and finish point. Participants 'radiate' out to visit one control at a time before returning to the centre for feedback. It is a system which gives good coach/instructor control.

Window Exercise An extension of the corridor idea described above, in which the map is blanked out apart from 'windows' of detail left round each control point. It can be used to test and reinforce distance judgement, compass work, control visualization and relocation skills. Like the corridor exercise, it is particularly useful for extending the difficulty of a familiar area.

Appendix 6

SPECIMEN JUNIOR ORIENTEERING TRAINING SCHEDULES

Winter Build-Up Dec–Jan

All sessions to include a 10–15 mins warm up and down
All sessions to include a 10–15 mins warm up and down

(a) AGE 17+
(b) AGE 17-

Session 1
(a) 45 mins fartlek including Hill Surges
(b) 35 mins fartlek

Session 2
(a) 60 mins long run, steady 4/5mins per km
(b) 50 mins long run, steady 5/6mins per km

Session 3
(a) 50 mins path run with 4 x 1km surges or 5 x 800 m or 6 x 600m not flat out, 5 mins jog between
(b) 30 mins pace run round set circuit. Regularly use as a test run with timing

Session 4
(a) Technical run with map and compass on map or course or competition, 60 mins
(b) 45 mins technical run with map and compass. Could be competition

(a) 40km a week
(b) 30km a week

Spring Sharpening-Up Feb–March, May – June

Session 1
(a) 45 mins fartlek on paths in terrain. Work hard up hills
(b) 35 mins fartlek with hard surges on hills

Session 2
(a) 50 mins pace run on paths
(b) 40 mins run on map line in terrain

Session 3
(a) Reduction run 1km, 800m, 600m, 400m, 200m, 3 mins jog between each one
(b) 30 mins pace run, continue as before monitoring times

Session 4
(a) Technical training as before – if possible in 'fine' terrain or competition, 60 mins
(b) 45 mins technical training as before if possible, Fine 'O', working on rhythm

(a) 35km a week
(b) 25km a week

Peak Competion Period – Tapering March – April, July, Aug

Session 1
(a) 30 mins easy run/jog
(b) 30 mins fartlek on paths or in terrain

Session 2
Rest

Rest

Session 3
(a) 6 x 600m or 4 x 800m – 3 mins rest between each, on paths
(b) 25 mins pace run + warm up and down

Session 4
(a) Technical control picking at slow speed or rest 30 mins
(b) Map run working on accuracy and rhythm – 25 mins

(a) 20km + race
(b) 15km + race

Points to Note

(1) Warm up includes stretching before and after each session as well as jogging for at least 5 mins. Work on concentration during technical sessions – never be sloppy.

(2) Stop running if you get a cold, infection or any injury. With twinges or minor injuries, such as tight calves, find out what produces no pain or aggravation and stay with this type of activity until free of pain or discomfort, for example running up hills or staying on flat surfaces with tight calves, or riding a bike with sore shins.

(3) Adjust schedules to allow for exams or special occasions (such as family holidays).

(4) With fartlek and intervals adjust rest interval according to tiredness – could be 2–3 or 5 mins – try to jog rather than standing still.

(5) Try not to be too competitive when training with others.

(6) Always monitor results carefully and discuss your progress with your coach.

(7) These schedules give guidance on content. Volume and balance will depend on sex, background ability and ambitions of individual youngsters – in discussion with teachers or coaches.

Appendix 7
ON SITE ORIENTEERING FOR SCHOOLS AND CLUBS

Following are some ideas for winter and summer activities within a school or centre complex. Scandinavians call orienteering the 'Forest Sport' but we have relatively few wooded areas in Britain and not many schools or clubs have direct access to those which we have. It is possible to do a lot with limited resources – particularly with some imagination. Many outdoor education centres are well placed to make good use of prime orienteering terrain, particularly if they have maps of the right scale and clarity. Some schools too have suitable countryside on the doorstep – even in urban areas. The map below was produced for a Telford Comprehensive School and so successful have been orienteering events planned on it that it now has a permanent course which is open to the public – with proceeds to school funds.

Here are some suggestions for school and community orienteering inside school or on the doorstep. Some have been tried at Madeley Court in co-operation with Wrekin Orienteering Club. More details on these and many others are given in publications like *Pathways to Excellence, Teaching Orienteering, Start Orienteering* and The National Curriculum Guides (all published by Harvey Map Services), *The Direct Compass Guide* (NCF/Silva), and *Orienteering Skills of the Game* (Crowood Press). Some will fit into class time, others into after school, evening and weekend sessions.

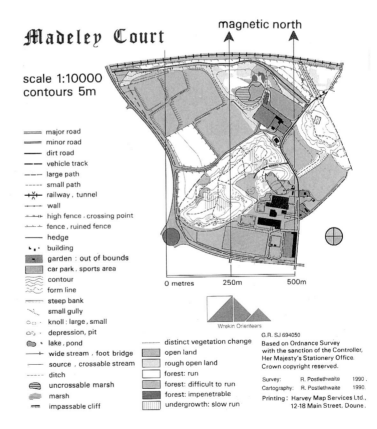

Madeley Court

magnetic north

scale 1:10000
contours 5m

═══	major road
═══	minor road
───	dirt road
─ ─	vehicle track
───	large path
-----	small path
	railway , tunnel
	wall
	high fence , crossing point
	fence , ruined fence
───	hedge
	building
	garden : out of bounds
	car park , sports area
	contour
	form line
	steep bank
	small gully
	knoll : large , small
	depression, pit
	lake , pond
	wide stream , foot bridge
	source , crossable stream
-----	ditch
	uncrossable marsh
	marsh
	impassable cliff

....	distinct vegetation change
	open land
	rough open land
	forest: run
	forest: difficult to run
	forest: impenetrable
	undergrowth: slow run

0 metres   250m   500m

Wrekin Orienteers

G.R. SJ 694050
Based on Ordnance Survey with the sanction of the Controller, Her Majesty's Stationery Office. Crown copyright reserved.

Survey: R. Postlethwaite   1990 .
Cartography: R. Postlethwaite   1990.

Printing : Harvey Map Services Ltd., 12-18 Main Street, Doune.

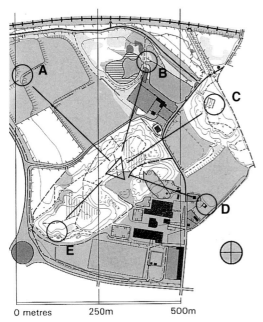
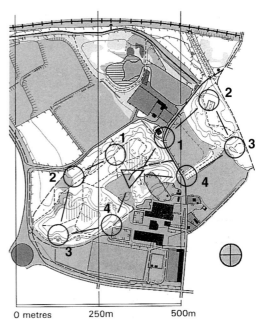

Daylight Outdoor Exercises – Winter and Summer

(1) Fun Competitions which Build Up Technique

(a) Star exercises – individual or relay.

(b) Sprint 'O' – two or four individuals at a time compete against each other on a knock-out principle. A final race can be arranged for the best two or four. The loops can also be used for team relays.

(c) Compass exercises on the open areas – blank maps, mini markers on the ground and pacing

(d) A variety of skills exercises – line, attack point, relocation, route choice, handrail – on a conventional school site at novice level or on areas like Madeley Court at more advanced levels.

(e) Pair exercises, for example drawing sketch maps to find each other's treasure.

(f) Street orienteering, but only in traffic-free areas.

(2) Physical Training for Orienteers

(a) Pack runs with 'follow my leader' on fartlek, interval or obstacle principle. Pitch markings can be used as handrails or mapped features like walls or fences.

(b) Warm up, stretching and jogging routines.

Indoor Exercises – Winter and Summer

(1) Technique Based

(a) 'O' Quizzes (e.g. pictorial descriptions, orienteering terms etc.).

(b) 'O' Bingo, 'O' Beetles, 'O' Snakes and Ladders, map drawing with dice and so on.

(c) Compass and orienteering games on self-drawn room or site maps.

(d) Indoor 'Night' events with mini markers – 'Night' events on site can also be fun.

(2) *Evaluation activities as follow up to competitions*

(a) Marking routes on maps and comparing with friends.
(b) Analysis of mistakes and good points – filling in log books.
(c) Goal setting and the drawing up of personal improvement programmes.
(d) Slide and video presentations.
(e) Teacher-led discussions on future plans for events and weekends away etc.

(3) *Technique with a Physical Element*

(a) Map symbol or map memory shuttle relays in hall or gymnasium.
(b) Timed circuits round a 'Gym Forest' comprised of a scatter of benches and obstacles with map tasks to do between each circuit.
(c) Punching relays – markers with punches scattered round the gym which teams of individuals have to dash round punching accurately in control card boxes.

(4) *Purely Physical – Timed Gym Circuits or Aerobics Sessions*

The detail on these exercises can be found in the publications mentioned earlier and teachers and coaches can of course devise variations of their own on basic themes. The important thing to remember is that orienteering does not demand large forests, and that small-scale activities in school or on the doorstep can give as much fun as major events. Even Scandinavian orienteers spend half the year enjoying this type of orienteering when snow and cold temperatures make forest orienteering impossible.

A regular programme of activities in winter and summer builds up experience and motivation as well as cementing social loyalties – a vital factor in sport and recreation for all ages.

Appendix 8
BOF COACHING AWARD SCHEME

BRITISH ORINTEERING FEDERATION

COACHING AWARD SCHEME

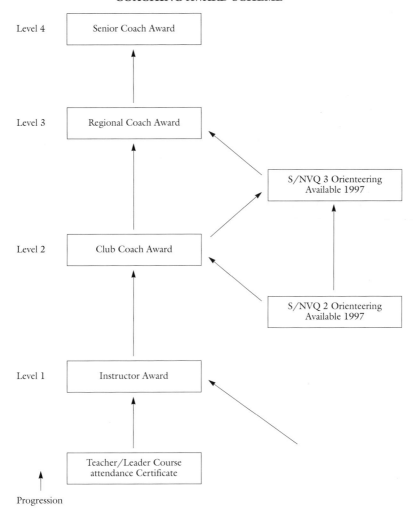

All awards and S/NVQs are assessed

COACHING AWARD SUMMARY

Teacher/Leader Certificate

Minimum age:17 for course attendance; duration: 7 hours.

The courses usually run over a full day or an equivalent number of evenings. They include basic instruction on the introduction of orienteering and National Curriculum requirements. An attendance certificate is issued and there is no assessment. The cost is determined by the organizing club or association.

Instructor Award

• (Valid for three years – renewable)

Minimum age:17 for course attendance; duration: 15 hours.

The courses usually run over one weekend or two separate days and include instruction on basic techniques (safety considerations, the introduction of orienteering and the coaching of beginners on simple courses). The cost is determined by the organizing club or association.

• A subsequent assessment of the candidate's ability to introduce and coach beginners on simple courses is required for successful completion.

Club Coach Award

• (Valid for three years – renewable)

Minimum age: 17 for course attendance; duration: 15 hours.

The courses run over one weekend or several separate days and include instruction on physical and technical training techniques applicable at club level and the planning of club training programmes.

• Valid First Aid Certificate is required, a further 15-hour weekend course or equivalent.
• As for the Instructor's Award, assessment must take place at a later date.

Regional Coach Award

• (Valid for three years – renewable)

Minimum age: 17 for course attendance; duration: 15 hours.

The courses run over one weekend or several separate days and include instruction on personal performance coaching, exercise physiology, fine technique training and the organization of club and regional coaching award and squad courses. Much of a coach's work could be in instructor and club coach tutoring and assessment at a regional level. The cost is determined by the organizing association or Federation Senior Coach running the course.

• Valid First Aid Certificate is required, a further 15-hour weekend course or equivalent.
• Attendance at some National Coaching Foundation course is mandatory for level 3.
• As for the other awards, assessment must take place at a later date.

Senior Coach Award

- (Valid for three years – renewable)

Minimum age: 21 for course attendance; duration: 11 hours.

Courses involve progressive assessment over several weekends or day courses depending upon the candidate's experience in the sport, which must be considerable. Courses include coaching explored in greater detail together with input on sport psychology, diet and coaching methodology. Assessment is geared to the candidate's area of specialization and qualification has to be confirmed by the National Coaching Committee on the recommendation of the Director of Coaching. Course costs are determined by the National or Regional Association.

- Attendance at some National Coaching Foundation courses is mandatory for level 4.

Members of the British Orienteering Federation only can take the above awards, except for the Teacher/Leader Certificate and Instructors Award. The Coaching Award booklet (free of charge) and the Complete Orienteering Manual (with which all coaching levels must be thoroughly conversant) are available from the National Office of the British Orienteering Federation.

The annual programme of courses is coordinated by the Director of Coaching and publicized to the membership through the Federation magazine and to coaches through Coaching Committee circulars and the National Coaching Newsletter. Details are available on application to the BOF National Office.

British Orienteering Federation

'Riversdale'
Dale Road North
Darley Dale
Matlock
Derbyshire DE4 2HX
Tel: 01629 734042.

Index